CRITICAL INSIGHTS

The Hunger Games Trilogy

CRITICAL INSIGHTS

The Hunger Games Trilogy

Editor

Lana A. Whited

Ferrum College, Virginia

SALEM PRESS

A Division of EBSCO Information Services, Inc.

Ipswich, Massachusetts

GREY HOUSE PUBLISHING

Publisher's Cataloging-In-Publication Data
(Prepared by The Donohue Group, Inc.)

Names: Whited, Lana A., 1958- editor.
Title: The Hunger Games trilogy / editor, Lana A. Whited, Ferrum College,
      Virginia.
Other Titles: Critical insights.
Description: [First edition]. | Ipswich, Massachusetts : Salem Press, a division
      of EBSCO Information Services, Inc. ; Amenia, NY : Grey
      House Publishing, [2016] | Critical insights | Includes
      bibliographical references and index.
Identifiers: ISBN 978-1-61925-844-0 (hardcover)
Subjects: LCSH: Collins, Suzanne--Criticism and interpretation. | Collins,
      Suzanne. Hunger Games (Series) | Young adult fiction, American--21st
      century--History and criticism. | Dystopias in literature.
Classification: LCC PS3603.O4558 Z68 2016 | DDC 813/.6--dc23

First Printing

PRINTED IN THE UNITED STATES OF AMERICA

Contents

Resources

About This Volume

Lana A. Whited

When plans for this book were in the very early stages, the number of people who wanted to write essays for it flabbergasted me. I was well aware of the popularity of The Hunger Games[1] series, but I really had no idea just how seriously the books were being taken by literature professionals—teachers, librarians, creative writers, employees of publishers, and graduate students in literature, film, popular culture, and other fields. I received thirty-eight proposals, enough for about three volumes of essays.

A number of important and interesting topics concerning The Hunger Games novels came up in the proposals but did not ultimately find space in this book. Several potential contributors wanted to write about gender, including the theme of motherhood: both real mother figures, such as Katniss' own (who are often ineffectual), and the mothering roles Katniss must adopt for the well-being of other characters (including her own mother, Prim, and, sometimes, Peeta). There is a tremendous amount of interest in what sort of girl Katniss is in the pages of Collins' novels, what sort of woman she might become, and how the hero myth applies to her. Some writers, including Meghan Lewit of *The Atlantic*, waited tensely as the first Hunger Games film was cast, to see which actress would play "the most important female character in recent pop culture history."

There were essays focusing on the theme of identity, including identity as a fluid construct that might be shaped or changed through the intensity of the arena; anticipating that intensity, Peeta says, "I want to die as myself ... I don't want them to change me in there. Turn me into some kind of monster that I'm not" (Collins 141). There were proposals for essays about technology and celebrity culture and materialism. There were comparisons of The Hunger Games novels with other works in which a government forces its own children into combat, such as *Battle Royale*. There were proposed discussions about how the series fits into the context of dystopic literature. There were allusions to the classical world—the myth of Theseus and the Minotaur, the story of Spartacus, the gladiators in the Roman Coliseum. There were thematic approaches about wildflowers and food and instruments of surveillance. There were pitches for articles about game theory. There were proposals about citizenship and presidents and power. And there were multiple proposals about several of these topics.

Choosing was hard, so I asked a colleague to read the proposals, too. As a primary criterion, we tried to choose proposals that did not merely repeat arguments already existing in the handful of Hunger Games-themed critical anthologies already published. In some cases of multiple proposals on the same topic, we opted for the best writing. We settled on the four essays in the Critical Contexts section, all of which, I'm happy to say, were obvious choices, as well as fourteen other essays that would comprise Critical Readings. We chose ten essays, and then I begged the editor for two more that I couldn't bear to exclude. Over the months of work, there were a few roster changes caused by unforeseen developments in contributors' lives.

The final result is a collection of fourteen essays that I would put up against any other volume in the arena of Hunger Games literary criticism. Reading only through the Critical Contexts section, a person would gain a sense of how the three novels have been appraised by book critics (Lana A. Whited), a deep familiarity with the series' literary lineage (Tina L. Hanlon), an understanding of the two predominant strands of dystopian fiction and how they appear in Collins' series (Amy H. Sturgis), and an illustration of how Reader-Response Criticism applies to *Mockingjay* (Jackie C. Horne).

The Critical Readings section comprises essays as diverse as their authors, whose day jobs cover territory that stretches from Thailand in the East to Michigan and Cincinnati in the Midwest, reaching as far north as Toronto and including the University of Hamburg. Katniss' inability to accept gifts from anyone but Prim and the role of "radical gifts" in the transformation of Panem are the subject of Amy Bennett-Zendzian's "'What I did was a radical thing': Panem's Corrupted Gift Economy." The gender discussion is handled deftly by Danielle Bienvenue Bray, author of "'You love me. Real': Gender in The Hunger Games Trilogy," who argues for Suzanne Collins' sympathetic presentation of any characters demonstrating traditionally feminine attitudes and behaviors, regardless of those characters' gender. In "Game Macabre: Fear as an Essential Element in The Hunger Games," Rebecca Sutherland Borah investigates Collins' use of horror and terror to achieve emotional resonance in her depiction of the oppression and debauchery of the Capitol and the monstrosity of war. Stephanie Dror discusses "The Nature of Consumerism" in the first novel from an ecocritical perspective, positing that Collins illustrates "the postmodernist claim that we inhabit a prosthetic [simulated] environment" rather than a natural one; thus, from an environmentalist standpoint, one of the dystopian author's cautions here is against humanity's destruction of the ecosystem via a cycle of consumerism like the Capitol's (Buell 5).

From concerns grounded in the natural sciences in Dror's essay, we move to the social sciences and Louise M. Freeman's essay "Pavlov, Peeta, and PTSD," a primer on the scientific principles underlying hijacking in which Freeman explains how Pavlovian conditioning models help clinicians understand post-traumatic stress disorder. Freeman's essay also accounts for the usefulness of a number of Peeta's therapies, including counterconditioning (rediscovered by Prim); the "real, not real" game; and art therapy. "'Where you can starve to death in safety': Appalachia and The Hunger Games" is the contribution of Elizabeth Baird Hardy, a resident of western North Carolina, where much of The Hunger Games filming took place. Hardy identifies the physical, cultural, and historical elements of Collins' narrative that allow readers to locate Katniss' home region on a real map, while also examining how traditional stereotypes of Appalachian people are manifested in the series.

The volume concludes with four essays, two each dealing with political aspects of the novels (Todd Ide and Sandra Via) and Collins' debt to classical culture and characters (Lars Schmeink and Amalia L. Selle). Ide applies theories of gaining, using, and holding power from Niccolò Machiavelli's 1517 treatise *The Prince* to President

Snow and President Coin, arguing that, given their situations, these presidents have no more effective option than following Machiavelli's guidelines. His essay will help the reader better understand both The Hunger Games novels and Machiavellianism. The final essay in the collection is Sandra Via's testimonial concerning her use of the series in the democracy, justice, and civic engagement classroom, with emphasis on how using the books strengthens not only her students' engagement in the course and comprehension of course concepts but also their academic skills.

Between Ide's and Via's essays is sandwiched an exploration of the labyrinth trope in the series, accompanied by a discussion of how Collins adapts the myth of Theseus and the Minotaur. Author Lars Schmeink focuses primarily on gaming theory and the use of "degenerate strategies" by Katniss and her allies to defeat the Gamemaker. To Amalia L. Selle falls the task of explaining Roman allusions in the narrative, first and foremost the myth of Spartacus, who, like Katniss, succeeds against the odds. Selle explores ways in which Katniss' character may appear to change in *Mockingjay*, encouraging readers to understand her motivation as evidence of the transformative power of war on the combatants and to question our own assumptions about war and our role in the world.

I hope that these essays will serve as a useful collection for Hunger Games readers eager to go beyond the narrative itself to larger questions of influence and interpretation, that they provoke insightful conversations among friends and colleagues, and that some of the students who use them for coursework will one day grow up to write book chapters of their own. My own preparation for editing this volume owes much to three experiences with my own students: teaching *The Hunger Games* in my course Harry Potter and the Hero Myth; directing Whitney Scott's independent study and honors thesis in feminist dystopian novels, "Perverse Piety: Criticism of Christian Extremism in *The Handmaid's Tale*, *The Gate to Women's Country*, and *The Fifth Sacred Thing* (Ferrum College, 2011); and supervising Harley Patterson's English senior thesis, "Eschatology and Dystopian Literature" (Ferrum College, 2014), a study of five dystopian novels, including *The Hunger*

Games. I am particularly grateful to Harley for introducing me to *We* (1924) by Yevgeny Zamyatin, widely considered the first modern dystopian novel. My work in dystopian fiction has been a reciprocal process, involving both what I have taught students and what they have taught me.

Note

1. This phrase is used in three ways in this volume. When it refers to the title of the first novel in this series, it is written in this way: *The Hunger Games*. When it refers to the entire series, it is written like this: The Hunger Games, often followed by the word "series" or "novels." When it refers to the competition, it is written as follows: the Hunger Games. Occasionally, a writer refers to "the Games," without the word "Hunger." In this case, we have elected to capitalize the "G" in "Games" because Collins capitalizes it in this usage in her novels.

Works Cited

Buell, Lawrence. *Environmental Imagination: Thoreau, Nature and Writing, and the Formation of American Culture*. Cambridge, MA: Belknap Press, 1996.

Lewit, Meghan. "Casting 'The Hunger Games': In Praise of Katniss Everdeen." *The Atlantic*. The Atlantic Monthly Group, 9 Mar. 2011. Web. 27 Nov. 2015.

THE BOOK
AND THE
AUTHOR

On Suzanne Collins' The Hunger Games Trilogy

Lana A. Whited

The forbidden fruit. The cave. The odyssey. The scarlet letter. The white whale. Never-never land. The yellow brick road. The grapes of wrath. The lottery. The spider web in the barn doorway. The Hogwarts Express. These are a few of the many recognizable literary tropes.[1] And thanks to Suzanne Collins, we can add another: The Girl on Fire.

Writing in *The Atlantic* when the first Hunger Games film was being cast, Meghan Lewit called Katniss Everdeen "the most important female character in recent pop culture history." By the time of the first film's release, she had become a one-name quantity: Katniss. She is a protagonist who points us both backward and forward. Her first name conjures the natural world, as she is named for an edible plant favored by her dead father; the practice of naming girls after flora and herbs is reminiscent of the Anglo-Saxon girls' names of bygone eras, such as Daisy, Violet, Hyacinth, and Rose (Katniss' sister is Primrose). Her habit of supplying her mother with ingredients for her remedies and poultices, practices she and Peeta much later record in a scrapbook illustrated with Peeta's drawings, is also an old-fashioned undertaking, as is her ability to keep her family fed through her hunting and foraging. Katniss' surname also connects her with the past, as it is borrowed from a feisty nineteenth-century Thomas Hardy heroine, Bathsheba Everdene. Bathsheba, protagonist of *Far from the Madding Crowd*, is an independent young woman who finds herself running a large agricultural estate in a climate of conventional gender expectations; she will avoid marriage if it means merely becoming the property of a man. Arguing for the importance of complex female characters, Clementine Ford says that Bathsheba knows "how to wield a strong will and a stronger wisecrack." Ford finds one of the strongest similarities between Bathsheba Everdene and her namesake is

The Hunger Games Trilogy 3

the fact that both characters are "rich with nuance. [Bathsheba's] decisions are not always right, nor is her motivation always clear. She is not always likeable—and it is this, above all else, that makes her so real and relatable." The reader's introduction to Katniss Everdeen includes Katniss' acknowledgment that she tried to drown her sister's cat. Suzanne Collins has said that despite Bathsheba and Katniss' differences, "both struggle with knowing their hearts" (qtd. in Ford). For example, both struggle with romantic choices involving men who signal very different futures. For more about Collins' indebtedness to previous works of literature, including Hardy's novel, see Tina L. Hanlon's essay in the Critical Contexts section of this volume. For more about gender dynamics in the series, see Danielle Bienvenue Bray's "'You love me. Real': Gender in The Hunger Games Trilogy."

At the same time that Katniss is in some ways an old-fashioned heroine, she is simultaneously a character whose story takes place in a futuristic landscape. Panem is located in the post-apocalypse remnants of North America, at least seventy-five years after a rebellion put down by the government that came to power and established the Capitol. For the tributes of District 12, visiting the Capitol is like visiting the future: they ride a high-speed train to a landscape of concrete and glass brimming with the flashiest technology. Food abounds, and residents can drink an elixir to make them vomit and have room for *more* food (Katniss' mother probably knows a plant with the same effect).

The tensions between these landscapes of the past and future and the value systems of each have not yet been properly assessed, but two essays in this volume can serve as a starting point for discussion: Amy Bennett-Zendzian's "What I did was a radical thing'": Panem's Corrupted Gift Economy" and Stephanie Dror's "As long as you can find yourself, you'll never starve'": Consuming Katniss in *The Hunger Games*."

The series has been adapted for educational purposes in many types of classrooms. The most obvious examples come from faculty teaching political science or related topics, such as citizenship and justice. For example, Sandra Via of Ferrum College (Virginia) uses the trilogy in an introductory course in practicing democracy, justice, and civic engagement. Via sought a means of presenting the course concepts in a manner "that would differ from a traditional American government or theory course." A challenge for Via is that most of her relatively young students have little experience of citizenship, the democratic process, or oppression. "Most have never experienced these types of injustices, nor do they imagine them happening in their own communities," Via says. She found that the series had an enticing effect for both students who struggled with course concepts and those who struggle with academic skills generally. (See Via's essay in the Critical Readings section of this volume.)

Working with pre-professional teachers in the Department of Curriculum and Instruction at the University of Illinois at Normal, Thomas Lucey and colleagues have adapted a module for using The Hunger Games trilogy to teach citizenship concepts. Lucey and colleagues note studies that "repeatedly show that social studies teachers lack understanding of social studies content and experience difficulties articulating its justification, particularly in environments that do require high-stakes standardized testing" (190–91). Models for citizenship in difficult contexts may be drawn from literature, drama, and art, Lucey et al. maintain, citing The Hunger Games books as providing a particularly good example of "social and political conditions that can make acting in certain roles as a citizen difficult, especially for youth" (190). If citizenship requires negotiation among various loyalties, such as government, community, and family, sixteen-year-old Katniss amply illustrates an individual with many, sometimes conflicting, loyalties. Learner activities in the citizenship module for middle schoolers include describing the function of sacrifice in citizenship and providing several examples of sacrifice from The Hunger Games and Auguste Rodin's sculpture The Burghers of Calais.

But applications of The Hunger Games novels in the classroom are far broader than studies of political science and government. In fall 2014, American University (AU) history professor Stef Woods launched an American cultural history course focused on the series. The course content includes "politics and class for one-third of the course, issues related to race, gender, food justice and feminism in the second third, and publishing, marketing and writing in the remaining third" (Sheffler). Samantha Theriault, a student in the AU course, said, "There's a fair amount of reading and a few larger projects that we'll get into later in the semester, but since it's all interesting, it doesn't feel like 'work'" (qtd. in Sheffler). An American studies Hunger Games-themed class is also offered at Macalester College in Minnesota, where Karin Aguilar-San Juan's course plan includes an archery lesson, a trip to a bakery accompanied by a discussion about food justice, and a visit from a guest artist whose work targets mountain top removal by the coal mining industry in West Virginia. Aguilar-San Juan call United Mine Workers activist Mother Jones "Katniss' political ancestor" (qtd. in Sheffler). Students also hear about post-traumatic stress disorder (PTSD) from a psychiatrist who is a Macalester alumnus and works with veterans (for more on PTSD and The Hunger Games, see Louise M. Freeman's essay in this volume). Will French, a recent Macalester alumnus, says that Aguilar-San Juan's course is "a demonstration of what liberal arts education can mean—you don't have to always stay in the classroom" (Kavish).

Of course, Katniss shows up on the syllabus of many literature and gender studies courses, such as those of the University of Nebraska at Lincoln (UN-L). There, lecturer Kathleen Lacey asks her students to discuss such gender issues as whether being a strong woman means demonstrating qualities ordinarily perceived as male-gendered characteristics. A recent freshman seminar at UN-L focused on similarities between Panem and the state of Nebraska. Planning service projects for homeless populations in Lincoln, first-year students realized, "Wow. I live in the Capitol," according to Rachel Droogsma, the course professor (qtd. in Howard).

One of the most interesting approaches to the lottery trope in The Hunger Games series is a statistics assignment designed by faculty at South Dakota School of Mines and Technology that invites students to investigate the possibility that the Gamemakers have rigged the system when Primrose Everdeen's name is drawn for the seventy-fourth annual event. At twelve and with no tesserae, with her name on only one slip of paper, Prim would seem practically out of danger of being selected: the odds, it would appear, are in her favor. To investigate how Prim might be selected, South Dakota School of Mines and Technology students use relevant data from the book, (age and number of tesserae) to do statistical analysis; they also use computer simulations to learn how to perform a "permutation goodness of fit test" (Caudle and Daniels). The project conclusion, based on some assumptions about the tesserae, is that "it seems there is evidence that the Gamemakers are fixing the lottery" (Caudle, and Daniels 40). Understanding *why* they might manipulate the odds, of course, is outside the scope of mathematics.

The series has even been used as a framework for a university program that trains pre-service teachers in teaching disciplinary literacy. Two members of the Department of Curriculum and Instruction at the University of Texas-San Marcos, Jane M. Saunders and Gwynne Ellen Ash, used The Hunger Games series in the preparation of pre-service teachers, both as a text for practicing disciplinary literacy and as a model for a professional development "arena" of achievements and rewards. The disciplinary literacy aspect of the program included a book club in which students read The Hunger Games novels as both disciplinary literacy practice and investigation of the qualities that contribute to Katniss Everdeen's persistence and success (tenacity, for example). The professional development "arena" features challenges in thirteen categories (modeled after the number of districts in Collins' novels) such as "Developing professional identity." Students must compile a portfolio of achievements, including at least one from each category to "survive" the semester. For example, a student can complete the "Developing professional identity" achievement by joining and becoming involved in a local, state, or national teachers' organization (Saunders, and Ash 493).

The premise of Saunders and Ash's plan is the idea that Katniss and the students in their teacher preparation program share an experience of crossing a threshold not fully prepared and not completely familiar with the world on the other side:

Just as Katniss faces unpredictable challenges as she enters the arena to compete in the Hunger Games, preservice teachers confront unanticipated obstacles as they leave the safety of the college classroom and enter into field-based experiences, where they will hone their skills and capacities as educators. Both are moving from one world to another—Katniss, from teenager to survivor; preservice teachers, from student to educator. Their transitions include vastly different, novel environments that require skills and talents not fully developed prior to entry into their puzzling new world. (Saunders, and Ash 190)

Of course, the "arena" system for collecting achievements could be adapted for any number of purposes.

Lesson plans for teaching the novels in middle school and high school classes are numerous on the Internet. It is obvious from these that the books lend themselves to as broad a range of academic subjects as the Harry Potter saga, including the mathematics example described above: using textual clues to make a map of Panem in geography class; drawing pictures of Hunger Games-related scenes in art; discussing how mutations might be made in biology; discussing Haymitch's struggle with alcoholism and the effects of alcoholism (or depression) on the body in health class; and, of course, connecting the series with other works of dystopian literature for young adults, such as William Golding's *Lord of the Flies* (1954). One teacher describes particular success in using the novels as the basis for assignments with remedial writing classes composed largely of boys, who often lag behind girls in verbal skills at the high school and early college level (Orman).[2]

At all educational levels, The Hunger Games books are an influence outside the classroom as well, particularly as the inspiration for community service projects. A notable example occurs at Carson-Newman University in Upper East Tennessee, which hosted its fifth annual Hunger Games-style event benefitting local nonprofits in fall 2015. The event was launched in 2012, and in the first year, participants raised $2,500 for local charities. But as the event rapidly became more popular, "tributes" were able to lure more sponsors, and the 2015 event brought in $18,000. As of November

2015, organizers had raised $55,000, despite a student body of just over 2,500. The two first-place winners each earned $4,000 for their charities and an additional $1,000 for working together to defeat the Head Gamemaker. Similar service projects have been undertaken in other communities, academic and nonacademic; most benefit organizations battling hunger or poverty. A particularly interesting one in Oregon, a canned food drive, focused around a roller derby event the weekend before Thanksgiving. It was the fourth annual event in the Salem area; the organizers' goal was to have participating "tributes" gather eight large barrels of food, and money raised in a raffle was also donated to charities. Another example of Hunger Games-inspired philanthropy comes from Syracuse University, where a chapter of the fraternity Phi Theta Epsilon partnered with sorority chapters to raise about $1,000 for the ALS Association in Central New York. About fifty tributes representing eight teams participated in twelve rounds of physical competition, sponsored by donors ("New York"). Some fundraiser consultants even have a Hunger Games template for potential philanthropists; for an example, see "Hunger Games fundraiser" at Fundraiserhelp.com.

Trend watchers have credited Collins' series with launching or fueling several developments in popular culture, foremost of which is the boom in the popularity of archery. Although the prowess of the beautiful elf Legolas in *The Lord of the Rings* screen adaptations and the various screen iterations of Robin Hood have caused incidental swells of increased interest, "Katniss has helped give archery a hip factor it's just never had before," said Teresa Iaconi, spokesperson for USA Archery, sponsor of the Olympic archery team (qtd. in Rubin). Prior to filming *The Hunger Games*, Jennifer Lawrence took fifteen lessons with US Olympic archer Khatuna Lorig,[3] who is herself no stranger to spectacle: Lorig carried the Team USA flag in the 2012 closing ceremonies (Rubin), just four months after the first Hunger Games film hit the big screen. Since late 2011, when that film was still in the editing room with a spring release anticipated, USA Archery individual memberships have increased by 25 percent and the number of affiliated archery clubs has increased from 279 to 540 (Rubin). By November 2012, when Courtney Rubin's article detailing the surge of interest in archery, "The Odds Are Ever in Their Favor," appeared in *The New York Times*, businesses such as Victors Archery on Staten Island were welcoming Girl Scout groups earning merit badges and hosting Hunger Games-themed birthday parties. Jim Belcher, whose Michigan-based archery company specializes in traditional bows, reported that orders of child-sized recurve bows quadrupled in 2012 (Rubin). Around the same time, a recreation department in suburban Baltimore had a waiting list for archery lessons of about 100 children, and archery instructor Patricia Gonsalves of Academie Duello Swordplay Training School in Vancouver reported that archery classes (including horseback archery) were filling up within twenty-four hours of being announced (Rubin). This trend was probably fed, at least in younger audiences, by the June 2012 debut of the animated archer Princess Merida, the spunky heroine of the Pixar film *Brave*, and for the remainder of the year, Disney stores couldn't keep plastic bow and suction cup arrow sets on the shelves. But *The Hunger Games* remained the primary influence, as illustrated in a question instructor Patricia Gonsalves heard regularly from young students: "Can you shoot an apple out of a pig's mouth like Katniss did?" (qtd. in Rubin). By the release of *Catching Fire* in November 2013, USA Archery wrote to Suzanne Collins to thank her for making archery a pastime with mass appeal (Rubin).

Another trend launched by The Hunger Games series is Katniss' pragmatic but stylish hair braid, designed by hairstylist Jennifer Flowers, who says the braid is about "both form and function" (qtd. in Rasmus). Obviously, the decision to bring the braid over Jennifer Lawrence's non-dominant shoulder was designed to keep it out of the bow. The hairstyle, Flowers says, was intended to be "a standout style that would make the character instantly recognizable onscreen, and would ensure Katniss never got lost in the fray." (qtd. in Rasmus). Concurrent with the release of the first film in March 2012, fashion and beauty sites began offering tutorials for emulating the heroine's hairstyle, described as "[e]qual parts sporty, functional, and beautiful" (McIntyre). By the release of *Catching Fire*, Jennifer Lawrence's hair braids had become considerably more elaborate, but the original side braid continued to drive the trend. Nearly two years after Lawrence's braid made its screen debut, vocalist Sarah Bareilles wore a "Katniss Everdeen-inspired braid" when she sang the nominated title song from the Pixar movie *Brave* at the 2014 Grammy Award ceremony. One commentator noted, "the braid trend isn't going anywhere anytime soon, thanks to *The Hunger Games*" (Popp).

Of course, Katniss and other characters' hair styles are only one aspect of the spectacle created by The Hunger Games competition, and just as television screens carry that spectacle outside the arena itself, certain real-life developments have taken Colllins' fictional world beyond book pages and film screens. These include an elaborate Hunger Games-themed exhibition in Time Square and plans for both a theatrical production and a theme park based on the series.

The successful Hunger Games film adaptations appear to have been only the beginning of the books' afterlife in auxiliary enterprises, plans for which escalated in late 2014. On Nov. 7, 2014, Lionsgate, distributor of the films, announced that it was developing a theatrical experience based upon Collins' novels, in partnership with Imagine Nation, a Dutch-based media company whose goal is "to create new intellectual properties through the use of innovative technology," and Triangular Entertainment (US). Lionsgate, a self-described "premier next generation global content leader," has new enterprises in "landscape-based entertainment" in the works at several locations, including the United Arab Emirates and China ("Lionsgate"). In the press release announcing the theatrical production—to be staged in a theatre in Wembley, England, built specifically for that purpose—Lionsgate called it the next step in the company's "global blockbuster Hunger Games franchise" and promised "innovative and immersive staging techniques" ("Lionsgate"). In The Netherlands, Robin de Levita, founder of Imagine Nation, has already staged a popular musical, *Soldier of Orange*, whose performances have been sold out four years running, and a new adaptation of Anne Frank's original and complete diaries. For the musical, audiences sit in a 360-degree auditorium and are rotated among sets. De Levita promises an equally "immersive" experience for The Hunger Games production ("Lionsgate"). Spectacle, indeed. The theatrical production plans to welcome audiences in 2016.

On July 1, 2015, Discovery Times Square opened an immersive Hunger Games exhibit, anticipating a six-month run. The exhibit was described by a *New York Times* reviewer as "a maze of seven galleries" (Shattuck), featuring about 1,000 movie props and about four dozen costumes, and by *The Guardian* as "a museum-quality show that mixes props, costumes and holograms with discussion of the series' weightier themes" (Hoffman). The Discovery exhibit was organized by The Thinkwell Group in partnership with Lionsgate. It includes a digital map of Panem, a Gamemaker's table replica, a costume sketchbook, a propaganda-designing kiosk, a video tutorial with the films' stunt coordinator, a green-screen stage where visitors can appear to be paraded by chariot around the Capitol, and, of course, a gift shop where visitors can buy Katniss' hunting cowl sweater for $129.99 (Shattuck). Visitors pay $29.50 each, enter in groups of about forty, and can download an app to enhance the experience and post "achievement badges" to social media (Hoffman). *The Guardian* reviewer described the exhibition as "well curated" and "more engaging and thought-provoking than might be expected from its origins" with "a noble and noticeable effort made to tie the Hunger Games [*sic*] franchise into relevant worldly themes" (Hoffman). Fans and curious spectators outside the New York region will have another chance to see the exhibit when it moves to San Francisco in early 2016.

In early November 2015, Lionsgate announced plans for more Hunger Games-inspired "location-based entertainment"—in other words, theme parks. Imagine a roller coaster simulating Katniss and Peeta's first journey to the Capitol. Current plans involve three locations: Atlanta, China, and the $3 billion "Motiongate" entertainment complex in the United Arab Emirates (Garber). Lionsgate says it also has parks in progress tied to the *Divergent* and *Twilight* series, as well as several other properties, most originally literary. Of course, a primary appeal of such "locations" for media conglomerates is that they provide alternate revenue streams in an era of technological change. NBCUniversal (owned by Comcast) and 21st Century Fox are also "investing billions of dollars in transferring movies from megaplexes to megaplaces" with properties such as Fox's *Planet of the Apes* (Garber).

How will devoted readers of Suzanne Collins' novels, those of us still enamored of words on paper, respond to the conversion of Collins' words to commercial immersive experiences? As ardent fans know, the spectacle of the Hunger Games arena was a political machination of the oppressive Capitol, not a thing to be admired by fair-minded and thinking people. In an article about Lionsgate's theme parks announcement, *The Atlantic* writer Meghan Garber compared the modern-day theme park environment to the launches of Disneyland and Walt Disney World, developments she views (particularly in their post-World War II timing) as "a testament not just to the various productions of the Walt Disney Company, but also to the accomplishments of the American experiment. It was brimming with optimism. It was a kind of permanent World's Fair." Another *Atlantic* writer, Alexis C. Madrigal, called the Disneyland of 1965 "the happiest landscape on Earth." But it is difficult to cultivate a similar attitude in the atmosphere of contemporary entertainment behemoths.

However much we might enjoy these multi-million (or multi-billion) dollar theme parks, fervent readers of The Hunger Games series may find it difficult not to view them as media mutations that have morphed off the pages of Suzanne Collins' novels. Collins herself has trained us to view spectacle suspiciously, even critically. If the excesses of Capitol-sponsored entertainment are intended to evoke readers' proletarian sympathies, it may be difficult in the face of the coming spectacle for ardent fans to reconcile their desire for a ticket with their simultaneous understanding that only citizens of the Capitol are allowed inside.

Notes

1.   A trope is "a figure of speech through which speakers or writers intend to express meanings of words that are different from their literal meanings...[a] metaphorical or figurative use of words in which

writers shift from the literal meanings of words to their non-literal meanings" ("Literary Devices"). Thus, in the trope of the forbidden fruit, which derives from the story of the Garden of Eden, the fruit is, in the story, literal (often represented by an apple), but it signifies knowledge that is the exclusive property of the gods, the knowledge of good and evil. What the trope *represents* is more important than what it *is*.

2. According to the book *Why Boys Fail* (2011) by Richard Whitmire, boys lag behind girls in the United States in almost every measure of scholastic achievement except math. A point particularly relevant to this discussion is that "[i]n federal writing tests, thirty-two percent of girls are considered 'proficient' or better. For boys, the figure is sixteen percent" (Kristoff).

3. Khatuna Lorig won a bronze medal as a member of a Soviet Union Unified Team in 1992, then competed for her native province of Georgia in the 1996 and 2002 Olympics. She was a member of the 2008 and 2012 US Olympic squads and carried the flag in the 2012 closing ceremonies.

Works Cited

Bloom, Peter. "Why the Message of the Hunger Games Films Is Dangerous." *The Conversation.* The Conversation US, Inc., 9 Dec. 2014. Web. 26 Nov. 2015.

Caudle, Kyle, and Erica Daniels. "Did the Gamemakers Fix the Lottery?" *Teaching Statistics.* 37.2 (2015): 37–40. PDF.

Collins, Suzanne. *Catching Fire.* New York: Scholastic, 2008; 2009.

_____. *The Hunger Games.* New York: Scholastic, 2008.

_____. *Mockingjay.* New York: Scholastic, 2008; 2010.

Ford, Clementine. "Literature's Feistiest Feminists: How Thomas Hardy Paved the Way for The Hunger Games' Katniss Everdeen." *The Telegraph.* 20 Apr. 2015. Web. 26 Nov. 2015.

Garber, Megan. "The *Hunger Games* Theme Park and the Death of the Disney Dream." *The Atlantic.* The Atlantic Monthly Group, 2 Nov. 2015. Web. 27 Nov. 2015.

Hoffman, Jordan. "The Hunger Games Exhibition Review—A Surprisingly Thoughtful Taste of Panem." *The Guardian.* The Guardian News and Media Limited, 1 Jul. 2015. Web. 27 Nov. 2015.

Howard, Kate. "How Katniss, 'Hunger Games' Give Meat to College Classes." (Omaha) *World-Herald* 20 Nov. 2014. Web. 26 Nov. 2015.

"Hunger Games Fundraiser." *Fundraiser Help*. FundraiserHelp.com, 2016. Web. 26 Nov. 2015.

"The Hunger Games." *Imagine Nation*. Imaginenation, 2016. Web. 26 Nov. 2015.

Kavish, Donovan. "Hunger Games: The Course." *Macalester College*. July 2013. Web. 26 Nov. 2015.

Key, Charles. "Carson-Newman's Fifth Hunger Games Event Raises Nearly $55,000 for Charity." *Kingsport Times-News*. 22 Nov. 2015. Web. 26 Nov. 2015. [*Editor's note*: This headline is misleading. The article indicates that Carson-Newman students have raised over $55,000 during the five years of their event, not that they raised over $55,000 in 2015 alone.]

Korn, Gabrielle. "A Katniss-Style Braid We'd All Volunteer For." *Refinery29*. Refinery29, 10 Dec. 2013. Web. 26 Nov. 2015.

Kristoff, Nicholas. "The Boys Have Fallen Behind." *New York Times*. The New York Times Co, 27 Mar. 2010. Web. 26 Nov. 2015.

Lewit, Meghan. "Casting 'The Hunger Games': In Praise of Katniss Everdeen." *The Atlantic*. 9 Mar. 2011. Web. 27 Nov. 2015.

"Lionsgate and Imagine Nation Form Partnership to Launch The Hunger Games on Stage." Press release. *Lionsgate*. Lions Gate Entertainment Inc., 7 Nov. 2014. Web. 19 Jan. 2015.

Lucey, Thomas A., Kara Lycke, James Laney, and Christopher Connelly. "Dimensions of Citizenship through the Lens of *The Hunger Games*: Fiction and the Visual and Performing Arts as Springboards for Citizenship Education." *The Social Studies* 10.4 (2013): 190-199. *EBSCO Host*. Web. 26 Nov. 2015.

McIntyre, Megan. "DIY Katniss Braid, No Hunger Games Required." *Refinery29*. Refinery29, 22 Mar. 2012. Web. 26 Nov. 2015.

Madrigal, Alexis C. "Disneyland, 1965." *The Atlantic*. The Atlantic Monthly Group, 15 Nov. 2013. Web. 26 Nov. 2015.

"New York Epsilon's (Syracuse) Hunger Games Philanthropy Raises Funds for ALS." *Phi Delta Theta*. Phi Delta Theta Fraternity, 4 Apr. 2014. Web. 26 Nov. 2015.

Orman, Tracee. "Top 7 Tips for Teaching *The Hunger Games*." *Novel Novice*. WordPress.com, 22 Mar. 2012. Web. 26 Nov. 2015.

Popp, Emily. "2014 Grammys: Sara Bareilles Wears Katniss Everdeen-Inspired Braids." *EOnline*. E! Entertainment Television, LLC, 26 Jan. 2014. Web. 26 Nov. 2015.

Rasmus, Tara. "The Katniss-Braid Creator Dishes on J-Lawr's Hair." *Refinery29*. Refinery29, 25 Feb. 2014. Web. 26 Nov. 2015.

Rubin, Courtney. "The Odds Are Ever in Their Favor." *New York Times*. The New York Times Co, 28 Nov. 2012. Web. 26 Nov. 2015.

Saunders, Jane M., and Gwynne Ellen Ash. "Entering the Arena: The Figured Worlds Transition of Preservice Teachers." *Journal of Adolescent and Adult Literacy* 56.6 (2013): 290–99. Web. 26 Nov. 2015.

Shattuck, Kathryn. "'The Hunger Games: The Exhibition' Allows Kids to Express Their Inner Katniss." Review. *The New York Times*. The New York Times Co., 2 Jul. 2015. Web. 26 Nov. 2015.

Sheffler, Bob. "AU Unveils New Course Based on 'The Hunger Games' Trilogy." *USA Today*. 11 Sept. 2014. Web. 26 Nov. 2015.

"Trope." *Literary Devices: Definitions and Examples of Literary Terms*. Literary Devices, 2016. Web. 26 Nov. 2015.

Suzanne Collins: One Life, Three Acts, Scripted by War

Laurie Adams

> I don't write about adolescence. I write about war. For adolescents.
> (Suzanne Collins qtd. in Dominus, *New York Times Magazine*)

Before there was a downtrodden District 12, a reluctantly valiant Katniss Everdeen locked in a gladiatorial death match called the Hunger Games, or a Machiavellian President Snow, there was the story of a moment: the precise moment when a little girl with an absent father came to the stunned understanding of the concept of war and the wrenching knowledge that her beloved parent was in the midst of this terrible danger. This devastating news struck from the impassive, flickering screen of a television accidentally left on, a messenger with no regard for the vulnerability of its audience. In that moment, young Suzanne Collins acquired not only a dreadful comprehension of the formerly abstract word "war," but an awe of the power of media and its potential to harm as well as inform. On this foundation, she would one day build the empires of Underland and Panem.

Suzanne Collins was born into a military family on August 10, 1962. The youngest daughter of Lieutenant Colonel Michael and Jane Brady Collins, Suzanne was the fourth of four children, following Kathryn, Drew, and Joan. Awareness of military life dawned early; Collins has noted some of her first memories were of drills being conducted on the parade grounds of West Point (Henthorne 13). Her father, a United States Air Force officer, taught at the Army's military academy only briefly, but his career and his intense interest in history, which was shared with his children at every opportunity, left a series of profound imprints on young Suzanne that would one day surface in her writing.

In 1968, Michael Collins was deployed to Vietnam. Collins recounted the progression of fear that characterized that period in her

2013 children's book *The Year of the Jungle*. First, there was the lack of understanding of why her father had to be away, accompanied by the anxiety that her mother would somehow vanish as well. Later, there would come a mirroring of adults' unease at the mention of her father's being in Vietnam and consternation when, well into his deployment, her father mistakenly sent a birthday card to Collins on her sister's birthday. In Collins' six-year-old mind, the cartoonish jungle she previously imagined Vietnam to be began warping into a place of nightmare—the only possible explanation for why her father would make such an error. Concern turned to serious worry when Collins' father sent her a postcard asking her to pray for him (Collins, *Year*).

In the following spring came the critical moment, a veritable dramatist's turning point: the television flashing the latest scenes from Collins' nightmare jungle: the weaponry, the explosions, the bodies. It was a moment that somehow slipped through a crack in Collins' mother's efforts to avoid exposing her children to coverage from the warzone (This is Teen "Part 3"). The TV was hurriedly turned off, but Collins had seen enough to make the connection that her father was in a place where he could be killed. She began to doubt he would ever come home, and over time—possibly as a defense mechanism—she began to forget what he looked like (Collins, *Year*). Collins' father returned from the war safely, but not unscathed, as he suffered recurrent nightmares "his whole life" (Dominus). After her father's return, Collins struggled to find words to express her experience. How could a six-year-old verbalize the intricate mix of love, fear, loss, and doubt to explain how having a deployed parent and confronting the specter of his possible death had affected her? The words to fully iterate that journey would have to wait.

Possibly due to his traumatic wartime memories, Collins' father, whom she described as "a historian, doctor of Political Science [and] military specialist," made a point of teaching his children to trace the underlying causes of wars and question their necessity, imbuing his lessons with grim reality (Dominus). In an interview with Rick Margolis with the *School Library Journal*, Collins said "[He] would

Critical Insights

discuss these things at a level that he thought we could understand and [was] acceptable for our age. But really, he thought a lot was acceptable for our age...." (Collins, "A Killer")

After a succession of moves to locations including Arlington County, Virginia, while Collins' father worked at the Pentagon, and Alabama, the Collins family relocated to Brussels when Michael Collins was given an assignment with NATO (Henthorne 14). Collins would complete seventh through tenth grades in Belgium, learning French and a smattering of Flemish (This is Teen, "Part 9").

In Brussels, her father often played tour guide for his children at various historical sites, which Collins, as a tween, anticipated as full of glamour—but which were quickly injected with stark fact. One outing to a castle, which Collins had rosily imagined would be "fairy-tale magical," became a lesson on how the fortification's arrow slits and spots for dumping boiling oil figured into its defenses (Dominus). Another such adventure gave Collins' father the opportunity to acquaint his daughter with the tragedies of World War I by likening a neighborhood poppy field to the mournful poem "In Flanders Fields." "[T]his moment becomes transformative, because now I'm looking out onto that field and wondering if it was a graveyard," she says (Dominus).

Collins was a highly literary child, with an affinity for the classics. Early favorites included D'Aulaires' *Greek Myths*, from which Collins would ultimately mine the myth of Theseus as a template for Katniss, and Madeleine L'Engle's *A Wrinkle in Time* (Henthorne 13). Later, she gravitated to works with strong social commentary, such as William Golding's *Lord of the Flies*, George Orwell's *1984*, and Kurt Vonnegut's *Slaughterhouse Five* (Henthorne 13). Not many of the titles amongst Collins' favorites could be described as fluff reading, and—given the competition for her attention from her father's gripping, if grimly pragmatic, history lessons—lighter fare likely would have paled by comparison. Throughout her young life, by chance exposure, nurturing, and her own choices, Collins' voice as a writer was being shaped to examine how people live, how people die, and how the stories of those events should be told.

Upon the family's return to the United States, Collins completed high school at the Alabama School of the Fine Arts in Birmingham, specializing in theater arts and graduating in 1980 (Henthorne 15). She followed this with a double major in theater and telecommunications at Indiana University, graduating in 1985 (Henthorne 15). At the university, Collins met actor Cap Pryor, whom she married in 1992. After attaining an MFA in dramatic writing at New York University's Tisch School of the Arts in 1989, Collins began her first forays as a dramatist, working with an Off-Broadway group called The Classic Stage Company and holding another job working with a film producer (Henthorne 15).

In 1991, Collins made the leap from playwright to screenwriter and began her working relationship with the Nickelodeon network, writing for shows including *Clarissa Explains it All*, *Little Bear*, and *The Mystery Files of Shelby Woo* (Suzanne Collins, *IMDb*). Nearly a decade later, while writing for a Warner Brothers series called *Generation O!*, Collins met author/illustrator James Proimos, who was struck by her talent. Spurred by Proimos' enthusiasm for her work, Collins set about writing her first series of novels: The Underland Chronicles, which follow the adventures of a young boy named Gregor who is plunged into peril in a mysterious subterranean city ("Suzanne Collins," *Authors*). Collins' father's military know-how became an invaluable resource as he helped Collins work out scenarios that made good real-world tactical sense for the books' battles between giant rats and roaches and their human allies. The first book in the series, *Gregor the Overlander*, was published in 2003. Sadly, Collins' father died in March of that year, just before the book came out. The Underland Chronicles were well-received, but Collins' next series, The Hunger Games trilogy, struck a major chord with readers, both the teenaged audience for which it was aimed and a surprise following of adult readers.

Beginning in 2008, with the release of *The Hunger Games*, Collins depicted characters whose lives allowed her to express the full scope of the emotional impact of war on both her father as an adult combatant and her former six-year-old self as a helpless spectator. Readers of the books were given a sense of the emotional turmoil and despair of home-front families helplessly watching warzone media coverage through the frustrated rage and disgust of Katniss and the Panem residents who were required to watch the broadcast of the Games that were taking their children's lives. Collins' father's nightmares and unwillingness to perpetuate needless violence echo in the character of Peeta, Katniss' fellow District 12 tribute and eventual love interest.

Collins had two very firm goals in mind for the books, the first being to challenge what she believed was the growing risk of desensitization of the media-consuming population to images of warfare in an age of blurring lines between information and entertainment. Collins' original inspiration for a story about children fighting in gladiatorial games came from channel surfing between reality shows like *Survivor* and actual news footage of the war in Iraq. She found the ease with which the two could become blended together for viewers "unsettling" and questioned the extent to which people differentiated between war footage and shows for entertainment (Bibliostar).

With the memory of her father's urgency in teaching young people to think critically about war, and being the mother of two children of her own, Collins felt her other goal was to address the concept of war and its costs to children at all reading levels. In an interview with *Time* magazine, Collins says,

> *The Hunger Games* is part of a larger goal I have, which is to write a war-appropriate story for every age of kids ... [I]f I took the 40 years of my dad talking to me about war and battles and taking me to battlefields and distilled it down into one question, it would probably be the idea of the necessary or unnecessary war ... In *The Hunger Games*, in most people's idea, in terms of rebellion or a civil-war situation, that would meet the criteria for a necessary war. These people are oppressed, their children are being taken off and put in gladiator games. They're impoverished, they're starving, they're brutalized. It would for most people be an acceptable situation for rebellion. And then what happens is that it turns back around on itself. If you look at the arenas as individual wars or battles, you start out in the first one and you have a very classic gladiator game. By

the second one it has evolved into what is the stage for the rebellion, because the arena is the one place that all the districts that cannot communicate with each other, it's the one place they can all watch together. So it's where the rebellion blows up. And then the third arena is the Capitol, which has now become an actual war. But in the process of becoming an actual war, in the process of becoming a rebellion, they have now replicated the original arena. So it's cyclical, and it's that cycle of violence that seems impossible for us to break out of. (qtd. in Grossman)

The public was receptive to Collins' message. *The Hunger Games* spent sixteen weeks at as the number one book on *USA Today*'s best-seller list and appeared on *The New York Times* best-seller list for over two hundred consecutive weeks. Over fifty million copies of the trilogy are now in print ("Scholastic"). On the strength of the books' success, Collins was selected as one of *Time* magazine's "100 Most Influential People" for 2010.

The trilogy also led to a four-part movie franchise, beginning in 2012 with *The Hunger Games*, which grossed nearly $690 million worldwide. ("*The Hunger Games*," *Internet Movie Database*). *The Hunger Games: Catching Fire*, released in theaters in 2013, earned a worldwide gross of over $864 million and was the highest grossing U.S. film of that year ("*The Hunger Games: Catching Fire*," *IMDb*). *The Hunger Games: Mockingjay—Part 1* was released in theaters in November 21, 2014 and earned a worldwide gross of over $752 million dollars. ("*The Hunger Games: Mockingjay—Part 1*," Internet Movie Database). The series finale, *The Hunger Games: Mockingjay—Part 2*, was released on November 20, 2015, generating over $646 million in worldwide box office sales.

With the 2013 publication of *The Year of the Jungle*, Collins completed her mission to present the subject of warfare to children in a way that would allow them to engage with it and open up discussion in a far less heart-wrenching and intimidating manner than her own experience. In this way, the story of a moment became a story that now belongs to the world.

Works Cited

"Award-Winning Books by Suzanne Collins." *Fiction DB*. FictionDB. com. n.d. Web. 16 Sept. 2015.

Bibliostar.TV. "Suzanne Collins on the Vietnam War Stories Behind The Hunger Games and *Year of the Jungle*." *Bibliostar.tv*. *YouTube*. 8 Oct. 2012. Web. 16 Sept. 2015.

Biography.com Editors. "Suzanne Collins Biography." *Biography.com*. A&E Television Networks, n.d. Web. 16 Sept. 2015.

Collins, Suzanne. *Year of the Jungle: Memories from the Home Front*. New York: Scholastic, 2013. Print.

Dominus, Susan. "Suzanne Collins' War Stories for Kids." *New York Times Magazine*. The New York Times Company, 8 Apr. 2011. Web. 16 Sept. 2015.

Grossman, Lev. "Writing 'War-Appropriate' Stories for Kids: A Conversation with Suzanne Collins and Francis Lawrence." *Time Magazine*. Time Inc., 19 Nov. 2013. Web. 16 Sept. 2015.

Henthorne, Tom. *Approaching the Hunger Games Trilogy: A Literary and Cultural Analysis*. Jefferson, NC: McFarland, 2012. Print.

"*The Hunger Games*." *Internet Movie Database*. IMDb.com, Inc., n.d. Web. 16 Sept. 2015.

"*The Hunger Games: Catching Fire*." *Internet Movie Database*. IMDb. com, Inc., n.d. Web. 16 Sept. 2015.

"*The Hunger Games: Mockingjay—Part 1*." *Internet Movie Database*. IMDb.com, Inc., n.d. Web. 16 Sept. 2015.

"*The Hunger Games: Mockingjay—Part 2*." *Internet Movie Database*. IMDb.com, Inc., n.d. Web. 16 Sept. 2015.

Hunter, Nick. *Extraordinary Women: Suzanne Collins*. Chicago: Raintree-Capstone Global Library, 2014. Print.

"Michael J. Collins Obituary." *The Montgomery Observer*. The Montgomery Observer, 19 Mar. 2003. Web. 26 Oct. 2015.

"Scholastic Announces Updated U.S. Figures for Suzanne Collins' Best Selling The Hunger Games Trilogy." *Scholastic*. Scholastic, n.d. Web. 16 Sept. 2015.

"Suzanne Collins." *Authors and Artists for Young Adults*. Vol. 86. Detroit: Gale, 2011. *Biography in Context*. Web. 16 Sept. 2015.

"Suzanne Collins (III)." *Internet Movie Database*. IMDb.com, Inc., n.d. Web. 16 Sept. 2015.

Suzannecollinsbooks.com. Scholastic, n.d. Web. 16 Sept. 2015.

This is Teen. "Suzanne Collins Part 3—Desensitization." *YouTube*. YouTube, 18 Aug. 2009. Web. 16 Sept. 2015

_____. "Suzanne Collins Part 9—Languages." *YouTube*. YouTube, 18 Aug. 2009. Web. 16 Sept. 2015.

CRITICAL
CONTEXTS

Lotteries and Scapegoats: Literary Antecedents and Influences on The Hunger Games

Tina L. Hanlon

When a series of novels becomes widely popular, readers are drawn to it partly because it reminds them of other stories they have known. As we enter a book's fantasy world, such as Oz, Middle Earth, or Hogwarts, or a futuristic society such as the Community in Lois Lowry's *The Giver* or Panem in The Hunger Games trilogy, part of the fun of walking around in that new place—or terror, more often, when imagining ourselves in Panem—involves comparing it with other places and events we have known, real or imaginary. In doing so, we learn more about the literary and legendary or historical traditions that the books we are reading grew out of, and marvel at the ways that a successful author creates something new by transforming patterns we have seen in works of the past. Author Jane Yolen wrote, "Stories lean on stories, art on art. This familiarity with the treasure-house of ancient story is necessary for any true appreciation of today's literature" (*Touch Magic* 15). It is especially true with fantasy and science fiction that the strangeness of their imagined societies, creatures, or inventions must be anchored to the familiar, to help us believe in the story we are reading.

Intertextuality is a term postmodern critics have used since the late 1960s for the variety of ways that texts interrelate. When we hear someone say in an advertisement, "May the odds be ever in your favor," we recognize that quotation as an intertextual link with *The Hunger Games*. We can find intertextuality in an author's choice of names, quotations and direct references to other texts, characterization, similar images or events, passages that echo or parody older texts, or general patterns or archetypes that books in the same genre seem to share. For example, two traditions that influence the fate of Katniss and Panem appear in both ancient and modern literature and culture: lotteries that determine who will die and scapegoats that are sacrificed in the belief that this action will protect others or avenge a wrong. Both occur in biblical passages (although casting lots was used for other kinds of decisions as well), such as God's command to Moses in Leviticus 16:8: "And Aaron shall cast lots upon the two goats; one lot for the LORD, and the other lot for the scapegoat" (*The Holy Bible*). While a text can be anything that uses words or other forms of communication, this chapter focuses on the intertextuality of books linked to The Hunger Games series, as well as myths and legends from ancient oral traditions.

Although the postmodern concept of intertextuality allows us to explore connections among texts without direct knowledge of an author's intentions or influences, some literary critics analyze what authors have read and experienced and said about their own works. Suzanne Collins has discussed her favorite books and sources of inspiration in several interviews, and the publisher's Hunger Games web site contains a discussion guide with a page on "Historical and Literary Connections" (Rockman). These sources and other published articles refer to more pre-texts (previous texts related to The Hunger Games) than this essay can discuss. Moreover, readers sometimes find links between texts that authors were not aware of, and as readers, our own interests are likely to guide us through the labyrinth of intertextual threads we might want to follow by comparing stories we read. For example, this chapter has sections on books about Appalachia and the Holocaust, although literature about mining districts, genocide, or totalitarian regimes in other places would work as well.

References to the ancient world appear throughout the trilogy, as Barry Strauss discusses in "The Classical Roots of 'The Hunger Games,'" especially in the many Capitol residents with Roman names and obvious similarities between the deadly "games" in Panem and contests in ancient Roman arenas. Collins explained,

> In keeping with the classical roots, I send my tributes into an updated version of the Roman gladiator games, which entails a ruthless government forcing people to fight to the death as popular entertainment.... Panem itself comes from the expression "Panem et Circenses" which translates into "Bread and Circuses." The audiences

for both the Roman games and reality TV are almost characters in themselves. They can respond with great enthusiasm or play a role in your elimination. ("A Conversation")

Characters who are most responsible for the decadent spectacles of The Hunger Games have names from historical literature about ancient Rome. Cinna, the stylist, transforms Katniss physically into the influential "girl on fire" and the Mockingjay figurehead. Caesar is the flamboyant pre-game interviewer. Plutarch replaces Seneca as head Gamemaker because Seneca is executed when the president, named Coriolanus, is dissatisfied with Katniss' first Hunger Games. Career tributes Cato, Brutus, and Enobaria are vicious fighters in the Games.[1] During the Victory Tour in *Catching Fire*, the party in President Snow's banquet room is much like a traditional Roman banquet, with wealthy guests reclining on couches, extravagant decorations and entertainments, and such an excessive display of foods, gluttony, and drinking that Katniss is sickened by the waste of food.[2] As Emily Gowers explains in *The Loaded Table*, Roman literary sources depicting lavish feasts don't reveal that most Romans actually "lived at subsistence level." Nevertheless, these banquets are "lingering souvenirs of Roman civilization" and "part of its mythology," although some writers, such as Plutarch, disapproved of focusing on bodily needs and pleasures rather than the life of the mind (Gowers 3).

Amalia L. Selle's chapter in this book compares Katniss and Spartacus, as the legendary rebellion of Greek slaves led by Spartacus was a major influence. Collins told *The New York Times Magazine*, "Katniss follows the same arc from slave to gladiator to rebel to face of a war" (Dominus). When asked about her favorite books as a child, Collins began, "I've had a lifelong love of mythology, so I'd have to top the list with *Myths and Enchantment Tales*, by Margaret Evans Price,... and *D'Aulaires' Book of Greek Myths*" ("Suzanne Collins on the Books"). In both books, Collins would have read about proud and independent Atalanta, the fastest runner on earth, who "stood poised like a graceful white bird about to fly" before a race with her suitors (Price 88). Katniss, who competes with men and is represented by bird images throughout the trilogy, is also associated with Artemis (named Diana by the Romans) in her love of hunting and extraordinary skill with bow and arrow. In *D'Aulaires' Book of Greek Myths*, Artemis "wanted to remain forever a wild young maiden hunting through the woods." After she turns an admirer into a stag for invading her private glade and his dogs kill him, she is seen as "a cold and pitiless goddess" (D'Aulaire 44). Although Katniss is not pitiless, she is hard on her male admirers as well as enemies. These same traits of skilled hunter and rebel also connect her with a later English folk hero, Robin Hood. According to legend, he led a band of outlaws in Sherwood Forest, poaching to steal game from the rich and provide food for the poor. Katniss preserves her love of hunting freely in the woods with her friend Gale as long as she can through the trilogy, but society forces her into such absurd and brutal types of hunting in artificial landscapes that all the killing and treachery nearly destroy her spirit.

Collins identified Theseus, a Greek hero who defeated many monsters, as a major influence on The Hunger Games, observing,

> The myth tells how in punishment for past deeds, Athens periodically had to send seven youths and seven maidens to Crete, where they were thrown in the Labyrinth and devoured by the monstrous Minotaur. Even as a kid, I could appreciate how ruthless this was. Crete was sending a very clear message: "Mess with us and we'll do something worse than kill you. We'll kill your children." And the thing is, it was allowed; the parents sat by powerless to stop it. Theseus, who was the son of the king, volunteered to go. I guess in her own way, Katniss is a futuristic Theseus. ("A Conversation")

This myth thus informed the structural outline of Collins' trilogy. Powerful rulers in the Capitol punish the districts for a past rebellion by forcing them to send a prescribed number of their children at specified times into the arena, where unpredictable conditions are as confusing as King Minos' labyrinth. All but one are condemned to certain death while their families and neighbors watch, and Collins adds an additional layer of horror by requiring these young scapegoats to kill each other as well as sending strange invented creatures to complicate their battles. The mythological Greek labyrinth is built by the extraordinary inventor Daedalus, while incredible futuristic technology enables Panem's Gamekeepers to trap the tributes in a variety of cruelly inventive ways. Only an exceptional hero such as Katniss, volunteering like Theseus to take her sister's place as tribute, can break the Capitol's sadistic tradition by saving Peeta as well as herself and later exploding the whole arena with her arrows at the climax of the Quarter Quell, with help from brilliant technicians such as Beetee, "an older inventor" (Collins, *Mockingjay* 11). To help Theseus escape with the other young victims and go on to further adventures as a reforming hero, the princess Ariadne also persuades Daedalus to devise a plan to get Theseus out of the labyrinth using a ball of string. Thus a love story affects the outcome, and Ariadne's price is a promise of marriage that Theseus is not destined to fulfill, just as Peeta and Katniss use their love relationship, with both real and artificial aspects, to thwart their rulers' plans. Lars Schmeink's chapter in this volume discusses other dimensions of Theseus and the labyrinth.

Many of the Roman references overlap with Shakespearean intertextuality, as William Shakespeare wrote plays about Julius Caesar, Coriolanus, and other historical characters who are alluded to in Panem, adapting ancient material from Plutarch's *Lives* and other sources. Barry Strauss, Adam Pulford, and other critics have discussed many names in the Capitol that come from *Julius Caesar*. In Panem, the rival presidents Snow and Coin are betrayed by their own people and killed, like Julius Caesar after he seized power to become a dictator in ancient Rome. Catherine R. Eskin devoted an essay to The Hunger Games series and other history plays by Shakespeare: "The PR Wars: The Hunger Games Trilogy and Shakespeare's Second Henriad." She discusses trilogies by Collins and Shakespeare as they involve political intrigue, propaganda, war, and problems of leadership. Shakespeare explored some of the same issues in *Macbeth* and *Richard III* as well (Rockman).

Some readers think Peeta and Katniss resemble Shakespeare's star-crossed lovers Romeo and Juliet, especially at the end of the first Hunger Games, when they threaten to eat poison berries and die together unless the Capitol lets them both live. Although Katniss never has a very passionate love affair with anyone and can't love either Peeta or Gale as they both love her, her story might be viewed as a kind of *Romeo and Juliet* turned inside out. In Shakespeare's play, Juliet pretends to die because the impulsive lovers are so eager to escape secretly from their feuding noble families to be together right away—and they do end up killing themselves because of mistakes in their plan made by well-meaning adults. Katniss and Peeta, on the other hand, pretend to be lovers to escape death, while adults trying to help them and hurt them encourage them to continue revealing their love affair, engagement, and even a feigned pregnancy for propaganda purposes. It's not pretense for Peeta, and the two do survive and have a marriage of mutual love in the Epilogue. However, it takes Katniss years of recovery from trauma to accept her own potential as a loving wife and mother.

Victorian literature provided Katniss Everdeen's last name (with a little respelling) through Bathsheba Everdene, the heroine of Thomas Hardy's nineteenth-century English novel *Far from the Madding Crowd*. Both characters are proud and independent young women who find themselves taking on responsibilities and physical labor traditionally handled by men. Both are fatherless, and after Bathsheba inherits her uncle's farm, she surprises everyone by deciding to manage it herself. She is also conflicted about several very different men who love and woo her. The awkwardness of her shifting roles and relationships is a little like Katniss' problems with Gale and Peeta, as they are at the same time partners with her in very serious business and potential lovers. Collins said Katniss and Bathsheba "are very different, but both struggle with knowing their hearts" ("Suzanne Collins on the Books"). Bathsheba ends up hiring Gabriel Oak, although she had scorned his marriage proposal before she had a farm and before he lost his own leased farm because of a disastrous mishap with his sheep. After some romantic misadventures and sorrows, followed by a period of isolation and reflection, Bathsheba happily marries faithful, good-hearted Gabriel. Katniss is not as happy when she returns home to live on the ravaged land, in seclusion at first and then with Peeta, who has loved her faithfully since childhood, but in Hardy's early novels such as *Far from the Madding Crowd*, comedy and romance prevail when conflicts are resolved in the rural English communities he depicted.

Hardy's last novels have more in common with Collins' dystopia, since in *Tess of the d'Urbervilles*, *The Woodlanders*, and *Jude the Obscure*, characters who live in more oppressive and unforgiving environments (although still in the same region of southwestern England) suffer much more from bad luck, poverty, unfortunate choices, and social injustice than Gabriel or other earlier characters. Across Europe, nineteenth-century authors wrote realistic novels and short stories that exposed the corruption of old hierarchies and imperialist regimes and revealed the oppression of children, women, and laborers at farms, factories, mines, and railroads as industrialization spread. Their novels were often long— sometimes massive—and many were published first in magazine or newspaper installments, which could be viewed as forerunners of today's fiction series. Many have been adapted in modern media as well, so that Victor Hugo's five-volume *Les Misérables*, for example, is well-known in one of the most popular stage musicals of the late twentieth century.

Some scenes in The Hunger Games seem Dickensian in their treatment of poverty, hunger, and the exploitation of workers, especially in the first book when Katniss introduces the class differences within District 12 and then experiences the outrageously luxurious lifestyle of the wealthy and powerful in the Capitol. Charles Dickens' nineteenth-century English novels exposed harsh working conditions and social inequities suffered by children and adults, some of which his family had experienced in his youth. In Collins' first chapter, Katniss explains that Madge has a relatively comfortable life in town as the mayor's daughter, while workers in the Seam go hungry and resort to black market dealings like London characters in a Dickens novel such as *Oliver Twist*. Katniss realizes that the cost of Madge's mockingjay pin could feed her family for a month, not suspecting that the pin later given to her in friendship would become her own symbol as leader of a sort of peasants' revolt. If there is Dickensian humor or exaggeration in the trilogy, it is mainly in the outlandish fashions and affected behaviors of Capitol residents, while their utter disregard for the lives of district families is abhorrent.

Also in the beginning, Katniss mutters in relation to the fence around Panem, "District Twelve. Where you can starve to death in safety" (Collins, *Hunger Games* 5). But her mother has taught her to hold her tongue to avoid trouble. Oliver Twist, born in a workhouse for the poor and most famous for daring to ask for extra gruel at the orphanage, also starves in places meant to protect him, where a misstep or careless word can bring further deprivations and beatings. The narrator freely expresses Dickens' indignation at adults "whose blood is ice, whose heart is iron" when, for example, Oliver tears "with all the ferocity of famine" into bits of food set aside for a dog, as he starts his new job and the undertaker's wife makes him sleep with coffins (34). Katniss' flashback to the cold day when she was so desperate and weak with hunger that Peeta risked a beating to give her some bread he burned deliberately in his parents' bakery seems most like a melodramatic scene in a Dickens novel. After feeding her family became her job at age eleven, Peeta's mother yelled at Katniss for looking in the trash and wanted the burned bread given to the pigs. While Katniss believed she would die on that day, a stranger saved her with an act of kindness that reverberates throughout their lives after the Hunger Games throw her and Peeta together.

Readers could compare Katniss and Gale's poaching for food, their constant fear of imprisonment or worse, the Peacekeepers' brutal beating of Gale in *Catching Fire*, President Snow's villainous campaign to destroy Katniss, and other injustices in Panem with Hugo's story in *Les Misérables* about Jean Valjean, the mistreated people he helps, and the 1832 student uprising in Paris. After stealing food for his sister and her starving children, Valjean is in and out of prison, even becoming a mayor and wealthy, benevolent factory owner. But his nearly superhuman physical strength betrays his identity when he helps others, while an obsessed police inspector, Javert, pursues him relentlessly as well as spying on the student rebels. Javert finally kills himself after Valjean saves him from execution by the revolutionaries because he can't bear living indebted to the man he has persecuted for years. Katniss encounters similar moral dilemmas and deadly conflicting loyalties in the Hunger Games and the rebellion. Hugo's idealistic student rebels, who nearly all die in Parisian streets, have parallels in the bloody climax of the Panem rebellion at the center of the Capitol.

Collins named another French masterpiece, Émile Zola's *Germinal*, as one of the novels she has read often ("Suzanne Collins on the Books"). Its widely influential depiction of the harsh environment and oppressive working conditions of a mining town in northern France, where the main characters are rescued from a long entrapment underground caused by a political enemy, has parallels in District 12. Since Katniss fears but does not enter the deep mines where her father died, *Germinal* has a different point of view, focusing on a young unemployed railroad worker who becomes a miner and part of a love triangle with a woman who also works in the mine. Étienne becomes a fiery socialist, leads an unsuccessful strike, and loses his job, but he believes that "his reason was ripening, he had sown the wild oats of his spite," and a better organized revolution would arise.

The title's reference to seeds is evoked in a famous passage at the end to express Étienne's faith that the many "mates" working below him, as he walks across the fertile land toward Paris in April, will burst forth like an "avenging army" and "their germination would soon overturn the earth." Collins' books are less optimistic, of course; at the end, the mines are buried, and the top of District 12's earth is turned over for a mass grave, where children play unaware years later. Katniss is disillusioned with organized revolt and avenging armies, but she does gradually plant seeds, literally and figuratively, by finding hope in home, married love, and children. Collins' use of botanical names such as Primrose, Katniss, and Gale Hawthorne, as well as the scruffy cat Buttercup—and Peeta, whose name suggests bread— symbolizes, from beginning to end, the District 12 natives who know how to live off the land with skills learned from their parents, and those who remain are able to rebuild their lives because "whatever has happened, this is our home" (Collins, *Mockingjay* 389).

The basic purposes and processes of the reaping and the Hunger Games remind us of two well-known twentieth-century stories with elusive and symbolic meanings. "The Lottery" by Shirley Jackson and "The Ones Who Walk Away from Omelas" by Ursula K. LeGuin are modern short stories about sacrificing scapegoats for the apparent purpose of benefiting society. LeGuin's 1973 story is sometimes called a work of philosophical fiction because it doesn't develop individual characters or plot as much as it describes circumstances that require us to consider a disturbing ethical question: would we knowingly sacrifice one child if that guaranteed complete happiness for everyone else? The story depicts a beautiful summer festival in a utopian city so perfect that the story asks us to use our own imagination to fill in details or it will sound "like a city in a fairy tale" (LeGuin 226). When they are old enough to understand, citizens learn that their eternal bliss depends on the abuse of one child, kept forever alone in a basement living in filth and torment. Some people walk away from this realization to an unknown place. Collins asks us to imagine a society in which each district is required to sacrifice two of its adolescents every year in order to keep the peace, in which the few who live in luxury make sport of these deaths, while others do as they are ordered and watch the Games on television. In *Mockingjay*, we learn that some citizens, in District 13 and even in the Capitol, have not just walked away but have secretly planned to rebel against this atrocity.

"The Lottery" has more direct links with specific scenes in *The Hunger Games*. Its setting seems so realistic—a traditional American small town—and the ending is so shocking that *The New Yorker* magazine received an unprecedented amount of mail after it was first published in 1948 (Franklin). Some readers asked where this barbaric town was, since the annual lottery described calmly throughout the story seems like an old-fashioned census of some kind, with careful recording of every citizen's name, but it ends with people of all ages stoning one of their neighbors to death, a woman whose name is drawn from slips of paper in a very old box. Conversations during the ceremony and the saying "Lottery in June, corn be heavy soon" hint that this custom might be a remnant of an ancient fertility ritual and that only the oldest citizens, such as Old Man Warner, remember that conducting the lottery faithfully was expected to bring a good harvest (Jackson 27). Calling Panem's lotteries "the reaping" in The Hunger Games suggests a link with agriculture as well, but it's an ironic one since Panem's citizens are not allowed to grow their own food and the purpose of the Hunger Games is to remind them not to rebel against the government that controls their meager food allowances and their lives.

One big difference in these rituals is that Jackson's lottery seems to be part of a democratic process—some bigger towns have discontinued it, although older citizens disapprove of such a change. Attendance is mandatory in both stories, but it is imposed on the citizens of all twelve districts by a ruthless totalitarian regime in The Hunger Games. As chilling as it is to realize at the end that children in "The Lottery" have been gathering rocks to throw at an innocent person, the reaping tradition seems all the more brutal because only young people are chosen and then have to kill each other in order to survive the "games." In "The Lottery," anyone might be selected, but in The Hunger Games, teenagers have increased chances of being chosen each year, and lower class children are more likely to become tributes because they are allowed to enter their names additional times in exchange for extra rations of food for their hungry families, as Katniss has done. Another difference is that "The Lottery" is narrated in a completely impersonal, impassive manner as if describing an ordinary day. Katniss is known for telling the horrors of her life in a matter-of-fact, understated tone, but she is narrator as well as heroine and she tells us how she feels, revealing from the beginning that reaping day could make you "scared out of your wits" and that it upsets Gale (Collins, *Hunger Games* 12). The stoning in "The Lottery" is shocking but ends quickly, unlike the long torturous ordeals of young tributes whose names are drawn in the Hunger Games reaping.

Two English novels written before and after World War II set the stage for many dystopias that followed them: *Brave New World* by Aldous Huxley (1932) and *Nineteen Eighty-Four* by George Orwell (1949). Huxley's title borrows an ironic phrase from Shakespeare's *The Tempest*, uttered in both works by naïve characters who are initiated into worlds where men fight over kingdoms, power, and love relationships. Huxley and Orwell both depicted futuristic worlds centered in England, where advanced technology is used to control the physical lives, minds, and emotions of citizens, enforcing a rigid caste system in *Brave New World* and a Party-based system of social classes in *Nineteen Eighty-Four*. The outsiders, who live more natural lives apart from Huxley's World State, are in a "Savage Reservation" in New Mexico. Thus Huxley used aspects of Native American history, while Collins used Appalachia, to represent sites of marginalized and persecuted traditional cultures that become sources of resistance. Orwell's novel, on Collins' list of books she has read most often, takes place in Airstrip One, established within a new world "superstate" amid the ruins of postwar England, as Panem was built on the ruins of North America after apocalyptic environmental disasters and wars. *Nineteen Eighty-Four* is probably most influential for its creation of the omniscient ruler Big Brother and posters saying "Big Brother is Watching You." The broadcast technology in The Hunger Games that provides surveillance of the districts and requires all citizens to watch whatever the Capitol orders, including the murderous games, is reminiscent of the giant telescreens throughout Airstrip One that monitor everyone's daily lives. Orwell does not reveal whether Big Brother is an actual person, while Katniss endures an increasingly personal struggle against the heartless Panem ruler called President Snow. Amy H. Sturgis' essay in this volume discusses these modern dystopias in more detail.

 Lord of the Flies is another mid-twentieth-century novel that Collins said she has read often ("Suzanne Collins on the Books"). William Golding's 1954 novel was published for adults long before anyone knew that young adults would read scads of dystopian novels written for them in the twenty-first century, and it became popular with young readers as an adventure story about English schoolboys stranded on a tropical island after a plane crash in wartime. It builds on one of the most popular traditions in world literature, the Robinsonnade, named after Daniel Defoe's 1719 novel *Robinson Crusoe*. When Crusoe is stranded on an island for twenty-eight years after a shipwreck and has to teach himself many survival strategies and domestic skills to make the island a good home for himself with crops and pets, he becomes a stronger person, a more devout Christian, and a good British colonialist, taming the wilderness and civilizing a native who becomes his servant. Multitudes of books and modern films and television shows have continued our fascination with this idea of surviving such an ordeal in a wild place. *The Coral Island* by Scottish author R. M. Ballantyne (1857) is the main pretext for *Lord of the Flies*. It's a traditional adventure novel, but it was unusual in its time for depicting a group of boys by themselves, and Golding parodied it by creating boys with some of the same names who don't stay so civilized on their island. As in *Robinson Crusoe*, Ballantyne's boys are depicted as morally superior to the cannibals and pirates they encounter. Golding challenged beliefs in childhood innocence and the goodness of nature's influence that were so strong from the Romantic period through the twentieth century, showing that boys in an unknown natural environment could become power-hungry, divisive, superstitious, and even sadistic and violent. After being rescued at the end by officers who disapprove of the poor "show" that "a pack of British boys" have made, Ralph, who tried to be a rational leader, "wept for the end of innocence, the darkness of man's heart, and the fall through the air of the true, wise friend called Piggy" (Golding 202).

The Hunger Games place the tributes in a vast arena where they struggle to survive in artificial wilderness settings, never knowing what environmental, manufactured, or human dangers they will encounter at any moment. They are cut off from their society like castaways in a Robinsonnade, except that all of Panem watches them on television and sponsors who decide they are worthy of help can send gifts, like castaways hoping for rescue. This futuristic technology makes the Games like an extreme, sadistic version of the long-running international television reality show *Survivor* (which began in Sweden with the title *Expedition Robinson* in 1997). Like *Survivor* contestants, stranded young victims in The Hunger Games and *Lord of the Flies* develop alliances and deadly enemies as their skills and inner nature are revealed and tested. Katniss grieving for the death of her ally Rue could be compared with Ralph mourning the loss of his supporter Piggy, an underdog who is killed in a struggle over his glasses. Tributes in the Hunger Games know going in that a corrupt government is forcing them to kill each other, while Golding was more interested in showing how evil within human nature would emerge when the boys were unexpectedly on their own in nature. Some of the boys develop paranoid beliefs in a monster they call "the beast" and make sacrifices to it. Since they find the corpse of a fighter pilot in a tree after a battle in the sky overhead and think it's the beast, this military image, along with the war references at beginning and end, suggests that adults and their political conflicts are to blame for stranding and perhaps corrupting these boys; however, before Simon is killed in the frenzy over this beast, he is Golding's mouthpiece for the realization that the beast is within.

In *Mockingjay*, when the rebellion organizers assign Katniss to squad 451, a sharpshooter and disinformation team, the squad number creates an intertextual link with another twentieth-century dystopia, *Fahrenheit 451* by Ray Bradbury. In Bradbury's futuristic society, firemen seek out and burn books, supposedly at the temperature of 451°F. In Panem, citizens are compelled to watch disturbing broadcasts to scare them into submission and squad 451 produces dramatic video promos to encourage all districts to rebel, while in *Fahrenheit 451*, citizens who are prohibited from reading to protect them from becoming discontented with their lives are kept docile with drugs and bland programming on their "parlor walls." These big-screen wall televisions were a science fiction novelty in the early days of broadcast media, the era in which this novel was published. Bradbury's main character, a fireman, does start hiding and reading books, just as Katniss and Gale break the rules to feed their families and then participate in a rebellion. In both works, the homes and cities of some of the people who rebel are burned and bombed.

Fire and birds are symbolic in both as well, with Bradbury's phoenix and Collins' mockingjay representing rebels. In Panem, headquarters for the rebellion are in District 13, which has managed to stay hidden in elaborate underground buildings for some years. Guy Montag, the fireman in *Fahrenheit 451*, finds his way to a secret society wandering in the countryside, where each person memorizes a book to ensure that it survives into the future. Although literature is not as important in Panem, the ballads Katniss memorized in childhood are essential to her survival from trauma, and books are part of the return to better lives. Characters mention that they want to revive their ancestors' representative government as recorded in books. Katniss carefully preserves her mother's book of medicinal plants—"the place where we recorded those things you cannot trust to memory"—and starts a memory book to honor all those killed from District 12 (Collins, *Mockingjay* 387).

Bradbury's images of book burning and nuclear war grew out of World War II, like the backdrop of *Lord of the Flies*. Many aspects of The Hunger Games are reminiscent of the Holocaust and wars fought in the past hundred years. From the beginning, the electric fence around District 12, where hungry people are essentially slave labor and are punished brutally for disobedience while those in power live in luxury, brings to mind Jewish ghettos, concentration camps, and Nazi domination in World War II. Other parallels include forcing citizens to betray each other and kill others or be killed, suppression of cultural traditions to protect one's family from persecution, political propaganda, underground resistance movements, spying and shifting alliances, bombings that create bleak wastelands in towns and cities, and mass graves for the victims. In *Mockingjay*, shuffling refugees in the Capitol expecting the president to find them a new residence are like Holocaust victims who were lied to when they were relocated, with millions sent to ghettos and death camps (338). As Susan Dominus discusses, Collins was heavily influenced by what she learned from and about her male relatives' experiences in war; her family lived in Belgium for five years, and her father's recitation of the World War I poem "In Flanders Fields" made her envision a poppy field she saw in Belgium as a possible gravesite rather than something out of *The Wizard of Oz*.

The complete destruction of District 12 as punishment for rebellion might remind us of Lidice, Czechoslovakia, a village destroyed by Nazis as an act of revenge in 1942 after erroneous accusations that linked it with the assassination of an important Nazi. The police are ironically called Peacekeepers in Panem, and the Nazi ruler who was murdered was a *Reichsprotektor* or "Reich Protector" in one of the occupied regions called Protectorates. *Someone Named Eva* by Joan M. Wolf is a novel about one child of Lidice. The men of her village are killed and most of the women and girls sent to concentration camps, but blond, blue-eyed Milada has very specific physical features preferred by the Nazis, so she is taken to harsh Lebensborn training centers where she is "Germanized": renamed Eva, she nearly forgets her native language and culture before being adopted by a German family. After the war, her mother finds her and helps her recover her identity. Although Milada is more naïve and compliant because she is younger, Katniss' struggles with alterations to her body and behavior for both the Hunger Games and the rebellion, as well as the Capitol's imprisonment and brainwashing of Peeta in order to destroy Katniss and the rebels, have some parallels with Nazi kidnappings and torture.

Uri Orlev, one of the first to write children's books about the Holocaust in the 1950s, has been a prolific and widely admired Israeli author since then. He was rescued from the Warsaw Ghetto during World War II after his mother died there, and later from Bergen-Belsen concentration camp. *The Man from the Other Side*, based on a true story from a man Orlev met, depicts a teenager who helps his stepfather smuggle food into the Warsaw Ghetto in Poland, where Jews are confined. The novel begins with these unlawful acts, like Katniss and Gale poaching to feed their families and dealing on the black market. In both stories, some people take advantage of secret transactions to make money, while others have good motives for helping the oppressed. Marek in Orlev's novel, like Katniss, misses his father, a Communist who believed everyone should have enough to eat and died working for the underground resistance. After finding out his father was Jewish, Marek gets involved in a rebellion as Katniss does—not exactly intentionally, but after helping a Jew find his way through the labyrinthine sewers, Marek is stranded in the ghetto and ends up fighting with guns in the famous Warsaw uprising of 1944. Some of the atrocities Katniss abhors are similar to Marek's repugnance at the cramped underground bunker where families hide, his ordeal with a young friend who is killed, the disappointing end of the brave rebellion, the smoke rising from ghetto ruins as bystanders watch while people die, and the brutality of Nazi conquerors with vast troops and weaponry. Like Katniss, Marek survives, disillusioned, and moves away to a quieter life.

Collins named *Boris*, a Dutch novel by Jaap ter Haar, as a favorite book of her childhood, saying "I still think [it] is one of the best war stories written for kids" ("Suzanne Collins on the Books"). Boris is a twelve-year-old during the Siege of Leningrad on the Eastern Front in late 1942. His story, like Katniss', begins with nightmares about the death of his father doing a dangerous job. While the city starves, men drive trucks over the frozen lake to get food. Because his father's truck went down, Boris is terrified of the ice, as Katniss hates thinking of mines and caves or having to stay underground. Some parts of The Hunger Games books were likely influenced by this novel's descriptions of frequent bombings, Boris ordeals to obtain meager food rations each day for his weak mother and himself, the deaths of friends from starvation and violence, mass graves, and postwar rebuilding. Somewhat like Katniss and Gale's illegal hunting, Boris and his friend Nadia are so desperate for food that they sneak into forbidden territory to dig for potatoes in No-man's-land between the Russian and German lines. When Nadia collapses in the cold and a German soldier risks capture to carry her back to the city, Boris' perceptions of the enemy and human nature are transformed, just as Katniss finds unexpected allies and acts of compassion during the Games and rebellion. Nadia's death is a blow to Boris as Prim's is to Katniss after all they suffered together, but they both control their bitterness and believe that life goes on.

Germinal was not Collins' only source of inspiration for depicting a coal mining region, as Katniss mentions early in the first book that District 12 used to be called Appalachia (even though other districts' locations are not identified so explicitly). Depictions of Katniss' home and family history are consistent with some of the cultural traditions and economic problems of Appalachian mining communities. Within the first few pages of *The Hunger Games*, we know that Katniss still has nightmares about her father being blown to bits in a mine accident when she was eleven, that he had taught her to hunt and sing ballads, and that the miners who work so hard at dangerous jobs live in a dingy area called the Seam, where their families go hungry and coal dust is "in every crack and crevice" (131). Many Appalachian books depict mining towns and mine accidents like the one Katniss relives in *Mockingjay* when the rebels' plan to blow up an army hiding inside a mountain reminds her of her father's death. In Lee Smith's compelling novel *Fair and Tender Ladies*, Ivy Rowe lives in a southwestern Virginia coal town during part of her youth, but when a mine disaster kills her friend's husband and makes her realize she loves a young man from home, they return to a farming life in their mountain homeplace. James Still's two novels, *River of Earth* for adults and *Sporty Creek* for children, contain some of the bleakest descriptions of coal camps that opened and closed during the Great Depression based on the needs of owners and markets far away.[3] In the ramshackle camp Low Glory, in *Sporty Creek*, no one cares to maintain the place decently as neighbors die of lung diseases, mine owners and thieves dismantle everything when the mines close, and neighbors throw rocks at the windows as soon as someone moves out.

In 1959, before social realism was common in children's books, Lois Lenski added *Coal Camp Girl* to her series of regional novels after visiting mines, coal companies, and homes in West Virginia. Her nine-year-old protagonist's family and neighbors don't have enough to eat when the mine closes; her uncle is injured in a mine accident and her father barely escapes from one. In *Catching Fire*, "things go from bad to worse" as the government uses mine closings, food shortages, more dangerous working conditions, pay decreases, and harsh punishments for minor offenses to discourage rebellion in District 12 (132). When real people rebelled in Appalachia, organization of unions resulted in violent "mine wars" in the first half of the twentieth century. In *Billy Creekmore: A Novel* by Tracey Porter, a boy and some men die in a mine accident clearly caused by the coal company's unwillingness to implement safety precautions in a deteriorating section mined by Polish workers. Katniss worries that something like this will happen to Gale in District 12. As soon as word of union organizing leaks out in Billy Creekmore's West

Virginia coal camp, he sees a family being evicted and sent away with no money or possessions, scapegoats persecuted to warn others suspected of joining unions; then Billy's uncle and another young friend are killed by hired gun thugs.

Mine closings also cause hardships in *The Miner's Daughter* by Gretchen Moran Laskas. The teenage protagonist finds an old woman who knows herbal medicine, like Katniss' mother, to help her mother with childbirth when the doctor won't help a miner's wife. Willa breaks the rules when her family is destitute by dressing as a boy to participate in harvesting in the fields. In their West Virginia town, hardly any plants or animals can thrive because trees were cut and mining pollutes, but Willa and her older brother feel most at home when they take refuge in the beautiful woods, like Katniss and Gale. Elizabeth O. Dulemba's recent novel *A Bird on Water Street* shows how copper mining destroyed the lives of all plants and animals and many humans throughout the middle of the twentieth century in an eastern Tennessee town. Other aspects of Appalachian culture reflected in The Hunger Games trilogy are discussed in Elizabeth Baird Hardy's chapter in this book.[4]

In *Approaching The Hunger Games Trilogy: A Literary and Cultural Analysis,* Tom Henthorne's section on "Sampling, Remix, and Intertextuality" contains a clever narrative summation of Collins' plot as a reworking or remix of many sources (including some not discussed here). Henthorne places considerable emphasis on contemporary debates about ideas of authorship and originality, and where to draw the line "between plagiarism and intertextuality" (153). There may be validity in his use of media theory to show that "digital age readers" are more accustomed to derivative creations (151–52), but postmodern literature since the middle of the twentieth century has experimented with intertextuality, multiple points of view, word play, fictionalizing history, magic realism, and other strategies that expose the instability and interdependence of texts. Thus extensive use of intertextuality is not new in the twentieth-first century and questioning the author's originality seems unnecessary. All the historical fiction discussed in this chapter has complex source materials. And last year was the 150th anniversary of a major landmark in the creation of fantasy for children, the publication of *Alice in Wonderland*. Lewis Carroll filled Wonderland with allusions to folklore, history, and English culture, including parodies of specific popular poems and songs. A masterpiece from the other end of the Golden Age of children's literature, *The Secret Garden* by Frances Hodgson Burnett (1911), has plotlines very similar to parts of beloved works of the previous century, *Heidi* and *Jane Eyre*. Louisa May Alcott built the plot, chapter titles, and themes of *Little Women* around Bunyan's *Pilgrim's Progress*, and the Robinsonnade tradition discussed above shows that imitation with variations continues to produce many excellent works of literature (as well as cheap imitations and rip-offs).

Without claiming that The Hunger Games trilogy will be ranked with these classic novels a hundred years from now, it can be said that Collins used intertextuality to create an intriguing story about atrocities of totalitarianism, economic injustice, and war by evoking some of the most outrageous aspects of popular culture and politics in our time and blending them with many echoes from the historical and literary past. In another version of Jane Yolen's comment on the storyteller's and writer's art cited earlier, Yolen wrote, "There is an eclecticism to modern telling. Stories lean on stories, art on art. I can only trace my own sources so far before I realize that, in the end, it is the story that matters, not the parts: the tapestry of the tale and not the individual threads" (*Tales of Wonder* xi–xii).

Notes

1. Lana A. Whited's review of the first Hunger Games film notes that "Unlikeable characters generally have names drawn from mythology," or from predatory and sterile aspects of nature, while "admirable characters have names derived from nature" (330).

2. See Raff for illustrated background on Roman banquets.

3. *River of Earth* has often been compared to John Steinbeck's *The Grapes of Wrath*. Some critics argue that Still's novel would be more widely known as an American masterpiece about economic injustice and struggles of poor workers during the Great Depression if *The Grapes of Wrath* had not been published a little earlier and received

such critical acclaim. Rockman recommends *The Grapes of Wrath* as a modern literary connection to discuss with *The Hunger Games*.

4.   See also my essay "Coal Dust and Ballads: Appalachia and District 12" and my online study guide, "Appalachia in The Hunger Games Trilogy by Suzanne Collins."

Works Cited

Ballantyne, R. M. *The Coral Island*. 1857. New York: Penguin, 1995. Print.

Bradbury, Ray. *Fahrenheit 451*. 1953. New York: Simon & Schuster, 2013. Print.

Carroll, Lewis. *The Annotated Alice in Wonderland*. Illus. John Tenniel. Ed. Martin Gardner. Rev. ed. New York: Penguin, 1970. Print.

Collins, Suzanne. *Catching Fire*. New York: Scholastic, 2009. Print.

_____. "A Conversation: Questions and Answers." Interview. *Scholastic.com*. Scholastic, Inc., 2015. Web. 31 Jul. 2015.

_____. *The Hunger Games*. New York: Scholastic, 2008. Print.

_____. *Mockingjay*. New York: Scholastic, 2010. Print.

_____. "Suzanne Collins on the Books She Loves." Interview by Tina Jordan. *EW.com: Entertainment Weekly*. Entertainment Weekly, 13 Aug. 2010. Web. 6 Feb. 2016.

D'Aulaire, Ingri, and Edgar Parin. *D'Aulaires' Book of Greek Myths*. Garden City, NJ: Doubleday, 1962. Print.

Defoe, Daniel. *Robinson Crusoe*. 1719. New York: Bantam, 1991. Print.

Dickens, Charles. *Oliver Twist*. 1838. New York: Quality Paperback Book Club, 1997. Print.

Dominus, Susan. "Suzanne Collins' War Stories for Kids." *New York Times Magazine*. The New York Times Company, 8 Apr. 2011. Web. 2 Aug. 2015.

Dulemba, Elizabeth O. *A Bird on Water Street*. San Francisco: Little Pickle Press, 2013. Print.

Eskin, Catherine R. "The PR Wars: The Hunger Games Trilogy and Shakespeare's Second Henriad." Pharr and Clark 179-89.

Franklin, Ruth. "'The Lottery' Letters." *The New Yorker*. Condé Nast, 25 June 2013. Web. 15 Nov. 2015.

Golding, William. *Lord of the Flies*. New York: Putnam Perigee, 1954. Print.

Gowers, Emily. *The Loaded Table: Representations of Food in Roman Literature*. Oxford, UK: Oxford UP, 1993. Print.

Hanlon, Tina L. "Appalachia in The Hunger Games Trilogy by Suzanne Collins." *AppLit: Resources for Readers and Teachers of Appalachian Literature for Children and Young Adults*. Ferrum College, 2015. Web. 10 Nov. 2015. Print.

_____. "Coal Dust and Ballads: Appalachia and District 12." Pharr and Clark 59-68.

Hardy, Thomas. *Far from the Madding Crowd*. 1874. London: Macmillan, 1974. Print.

Henthorne, Tom. *Approaching The Hunger Games Trilogy: A Literary and Cultural Analysis*. Jefferson, NC: McFarland, 2012. Print.

The Holy Bible: Containing the Old and New Testaments Translated Out of the Original Tongues. Cambridge, UK: Cambridge UP, 1995. Web. 2 Aug. 2015.

Hugo, Victor. *Les Misérables*. 1862. Transl. Charles E. Wilbour. New York: Modern Library, 1992. Print.

Huxley, Aldous. *Brave New World*. 1932. New York: Harper & Row, 1969. Print.

Jackson, Shirley. "The Lottery." *The New Yorker* 26 June 1948: 25–28. Print.

Laskas, Gretchen Moran. *The Miner's Daughter*. New York: Simon & Schuster, 2007. Print.

LeGuin, Ursula K. "The Ones Who Walk Away from Omelas." 1973. *The Broadview Anthology of Short Fiction*. Ed. Julia Gaunce, et al. 2nd ed. Buffalo: Broadview Press, 2012. 224–30. Print.

Lenski, Lois. *Coal Camp Girl*. Philadelphia: Lippincott, 1959. Print.

Lowry, Lois. *The Giver*. New York: Bantam Doubleday Dell, 1993. Print.

Orlev, Uri. *The Man from the Other Side*. New York: Puffin, 1989. Print.

Orwell, George. *Nineteen Eighty-Four: A Novel*. 1949. London: Penguin, 1954. Print.

Pharr, Mary, and Leisa A. Clark, eds. *Of Bread, Blood, and The Hunger Games: Critical Essays on the Suzanne Collins Trilogy*. Jefferson, NC: McFarland, 2012. Print.

Porter, Tracey. *Billy Creekmore: A Novel*. New York: Joanna Cotler Books, 2007. Print.

Price, Margaret Evans. *Myths and Enchantment Tales*. New York: Rand McNally, 1956. Print.

Pulford, Adam. "'May the odds be ever in your favour': The Language of The Hunger Games." *Oxford Dictionaries*. Oxford UP, 5 Sept. 2012. Web. 5 Aug. 2015.

Raff, Katherine. "The Roman Banquet." *The Metropolitan Museum of Art*. The Metropolitan Museum of Art, 2015. Web. 3 Aug. 2015.

Rockman, Connie. "Discussion Guide: The Hunger Games Trilogy." *Scholastic.com*. Scholastic, Inc., 2015. Web. 29 July 2015.

Shakespeare, William. *Julius Caesar*. New York: Bantam, 1988. Print.

_____. *Romeo and Juliet*. New York: Bantam, 1988. Print.

Still, James. *River of Earth*. 1940. Lexington: UP of Kentucky, 1978. Print.

_____. *Sporty Creek*. 1977. Lexington: UP of Kentucky, 1999. Print.

Smith, Lee. *Fair and Tender Ladies*. New York: Putnam, 1988. Print.

Strauss, Barry. "The Classical Roots of 'The Hunger Games.'" *The Wall Street Journal*. Dow Jones, 13 Nov. 2014. Web. 31 July 2015.

ter Haar, Jaap. *Boris*. 1966. Trans. Martha Mearns. New York: Harcourt Brace, 1994. Print.

Whited, Lana A. "Rev. of *The Hunger Games*. Dir. Gary Ross." *Journal of Appalachian Studies* 18 (2012): 326–31. *Academic Search Complete*. Web. 12 Nov. 2015.

Wolf, Joan M. *Someone Named Eva*. Boston: Houghton Mifflin Harcourt, 2007. Print.

Yolen, Jane. *Tales of Wonder*. New York: Schocken Books, 1983. Print.

_____. *Touch Magic*. 1981. Rev. ed. Little Rock: August House, 2000. Print.

Zola, Émile. *Germinal*. 1885. Trans. Havelock Ellis. Amazon Digital Services, 2014. Ebook.

Dystopian Copycat or YA Lit on Fire? The Critical Reception of The Hunger Games Novels

Lana A. Whited

Critical Reputation: A Primer

As this is a volume intended primarily for undergraduate and advanced high school students, it may be useful to discuss how critical reputation is assessed. Who are the players in the overall act of assessing a book, and what are their roles? What is the difference between a book critic and a literary scholar?

Even before a book is released, the publisher (Scholastic, in the case of *The Hunger Games, Catching Fire*, and *Mockingjay*) develops a marketing plan that includes sending out advance copies to people in a position to recommend books to others, especially if they will recommend them to large audiences in a publication such as a newspaper, magazine, or journal. Publishers provide free copies to these publications.

Reviewers generally fall into two categories. Some are staff members at newspapers or magazines (print, online, or both) and usually have at least an undergraduate degree in a field involving writing, such as journalism or English; they may also have expertise in a certain area and write reviews about that area, such as food or film. If they are specifically assigned to write reviews, they may write many each month. A well-known and well-respected writer at a major publication can really boost a book's sales with a positive review. In July 2014, former *Roanoke Times* reporter Beth Macy published her first book, *Factory Man*. The book got much attention early on, and Macy got a number of national interviews because of high praise from *New York Times* reviewer Janet Maslin, who wrote in her Summer Books Survey, "Early warning: 'Factory Man' (coming July 15) is an illuminating, deeply patriotic David vs. Goliath book. They give out awards for this kind of thing." Some reviews are written by other authors, and some of the early reviews of *The Hunger Games* were written by very prominent authors: John Green (*The Fault in Our Stars*), horror novelist Stephen King, and Rick Riordan (the Percy Jackson and Kane Chronicles series).

Although scholars also write reviews sometimes, their work has less impact on a book's success because scholarly reviews are seldom published close to the time of the book's publication; scholars usually write for professional journals published one, two, or four times a year. Scholars have graduate degrees (a master's and perhaps also a doctorate) and are generally asked to review new books only in their specific areas of expertise. Of greater significance than their reviews is the original writing scholars produce, based on their own research questions; just as a medical researcher might examine tissue samples to look for the presence of a particular disease, a literary researcher might examine a book to look for the presence of certain ideas or patterns. Writing based on this research is called literary scholarship or literary criticism, although "criticism" in this context can be misleading. To say that a scholar writes literary criticism does not mean that he or she only makes negative comments about a book; rather, it suggests that the scholar makes a thorough examination of a text with a goal in mind, such as discussing what attitudes toward slavery Mark Twain includes in *Adventures of Huckleberry Finn*. Combining the work of many literary scholars writing about the same book (or series) can help to determine its overall value.

Artistic works, including books, are judged according to two criteria: literary quality and popularity. Quality evaluations involve scholarly criteria and are generally made by experts, and assessments of popularity involve everyone who buys, reads, or recommends a book. In addition to reviews, criteria used to determine quality include awards and prizes given by boards and organizations, most private, and based on a pre-established set of criteria (such as the aspects of literature taught to students in a literature course). In the United States, the major literary awards are the Pulitzer prizes, which are awarded in a variety of categories (some non-literary) and the National Book Awards. For the most part, these awards and prizes are qualitative measures of a book's success, but some, such as the Costa Award in the United Kingdom, also take into account a book's popularity.

Lists of notable books are usually measures of popularity when they are based exclusively on sales or polls of readers. (They may also be compiled by reviewers; Janet Maslin compiles a "Best Books of—" list at the end of every year.) Lists are usually published by organizations and publications, and the most prestigious such list in North American publishing is the "*New York Times* Best Sellers," for which books are chosen in several categories. On special occasions, an organization or publication may compile a special list, such as the Modern Library list of Top 100 Books of the Twentieth Century, released at the turn of the twenty-first century.[1] In a contrast of qualitative and populist assessments, Modern Library compiled both a list voted on by its editorial board and a list selected by readers. The board selected Irish writer James Joyce's *Ulysses* as its top selection, while readers chose Ayn Rand's *Atlas Shrugged*. Rand had three novels on the top ten in the reader's list; Joyce's *Ulysses* was number eleven. No Ayn Rand novel appeared on the editorial board's top one hundred. Thus, a book's critical success and its popular success may be very different.

Another group of people who influence a book's reputation are those who put books in readers' hands or recommend them, including librarians, teachers, and bookstore employees. An example described later in this essay involves a middle school English teacher who was urged to read *The Hunger Games* by a bookstore clerk. This category reflects measures of both quality and popularity, as teachers, librarians, and bookstore employees have opinions about books shaped by both sets of criteria and may also have varying levels of expertise. They may read reviews or the recommendations of professional organizations such as the American Library Association, but they also pay attention to book lists and to what young readers are buying or borrowing.

Thus, a critical reputation is a stew containing ingredients from many sources, some experts and some not. What, then, are the elements of The Hunger Games series' critical reputation?

The Hunger Games and the Dystopian Surge

It is both common knowledge and common sense that the trend in dystopian novels for middle grade and young adult readers surged in the aftermath of the Sept. 11, 2001 terrorist attacks on the United States, as adults considered how to discuss with young people the dark themes resonating from those events. In "Engaging 'Apolitical' Adolescents: Analyzing the Popularity and Educational Potential of Dystopian Literature Post-9/11," Melissa Ames writes, "the popularity of young adult dystopian literature, which is ripe with these political themes, suggests that this group is actually quite interested in these topics, although they often turn to the safe confines of fiction to wrestle with them." Reviewing *The Hunger Games* and another novel in November 2008 in *The New York Times*, John Green notes that more than a dozen post-apocalyptic novels for young readers were published in that year alone and cites *The Hunger Games* and Susan Beth Pfeffer's *The Dead and Gone* as among the best. In *Publisher's Weekly*, Megan Whalen Turner writes that the series follows "a long tradition of Brave New Worlds." Coming somewhat late to the Hunger Games series after all the novels were published, Charles de Lint writes in *The Magazine of Fantasy and Science Fiction*, "dystopian fiction is really on the upsurge (we probably have Suzanne Collins to thank for that with the success of The Hunger Games)" (38).

Suzanne Collins herself downplays her own role in the dystopian fiction trend. Asked about her contribution to that trend by fellow author Lev Grossman (author of The Magicians trilogy) when the *Catching Fire* film was released, Collins said,

> I just think the dystopian stories are striking a nerve with people right now, and *The Hunger Games* contributed somewhat to that, but that can't be the whole explanation for it.... I think people respond to dystopian stories because they're ways of acting out anxieties that we have and fears that we have about the future. (Collins, and Lawrence, "Gamekeepers")

The average person now processes so much information about the world coming from so many sources, says Collins, that "your brain gets overloaded," and one way of processing the issues involved is to read a story depicting those issues (Collins, "Gamekeepers").

In an essay for *Utopian and Dystopian Writing for Children and Young Adults* (2013), Kay Sambell writes that the difference between dystopian writing for young readers and dystopian writing for adults is that authors of the former are "reluctant to depict the extinction of hope within their stories" (qtd. in Miller). Authors writing dystopia for adults, on the other hand, know that "The more utterly the protagonist is crushed, the more urgent and forceful the message" of warning about "how terrible things will become if our deplorable behavior continues unchecked" (qtd. in Miller). Thus, if a protagonist such as Katniss, who has received what mythologist Joseph Campbell would term "the call to action," can engage the forces darkening the human landscape and return it to something better than her life before the call, then maybe the apocalypse wasn't completely bad after all.

In her *New Yorker* exploration of the success of Collins' saga, "Fresh Hell," Laura Miller articulates why dystopia resonates particularly with the tween and teen set. "Dystopian fiction may be the only genre written for children that's routinely less didactic than its adult counterpart," Miller writes. "It's not about persuading the reader to stop something terrible from happening—it's about what's happening, right this minute, in the stormy psyche of the adolescent reader." Miller notes that author Scott Westerfield has attributed the success of his "Uglies" series to the fact that the high school experience is largely a dystopia. The same notion applies to the actual Hunger Games—the competition—according to Miller, who argues that only if a reader views the experience of the participants as "a fever-dream allegory of the adolescent social experience" does it really become "intelligible." Viewed in other ways—as "totalitarian spectacle," for example—the Games lack "ideological coherence," as no regime should really hope to degrade and dehumanize its subjects by turning twenty-four young people into media celebrities every year or hope to hold off rebellion by forcing its subjects' children into mortal combat. If psychologist Bruno Bettelheim was right that children view the disturbing aspects of folk tales differently from adult listeners or readers, and if Christina Chant Sullivan, an English teacher who has taught *The Hunger Games* to seventh-grade boys in a private school setting, is right that "tweens" view the difficult aspects of "real" life—including violence—differently from adults, then perhaps Laura Miller is right that tween and teen readers so identify with Katniss because her quest is truly "a fever-dream allegory" of their journey from childhood to adulthood. What theme is more native to adolescence, after all, than figuring out how to deal with the authority figures threatening to ruin one's life? Says Miller: "The typical arc of the dystopian narrative mirrors the course of adolescent disaffection."

On another level from the allegory of adolescence, of course, these dystopian narratives constitute indictments—and not only of autocrats and dictators; the scope of the social criticism in dystopian fiction is generally broad enough to include the audience. Indeed, in the Hunger Games trilogy, Suzanne Collins foregrounds the audience, first and foremost in the citizens of the Capitol who serve as spectators for the Games and, in a secondary manner, in the audience for the narrative itself. (Of course, the citizens of the districts are also spectators, but they have little choice.) If the function of literature is, as Aristotle wrote in the *Poetics*, imitation, or, in Hamlet's words, "to hold, as 'twere, the mirror up to nature" (III.2), the purpose of dystopian literature appears to be holding something like a funhouse mirror up to life, so that the viewer sees everything in disturbing distortion. Ian Chipman writes that while the Hunger Games novels are, for young readers, "excellent escapist fare rife with survivalist adventure and grim imaginings of future worlds," they also provide "an opportunity to reflect on how the issues in their own lives and societies are mirrored in these worlds gone horribly wrong." Megan Whalen Turner explains that every culture projects its fears through its popular culture; reality television is this generation's means of transmission. Thus, says Turner,

> It's no accident that these games are presented as pop culture…. The State of Panem—which needs to keep its tributaries subdued and its

citizens complacent—may have created the Games, but mindless television is the real danger, the means by which society pacifies its citizens and punishes those who fail to conform.

Turner questions whether this connection with reality TV will eventually date The Hunger Games series, "but for now," she says, "it makes this the right book at the right time." Turner cautions about "what happens if we choose entertainment over humanity…. It isn't just the contestants who risk the loss of their humanity. It is all who watch."

Part of the success of Collins' fictional "world gone wrong," says Katie Roiphe, a *New York Times* reviewer, is that Suzanne Collins can view her fictional universe dispassionately; Collins, Roiphe writes, is "not an author to delicately avert her gaze." Other reviewers have praised Collins' emotional steadiness. Reviewers such as Andrew Stuttaford (*National Review*) and Gabrielle Zevin (*New York Times*) note that Collins' willingness to write the brutal beatings of sympathetic and popular characters (e.g., Cinna and Gale) and even their deaths (e.g., Finnick Odair, Primrose Everdeen) is a compelling aspect of the series' realism: "The brutality is inclusive. Sympathetic characters do not escape Collins' chopping block" (Stuttaford 44-5). Zevin writes in her review of *Catching Fire* that this aspect of Collins' method contributes to the suspense for readers: "Panem feels like a place where anything might happen, and where a reader will want to return to see what happens next." Perhaps the best example of the author's steely-eyed approach is the story's basic premise; as James Delingpole describes it, "When you start the book you say to yourself, 'Nah. It's never going to happen. No way in a children's book is the author going to allow 23 kids between 12 and 17 to die in myriad horrid ways…' But then, one by one, they do."

Suzanne Collins as Gamemaker
Interviewing Suzanne Collins just as the *Catching Fire* film adaptation was released, author Lev Grossman asked the author which *Hunger Games* character she relates to best. Collins says that whereas

she feels that she and Katniss share some traits, the character she most identifies with is Plutarch Heavensbee, the Gamemaker. Her explanation is entirely logical: a novelist is essentially a Gamemaker, calling all the shots with regard to the characters. "[I]f you look at it from a creative perspective," Collins says, "we're really doing the same job."

Collins' plotting and pacing ability as fictional "gamemaker"— the fabler behind the series—is one of the most frequently praised aspects of her novels' reviews. John Green calls *The Hunger Games* "brilliantly plotted and perfectly paced." In an otherwise tepid review (more on that later), author Stephen King writes, "I couldn't stop reading." "Reading *The Hunger Games* is as addictive," King says, "as playing one of those shoot-it-if-it-moves videogames in the lobby of the local eightplex; you know it's not real, but you keep plugging in quarters anyway." James Delingpole recognizes the addictive quality of Collins' narrative: "*The Hunger Games* is the kiddie-lit equivalent of crack cocaine: whoof, one taste, and that's it—your next twenty-four hours are wiped out in a frenzy of page-turning." Delingpole praises the plot, although his overall review is as lukewarm as King's: "it's not literature at all. But you only realise this when you've reached the increasingly feeble second and third books in the trilogy. With the first one you're too gripped by the storyline to care."

Unlike Delingpole, many reviewers feel that the series only improved with the publication of *Catching Fire*. In a *Horn Book* review, Jonathan Hunt writes that *Catching Fire* is "a page-turning blend of plot and character with an inventive setting and provocative themes." Susan Carpenter writes of *Catching Fire*, "Beyond the expert world building, the acute social commentary and the large cast of fully realized characters, there's action, intrigue, romance and some amount of hope in a story readers will find completely engrossing." "The first book was more of a thrill ride, definitely," writes Heather O'Roark, "but I felt that [*Catching Fire*] had a bit more substance mixed in with the crazy, twisting plot." And in *The New York Times*, Gabrielle Zevon declared, upon the second novel's release, that "Collins has done that rare thing. She has written a sequel that improves upon the first book." One particular aspect of *Catching Fire* that reviewers consistently find superior to the first novel is the cliffhanger ending, when the depth of the revolutionary plot is revealed as extending all the way to the Gamemaker himself.

Of the three novels, *Mockingjay* has drawn the most mixed reviews, a fact that may be accounted for, in part, because it "features less action and more introspection than the earlier books" and because some readers "may wish for a different resolution, particularly where romance is concerned" (Hunt, *Mockingjay* 87). Hunt also argues that because the events of *Mockingjay* "play out on a much more epic scale (rapid changes in time and place and a larger cast of characters)," it almost "demand[s] more than the single point of view (Katniss') Collins employs" (*Mockingjay* 87). (Although Hunt has a point about the enlarged scope of the *Mockingjay* arena, there is frankly something strange about suggesting a change in point of view in the third volume of a trilogy.) Katie Roiphe writes that *Mockingjay* is "not as impeccably plotted as *The Hunger Games*, but nonetheless retains its fierce, chilly fascination."

But other reviewers, such as Susan Carpenter, like *Mockingjay* best, citing some of the qualities that Hunt criticizes: "less action and more introspection." Carpenter writes that *Mockingjay* is her favorite *Hunger Games* novel, "[d]ifficult as it would seem to top the ingenuity and action-packed, edge-of-your-seat storyline of *The Hunger Games* or the continued, in-the-ring thrill ride of its follow-up, *Catching Fire*."

The Girl on Fire

Reviewing the first novel in *The New York Times*, author John Green attributes the success of the novel not only to Collins' "crisp plotting" but also to its "fascinating heroine." Asked by fellow author Lev Grossman to account for readers' identification with Katniss Everdeen, Suzanne Collins said that her protagonist is recognizable as "a flawed character" from the outset, when she explains that she once tried drowning a kitten in front of her little sister. Says Collins, "you're on page 1 and you don't have to worry that this character's going to feel morally superior to you for three volumes."

In his *New York Times* review of *The Hunger Games*, novelist John Green describes a similar reaction to Katniss' explanation about why she had to kill the lynx that kept her company in the woods: "We are put on notice that Katniss is something different" from the typical protagonist, for whom the lynx would likely become a pet. In *Publisher's Weekly*, Megan Whalen Turner writes, "It's a credit to Collins' skill at characterization that Katniss, like a new Theseus, is cold, calculating and still likable." Says Gabrielle Zevin, reviewing *Catching Fire* in *The New York Times*, "at the heart of this exotic world is a very real girl, the kind lacking even a single supernatural gift. (Those 'real' types seem to be in short supply in children's books lately.)"

Upon the release of the first film adaptation, *New York Times* chief film reviewers A. O. Scott and Manohla Dargus published a dialogue on Katniss' character, whom they term "one of the most radical female characters to appear in American movies" and "one of the truest feeling, most complex female characters to hit American movies in a while." Much of their analysis applies equally to the print Katniss, as the character is their primary focus. Dargus discusses Katniss as an example of an archetype that American literature scholar R.W.B. Lewis calls "the American Adam," a figure which Lewis discusses in the context of nineteenth-century American characters such as James Fenimore Cooper's Natty Bumppo. Although Katniss is connected to her own history and ancestry in ways that strengthen her, she does fit the remainder of Lewis's prototype: "an individual standing alone, self-reliant and self-propelling, ready to confront whatever awaited him with the aid of his own unique and inherent resources" (Scott, and Dargus).

But Katniss defies easy categorization as a recognizable type. Scott enumerates her "multiple symbolic identities":

> She's an athlete, a media celebrity and a warrior as well as a sister, a daughter, a loyal friend and (potential) girlfriend. In genre terms she is a western hero, an action hero, a romantic heroine and a tween idol. She is Natty Bumppo, Diana the chaste huntress of classical myth, and also the synthesis of Harry Potter and Bella Swan—the Boy Who Lived and the Girl Who Must Choose. (Scott, and Dargus)

In a review of *Mockingjay*, Katie Roiphe echoes the praise for the multifaceted nature of Katniss' characterization:

> She is both murderer and victim, somehow representing female strength and female vulnerability all mingled and entwined, dangerously, ambiguously, into one. She is Pippi Longstocking. She is the girl with the dragon tattoo. She is mesmerizing in her way of defying authority, antisocial, courageous, angry, self-involved and yet somehow sweepingly sympathetic.

Scott and Dargus discuss two other distinctions of Katniss' character: her defiance of typical notions of gender and her appeal to viewers of both genders. In her own family, she must assume both the nurturing role of the mother and the providing role of the father, but rather than shifting between these roles, Scott writes, "she inhabits both, which may mean that neither really fits." Perhaps this gender fluidity helps to account for the second distinction: her appeal to both female and male viewers. Scott contends that while it is common and perfectly acceptable for girls to aspire to be Harry Potter or Spider Man, "it is an article of faith that boys won't pretend to be princesses. Unless the princesses are armed." In this respect, says Scott, *The Hunger Games* "allows—or maybe compels—a kind of universal identification that is rare, or maybe even taboo." Christina Chant Sullivan, a seventh-grade English teacher, took home *The Hunger Games* at the urging of a bookstore clerk who found out Sullivan's private school students were all boys. Sullivan began reading the book, mentioning tidbits to her students, some of whom grew curious, bought the book, and began sharing it. "In my experience," wrote Sullivan in a *Horn Book* review, "few young men that I teach have read such classics as *Little Women, A Tree Grows in Brooklyn*, or *I Know Why the Caged Bird Sings* (and, in my experience, very few will choose on their own to read a book with a female protagonist)." The book was so successful with Sullivan's boys that, the following summer, she assigned it as required summer reading and asked students to write the first chapter of *Catching Fire*, which had not yet appeared. The result, Sullivan writes, was "the perfect writing prompt.... The writing that came in that September was some of the best I have seen from a group of students over my twenty-plus years of teaching."

Reviewers of *Catching Fire* and *Mockingjay* have praised Katniss' maturation over the course of the series. Reviewing *Catching Fire*, Gabrielle Zevin writes, "Katniss is more sophisticated in this book, and her observations are more acute ... she notices how much more difficult it is to kill people once you know them," and she gradually realizes "that she may just stand for something greater than herself."

Collins' skill at complex characterization is recognized by reviewers as extending also to secondary characters, with Finnick Odair and Johanna Mason frequently cited as examples. Particularly in *Catching Fire,* Collins acquaints the reader with additional Hunger Games victors, and she adeptly depicts them as people brutalized but not entirely devastated by their participation in the arena. Finnick and Johanna have been further exploited and abused by the Capitol powers-that-be following their victories, but at the core of each remains something vulnerable. In the interview with Lev Grossman upon the release of *Catching Fire,* Collins refers to Finnick and Johanna as "onion characters." Actors Sam Claflin (Finnick) and Jena Malone (Johanna) have been praised by movie reviewers for their success at suggesting those emotional layers in the film adaptations.

Bones of Critical Contention

If there is disagreement in the reviews, some of it focuses on Collins' style, although reviewers note not so much flawed writing as the fact that nothing about the style particularly stands out—which one might call a strength. Green says of Collins' writing, "by not calling attention to itself, the text disappears in the way a good font does: nothing stands between Katniss and the reader, between Panem and America." Author Stephen King says Collins is "an efficient no-nonsense prose stylist." Gabrielle Zevin writes of *Catching Fire* that Collins writes about weighty themes "with the light touch of a writer who truly understands writing for young people: the pacing is brisk and the message tucked below the surface."

Stephen King is one of several prominent authors who have written about the series; in one of the most lukewarm reviews Collins received, King lists these complaints: Katniss has a "lame name," and it is worse when Gale calls her "catnip." Collins is guilty of some "displays of authorial laziness that kids will accept more readily than adults," such as the fact that the burn medicine Peeta needs "floats down from the sky on silver parachutes," or the fact that despite Katniss' awareness that cameras are everywhere in the arena, she never mentions seeing one. King also finds Peeta "clueless" and says that Katniss "more or less babysits [him] during the second half of the book." He also finds the love triangle to be "fairly standard teen-read stuff" and finds the overall premise derivative of earlier novels, such as *Battle Royale* and two of his own novels, published under the pen name Richard Bachman. Readers of these other books, King says, "will quickly realize they have visited these TV badlands before." However, King ultimately acknowledges that the series will succeed or fail with readers based on the storyline, which he finds more than sufficient: "since this is the first novel of a projected trilogy, it seems to me that the essential question is whether or not readers will care enough to stick around and find out what comes next for Katniss. I know I will."

The question Stephen King raises regarding the series' originality, or lack thereof, is a common point of discussion in reviews, with most coming down on the side of originality. Directly addressing the complaints of imitation, Charles de Lint calls the first novel "fresh and original." Collins repeats the old adage that "while you can give ten writers the same idea, if they're any good at their craft, you'll get ten entirely different stories" (qtd. in de Lint 37). Understandably, The Hunger Games series has been compared to a long list of novels in a similar, generally dystopian, vein: *Brave New World*; *1984*; *Battle Royale*; *Lord of the Flies*; and, less frequently, *We* and *Animal Farm*. The plot of *Battle Royale* (1999) revolves around the notion of a fictitious Japanese government that, "in an alternative universe ... was victorious in the Second World War, making it an authoritative world power" but has experienced social decline and, as a response to problems of juvenile delinquency, forces its children to engage in combat against each other (Nishimura). Due to the obvious similarities in plot of a government's forcing children to fight one another, reviewers' allegations of imitation point most frequently to Kōshun Takami's novel, with some "going so far as to call it a bold-faced ripoff" (Nishimura). But Collins insists that she had not even heard of *Battle Royale* until she had submitted her first manuscript (Dominus), and her only deliberate imitation, according to her, was from the story of Theseus and the Minotaur in Greek mythology. Robert Nishimura appears to describe the position on this controversy of most reviewers when he writes that Collins "just happened to tap in to the creative collective consciousness, drawing on ideas that have played out many times before." A quick survey on Amazon.com reveals that *Battle Royale* has been published in a new edition since the appearance of the first Hunger Games novel; it is difficult not to credit Collins' series with the Japanese novel's revival.

Arguments about Readers

From the very beginning, questions of appropriate audience and the inherent difficulty of the material have been a controversial aspect of The Hunger Games phenomenon. Stephen King addresses the violence of the Games, concluding that "[t]he only 'unspoken rule' . . . [is that] you can't eat the dead contestants." King declares, "Let's see the makers of the movie version try to get a PG-13 on this baby." Remarkably, they did. And speaking of the makers of the movies, upon reading the first Hunger Games novel, *Catching Fire* and *Mockingjay* (Parts 1 and 2) director Francis Lawrence had a reaction quite similar to King's: "I'm thinking, *Gosh, child endangerment is a tricky thing with the ratings board, and showing kids killing other kids is tricky.*" But Lawrence's task in directing the second and third installments was made easier, he explained in the interview with Lev Grossman, "because there's far fewer children in *Catching Fire* than in the *Hunger Games* [sic]. You're now dealing with an arena full of victors, so now we have an eighty-year-old woman, and Katniss and Peeta, I think, are the youngest ones…. I was really far less worried than I would have been had I been making the first film" (Collins, and Lawrence, "I Was Destined"). On this point, Suzanne Collins adds that in the second arena, Katniss and Peeta are "the only two that are still technically minors. They're seventeen, and the next youngest is probably Johanna and she's twenty-one."

Some reviews of the novels have listed the recommended readership age as "eleven and up," while others use imprecise labels (such as *Christian Century*'s "fourteen and under"). The majority, such as Jilaine Johnson in *Reading Time* have felt that these novels are *not* for younger readers: "because of the inevitable violence [the series] is more suitable for teens or mature twelve year old readers." *Teacher Librarian* recommends the series for readers in grades six through ten, and *School Library Journal* says grade seven and up. Library-themed publications have a tendency to affect public school library collections more than mainstream reviews, so many young people will first encounter the books in middle school. As James Blasingame has noted, the question of appropriateness may not be the same for all three novels: reviewing *Mockingjay*, he writes, "The first two novels may have been more appropriate for younger readers than this final installment, which is probably best for upper middle school, high school, and adult readers due to violence." Some reviewers played up the incongruity of such weighty subject matter being intended for young readers: James Delingpole's *Spectator* review is called "A Gorefest in Which Everyone Dies Horribly: Here's My Book Recommendation for Kids."

Christina Sullivan, the seventh-grade English teacher discussed earlier, did not have an entirely conflict-free experience using *The Hunger Games* in her classroom; despite the academic success, Sullivan found herself explaining to her principal why she chose a book about teenagers killing teenagers for her mostly thirteen-year-old students. She was also confronted in the hallway on the day before students returned to school by the mother of one of her best student writers, a boy whose maternal grandmother had refused to sell Collins' novel in her independent bookstore. The mother had substituted another book for her son's summer reading.

But Christina Sullivan believes "these pubescent boys were experiencing [the novel] differently from us midlife mothers," citing her experience with another disturbing novel for adolescents, Andy Mulligan's *Trash*. The three main characters in *Trash* live at the edge of a trash dump and spend their days picking through garbage. The novel is slightly futuristic but set in a realistic modern city. But whereas Sullivan expected her privileged private school students to recognize the disparity between their own lives and the characters' lives and pity the fictional boys, the class "not only embraced but also envied the independence of the trash boys. To them, the dumpsite setting was just as fantastical as Hogwarts." Similarly, she found that her students envied Katniss' independence and reveled in her opportunity to outsmart adults intent on oppressing her. "In the end," Sullivan writes, "no matter how realistic these novels seemed, my boys recognized them as fiction." Sullivan believes that the "tweeners," whom most reviewers have identified as the target for The Hunger Games series "intrinsically know what is pretend and what is not." They "can handle graphic violence, injustice, and horror that is fabricated, as long as there is the idealistic promise of the good guy winning in the end" (Sullivan).

Whatever publishing houses and reviewers may think is the approximate appropriate age for reading The Hunger Games novels, most acknowledge that *Mockingjay* may require a slightly older audience, due to its more introspective and philosophically darker nature. When *The Hunger Games* was initially reviewed in *The New York Times*, the review, by Katie Roiphe, appeared in the "Children's Books" section of the *Sunday Book Review*. Just a few years later, Roiphe writes that *Mockingjay* "is the perfect *teenage* story with its exquisitely refined rage against the cruel and arbitrary power of the adult world" (emphasis mine). Despite the difficult nature of the material, nearly all reviewers accept the premise that the series is beneficial and socially instructive reading for young people as early as they are ready. James Delingpole says children should read The Hunger Games novels because they "teach them from the off that life is going to be pure hardship and misery with death the only release and you've given them a vital head start over the competition." Suzanne Collins told Lev Grossman, "I think we put our children at an enormous disadvantage by not educating them

in war, by not letting them understand about it from a very early age"
(Collins, and Lawrence, "Gamekeepers"). However, it also seems
that it would have been a blessing if Collins could have postponed
her own acquaintance with war significantly beyond the age of six.

The Ideology of The Hunger Games Trilogy

If there is general agreement that children should be helped to
understand something about war (the exact age depending on one's
viewpoint or perhaps on the child), it still seems unclear—or perhaps
open to debate—exactly what point about war Suzanne Collins wants
to convey. In the Collins biography in this volume, Laurie Adams has
detailed Collins' experience of having her father away in Vietnam
and coming to understand from television depictions something
about the horrifying nature of armed conflict and the jeopardy her
father faced. In "Why the Message of the Hunger Games Films Is
Dangerous," Peter Bloom contends that the series—and *Mockingjay*
in particular—might suggest to young readers that putting an end to
government oppression is as simple as assassinating the president:
"all that is needed is to destroy the tyrant and therefore end tyranny."
Bloom writes:

> There is a continual refrain from these leaders that all can be solved
> by "getting rid" of the most threatening adversaries. From Saddam
> Hussein to Osama Bin Laden to the current bogeyman of Islamic
> State, Abu Bakr al-Baghdadi, complex socioeconomic and political
> problems are reduced to a simplified narrative of killing the 'bad
> guys.' It is not surprising then that while these discourses can inspire,
> they in no way provide long-term solutions. (par. 10)

This oversimplification of the causes of governmental oppression
encourages a sort of "us-versus-them" thinking, Bloom says,
in which we and our "enemies" are polarized and our endurance
is predicated upon their extinction. However, Bloom finds this
paradigm "completely understandable in the context of children's
entertainment." What concerns him more is that maturity should
bring the more complex perspective that worlds go wrong because
of entire systems, not individuals, but Bloom fears that "current

political discourse in the real world ... closely mirrors" the us-versus-them paradigm. In other words, due to the developmental status of her youthful target audience, Collins may oversimplify social change, not sufficiently clarifying "the difference between an angry rebellion and a transformational revolution" (Bloom).

I recently stood in the hallway of a movie theatre while two of my colleagues—English professors with PhDs who had just seen the *Mockingjay 2* film—argued about whether Collins is an anti-war novelist. Certainly Collins presents the viewpoint that war is hell, which, Andrew Stuttaford has pointed out, is both a theme shared with Collins' Underland Chronicles and "unoriginal," though "commendable." But my colleagues disagreed over whether Collins oversimplifies solutions to state-sponsored conflict. Stuttaford argues,

> Sometime in the course of *Mockingjay*, sermon overwhelms story. The tale of the Capitol's fall offered an ideal opportunity for a deeper exploration of the principle of morally legitimate violence that, from Katniss' arrival in the arena, forms one of a number of this trilogy's more interesting subtexts. That opportunity is at first grasped but then thrown away in favor of a dull plague on-both-your-houses world-weariness that is more evasion or tantrum than an attempt at an answer." (45)

Stuttaford may have a point that, in the *Mockingjay* climax, Collins appears to abandon the introspective approach to the question of legitimized violence in favor of a neat and satisfying resolution. After all, Katniss has just seen the person she loves most in the world—Prim—blown to pieces before her own eyes. When Katniss sends her arrow through the chest of Alma Coin rather than Coriolanus Snow, she is making the point that tyranny itself must go, not just the tyrant. What follows—the prospect of a democratically elected leader—is not "transformative" but will perhaps lead to transformation. It is certainly an improvement over the post-apocalyptic world in which the reader is introduced to Katniss.

Suzanne Collins has made her own answer to this question very clear: she wants young readers to understand that war is brutal but that violence may sometimes be necessary to end oppression at the hands of those Machiavellian "princes" who rule by instilling fear in their subjects. Upon the release of *Catching Fire*, Collins summarized what she learned from growing up with a father who was both a war veteran and a history professor:

> [I]f I took the 40 years of my dad talking to me about war and battles and taking me to battlefields and distilled it down into one question, it would probably be the idea of the necessary or unnecessary war. That's very much at the heart of it....
>
> In *The Hunger Games*, in most people's idea, in terms of rebellion or a civil-war situation, that would meet the criteria for a necessary war. These people are oppressed, their children are being taken off and put in gladiator games. They're impoverished, they're starving, they're brutalized. It would for most people be an acceptable situation for rebellion." (Collins, "Writing")

Andrew Stuttaford also points out that The Hunger Games trilogy made its debut just "as Lehman [Brothers][2] went down" and that maybe some of its appeal is in capturing the Zeitgeist[3] of that period. (The novel was released in hardback on Sept. 14, 2008, and Lehman Brothers filed for bankruptcy the next day.) Writing in *The Atlantic*, Nicole Allan calls Katniss "the populist hero the Occupy movement wasn't able to deliver." Stuttaford (writing in the conservative-leaning *National Review*) says "it's easy to see how this trilogy could be cast as a manifesto for the ninety-nine percent" (45).[4] If the *Hunger Games Wikia* is accurate and Panem has about 4.5 million residents with about 96,500 living in the Capitol, that would make residents of the districts the 98 percent. But the economic disenfranchisement of the districts in The Hunger Games series is only one particularly compelling example of the larger social problem: the exclusion of citizens from the decision-making process and the denial of personal autonomy. This theme resonates with teens, says Geri Diorio, because they "feel as though their rights are being stomped on."

Among *The Hunger Games* themes that reviewers find useful for young adult readers is the series' "satire of celebrity culture, mindless tabloidism and decadence" (Roiphe). That the Hunger Games competition is broadcast on national television means both exploitation and advantage for the tributes: any pain and suffering they experience or inflict is transmitted to every screen in Panem, but their potential sponsors can assist them much better than if the arena were blacked out. Katniss resents the ever-present cameras tracking her movements, especially when she is breaking the Capitol's rules, but she subsequently has to learn to use them to her advantage as both a tribute and a revolutionary. The notion of constant surveillance is the government's means of both forcing compliance, through its potential to transmit the fate of those who transgress, and diverting defiance, by providing the people with violent "entertainment." Amalie Selle's essay in this volume explores Collins' use of "bread and circus" or *panem et circenses* as the concept was employed in the age of the Holy Roman Empire. In the era of reality television and a culture saturated with mass media, it seems more important than ever for teenagers to consider how they are impacted by media and, most important, how media might be used for nefarious purposes.

"Where literature goes, scholars follow," writes Leisa A. Clark in the introduction to *Of Bread, Blood, and The Hunger Games* (July 2012), one of the first published volumes of Hunger Games literary criticism. McFarland, a North Carolina-based publisher, got a head start on other providers of academic books with three volumes appearing less than two years after the series' completion, the first of which was edited by Clark and Mary F. Pharr. The other two are Tom Henthorne's *Approaching the Hunger Games Trilogy: A Literary and Cultural Analysis* (also July 2012) and *Space and Place in the Hunger Games: New Readings of the Novels* (2014), edited by Deidre Anne Evans Garriott, Whitney Elaine Jones, and Julie Elizabeth Tyler. The McFarland titles were preceded by about five months by a book in the Wiley-Blackwell company's Philosophy and Popular Culture series, *The Hunger Games and Philosophy: A Critique of Pure Treason* (February 2012), edited by George A. Dunn and Nicolas Michaud. Leisa A. Clark might be describing the primary purpose of any of these four books when she writes that she and coeditor Pharr sought "to enable students of the series to begin their research on any or all three of the novels with an anthology that is scholarly *and* readable" (3).

Of Bread, Blood, and The Hunger Games is divided into four sections. The "History, Politics, Economics, and Culture" section contains essays about crisis economics, power, spectacle, the gluttony and waste of the Capitol, connections between District 12 and Appalachia, and Collins' use of food to reveal society and culture. Section two, "Ethics, Aesthetics, and Identity," focuses on Katniss' characterization and issues of gender, including the ways in which Collins defies gender norms. The third section, "Resistance, Surveillance, and Simulacra," contains essays concerning costumes, the role of the audience in the Games, and how both the Capitol and District 13 use spectacle and surveillance as a management technique. The final section focuses on connections—thematic and otherwise—with other works of literature, including *Ender's Game*, Shakespeare's *Henry V*, *Twilight*, and the Harry Potter series. For example, one writer discusses the child soldier in both The Hunger Games series and *Ender's Game*. Reviewer Jacob Jedidah Horn's praises Pharr and Clark's volume for its overall breadth or "variety of voices" and declares, "Even when a particular essay is less successful than others, the range of subjects under discussion encourages continued reading, and the overall quality of the material here rewards such persistence" (Horn 410). Despite unevenness in the quality of the essays, Horn singles out for praise two essays that "do not have a completely favorable view of Collins' trilogy": Anthony Pavlik's "Absolute Power Games," about the series' treatment of violence, and Tina Hanlon's "Coal Dust and Ballads," about the District 12-Appalachia correspondence. "Such willingness to engage critically—and sometimes negatively—with *The Hunger Games* and its sequels demonstrates a refreshingly rigorous level of scholarship," Horn writes (411).

Horn finds Henthorne's *Approaching the Hunger Games Trilogy* the less impressive of the two books, feeling that while the single-author approach should provide improved focus, the volume is disjointed overall: "the reader may be impressed with the variety of bright spots but will have difficulty locating an organizing structure

---

holding all of the material together" (Horn 408). The "bright spots" include Henthorne's explanations of the literary theories he uses, which Horn recommends particularly for novice literature students. Horn also praises Henthorne's analysis of the difference between Gale and Peeta as love interests for Katniss and his exploration of the distinction between survivor and victim, using for demonstration President Snow's treatment of Katniss. But Horn notes that strengths can also be frustrations, as they suggest the book's potential for "for longer, more carefully organized analysis" (408) he would have preferred.

As The Hunger Games novels began appearing less than a decade ago and the series was completed only about five years ago, assessment of the works by literary scholars is just getting underway. In addition to the volumes of serious literary criticism discussed here, a few companion-type books exist, including *The Panem Companion* (2012), *The Hunger Games Tribute Guide* (2012), and *Katniss the Cattail* (2012) by Valerie Estele Frankel, author of many books on popular culture topics. Frankel is the author of two books on The Hunger Games series, both focusing on Katniss, and Frankel's work in popular culture tends to focus on gender, as in *From Girl to Goddess: The Heroine's Journey through Myth and Legend* (McFarland, 2010). In all, these early examples of literary analysis (for some) and popular culture coattail-riding (by others) bear out Leisa A. Clark's comment that the perspectives in *Of Bread, Blood, and the Hunger Games* "will not be the last word" on the world of the Girl on Fire.

Notes

1. Modern Library is an "imprint" or brand of Random House publishing company.

2. Lehman Brothers is a Wall Street investment firm that filed for bankruptcy on Sept 15, 2008. At the time of the bankruptcy, the company had $639 billion in assets and $619 billion in debts. This was a particularly shocking development because Lehman Brothers was founded in 1850 by Henry, Emanuel, and Mayer Lehman and was a Wall Street fixture. The bankruptcy filing was the major topic of discussion in the international finance community for months, and

many experts questioned why the U.S. government did not intervene ("Case Study").

3. Zeitgeist is the prevailing spirit of the age or the time period.

4. The Occupy movement began in 2011 as "Occupy Wall Street" and became an international effort protesting social and economic equality. Based on the claim that one percent of the U.S. population holds the vast majority of wealth, the Occupy movement adopted the slogan "We are the 99 percent."

Works Cited

Allan, Nicole. "'The Hunger Games' Crosses Child Warfare With Class Warfare." *The Atlantic*. The Atlantic Monthly Group, 23 Mar. 2012. Web. 28 Nov. 2015.

Ames, Melissa A. "Engaging 'Apolitical' Adolescents: Analyzing the Popularity and Educational Potential of Dystopian Literature Post-9/11." *The Keep*: *Faculty Research and Creative Activity*. Eastern Illinois UP. 1 Oct. 2013. PDF. 1 Dec. 2015.

Blasingame, James. "*Mockingjay*." Review of *Mockingjay* by Suzanne Collins. *Journal of Adolescent & Adult Literacy* 54.6 (2011): 464–5. Web. 20 Nov. 2015.

Bloom, Peter. "Why the Message of the Hunger Games Films Is Dangerous." *The Conversation*. The Conversation US, Inc., 9 Dec. 2014. Web. 26 Nov. 2015.

Carpenter, Susan. "Shocking Conclusion—With 'Mockingjay,' Suzanne Collins Ties up the Trilogy That Started with 'Hunger Games' and Raced through 'Catching Fire.'" *St. Paul Pioneer Press*. Digital First Media, 26 Sept. 2010. *Newsbank*. Web. 29 Nov. 2015.

"Case Study: The Collapse of Lehman Brothers." *Investopedia*. Investopedia, LLC, 2016. Web. 2 Dec. 2015.

"*Catching Fire*." Review. *Kirkus*. Kirkusreviews.com, 1 Sept. 2009. Web. 29 Nov. 2015.

Chipman, Ian. "Core Collection: Dystopian Fiction for Youth." *Booklist* 15 May 2009: 50. Web. 28 Nov. 2015.

Collins, Suzanne, and Francis Lawrence. "'Come for the Love Story, Stay for the War': A Conversation with Suzanne Collins and Francis Lawrence." Part five of a five-part interview with Lev Grossman. *Time*. Time Inc., 22 Nov. 2013. Web. 28 Nov. 2015.

_____. "The Gamekeepers: A Conversation with Suzanne Collins and Francis Lawrence." Part two of a five-part interview with Lev Grossman. *Time*. Time Inc., 25 Nov. 2013. Web. 28 Nov. 2015.

_____. "'I'm More Like Plutarch than Katniss:' A Conversation with Suzanne Collins and Francis Lawrence." Part four of a five-part interview with Lev Grossman. *Time*. Time Inc., 21 Nov. 2013. Web. 28 Nov. 2015.

_____. "'I Was Destined to Write a Gladiator Game:' A Conversation with Suzanne Collins and Francis Lawrence." Part three of a five-part interview with Lev Grossman. *Time*. Time Inc., 20 Nov. 2013. Web. 28 Nov. 2015.

_____. and Francis Lawrence. "Katniss is 'A Wreck': A Conversation with Suzanne Collins and Francis Lawrence." Part one of a five-part interview with Lev Grossman. *Time*. Time Inc., 18 Nov. 2013. Web. 28 Nov. 2015.

_____. "A Killer Story: An Interview with Suzanne Collins, Author of 'The Hunger Games.'" Interview by Rick Margolis. *School Library Journal*. Media Source. 1 Sept. 2008. Web. 14 March 2013.

_____. "Writing 'War-Appropriate' Stories for Kids: A Conversation with Suzanne Collins and Francis Lawrence." Part two of a five-part interview with Lev Grossman. *Time*. Time Inc., 18 Nov. 2013. Web. 28 Nov. 2015.

Delingpole, James. "A Gorefest in Which Everyone Dies Horribly: Here's My Book Recommendation for Kids." *The Spectator*. The Spectator, Ltd. 11 Feb. 2012. Web. 28 Nov. 2015.

de Lint, Charles. "Books to Look For." Review of *The Hunger Games*, *Catching Fire*, and *Mockingjay*. *Magazine of Fantasy and Science Fiction*. 1 Nov. 2011: 29–38. Web. 29 Nov. 2015.

Diorio, Geri. "Big Brother is Watching You Read." *Voice of Youth Advocates* 34.2 (June 2011): 114. Web. 20 Nov. 2015.

Dominus, Susan. "Suzanne Collins' War Stories for Kids." *The New York Times*. 8 April 2011. Web. 30 Nov. 2015.

Green, John. "Scary New World." Review of *The Dead and Gone* by Susan Beth Pfeffer and *The Hunger Games* by Suzanne Collins. *New York Times*. The New York Times Company, 7 Nov. 2008. Web. 27 Nov. 2015.

Horn, Jacob Jedidah. *"Approaching the Hunger Games Trilogy: A Literary and Cultural Analysis* by Tom Henthorne and *Of Bread, Blood, and The Hunger Games* by Mary F. Pharr and Leisa A. Clark." Review. *Journal of the Fantastic in the Arts* 25.2–3 (2014): 406–12. One Search. Stanley Library. Ferrum College. 20 Nov. 2015.

"The Hunger Games." Hollywood Reporter. The Hollywood Reporter, 1 Feb. 2012. Web. 29 Nov. 2015.

"The Hunger Games." Review. *Kirkus.* 1 Oct. 2008. 20 May 2010. Web. 27 Nov. 2015.

Hunt, Jonathan. "Suzanne Collins['] *Catching Fire*." Review of *Catching Fire. The Horn Book Magazine* Sept./Oct. 2009: 555. Web. 30 Nov. 2015.

_____. *"Mockingjay."* Review of *Mockingjay. The Horn Book Magazine* Nov./Dec. 2010: 86–7. Web. 30 Nov. 2015.

Johnson, Jilaine. Review of *The Hunger Games* by Suzanne Collins. *Reading Time* 57.1 (2009): 30. Web. 28 Nov. 2015.

King, Stephen. *"The Hunger Games."* Review of *The Hunger Games* by Suzanne Collins. *Entertainment Weekly.* Entertainment Weekly Inc., 12 Sept. 2008. Web. 30 Nov. 2015.

Miller, Laura. "Fresh Hell." *The New Yorker.* Condé Nast, 14 Jun. 2010. Web. 29 Nov. 2015.

Nishimura, Robert. *"Battle Royale,* a Hunger Games for Grownups." *Press Play.* Indiewire.com, 20 Mar. 2012. Web. 30 Nov. 2015.

Odean, Kathleen. "Struggling with Tough Questions." Review of *The Hunger Games* by Suzanne Collins. *Teacher Librarian* 36.4 (2010): 17. *EBSCOHost.* Web. 29 Nov. 2015.

O'Roarke, Heather. "Book Review: *Catching Fire* by Suzanne Collins." Review. *Basil & Spice* 24 Dec. 2009. *EBSCO Host.* Web. 29 Nov. 2015.

Pharr, Mary F., and Leisa A. Clark. *Of Bread, Blood, and The Hunger Games: Critical Essays on the Suzanne Collins Trilogy.* Jefferson, NC: McFarland, 2012. Print.

Roiphe, Katie. "Survivor." Review of *Mockingjay* by Suzanne Collins. *New York Times Sunday Book Review.* The New York Times Company, 8 Sept. 2010. Web. 27 Nov. 2015.

Russell, Mary Harris. *"The Century Recommends." The Christian Century* 16 Dec. 2008: 27. Web. 20 Nov. 2015.

Scott, A. O., and Manohla Dargus. "A Radical Female Hero from Dystopia." Review of *The Hunger Games* (film*). New York Times*. The New York Times Company, 4 April 2012. Web. 27 Nov. 2015.

Stuttaford, Andrew. "Quidditch, It's Not." *National Review* 30 Jul. 2012: 44–5. Web. 28 Nov. 2015.

Sullivan, Christina Chant. "Disturbing (or Not?) Young Adult Fiction." Review of *The Hunger Games* by Suzanne Collins. *The Horn Book Magazine*. The Horn Book, 14 Aug. 2013. Web. 29 Nov. 2015.

Turner, Megan Whalen. "*The Hunger Games*." Review. *Publisher's Weekly*. 3 Nov. 2008: 58. Web. 28 Nov. 2015.

Zevin, Gabrielle. "Constant Craving." Review of *Catching Fire* by Suzanne Collins. *New York Times*. The New York Times Company, 9 Oct. 2009. Web. 30 Nov. 2015.

Rebelling Against the Rebellion: Frustrating Readerly Desire in Suzanne Collins' Mockingjay

Jackie C. Horne

Fans of Suzanne Collins' bestselling dystopian fantasy novels *The Hunger Games* (2008) and *Catching Fire* (2009) waited for the arrival of the trilogy's concluding volume not only with bated breath, but also with enormous expectations about how the final book would and, perhaps more importantly, *should* end. With the publication of *Mockingjay* in August of 2010, said readers could finally breathe again. But many found themselves struggling with expectations that were far from met in the series' final installment. While some readers found themselves well-satisfied by *Mockingjay's* cynical, even nihilistic, attitude towards warfare, many others were left frustrated, decrying what they perceived to be the novel's seriously flawed character construction and plotting, in comparison to the trilogy's first two volumes. "The Fire Went Out," "Cheated, Disappointed and Dismayed," and "Ms. Collins, write a NEW third book and throw this OUT" are just a few of the kinder headlines attached to Amazon.com reviews written by *Mockingjay's* many disappointed readers.

Although such readers typically write that *Mockingjay* is "bad," readers' comments on Amazon.com about *Mockingjay* reveal that their dissatisfaction stems less from any technical flaws in Collins' writing and more from the way the novel frustrates its readers' desires. *The Hunger Games* and *Catching Fire* deliberately offer and, to a large extent, satisfy very specific desires: the desire to read about or identify with a "kick-ass heroine"; the desire to participate vicariously in, or thrill voyeuristically to, the violent competition of the Hunger Games; and the desire to believe that fighting oppression can come without severe, even debilitating loss. Though both *The Hunger Games* and *Catching Fire* include a simultaneous critique of the very readerly desires they evoke, this critique is far easier for readers to overlook or ignore in the first two volumes than it is in *Mockingjay*. Collins has noted "disturbing" and "desensitizing" aspects of some readers' response to the first two books of the trilogy; because much of Collins' readership is more familiar with the triumphalism of the Harry Potter series and other high fantasy fiction than with the "apocalyptic despair" of the true dystopian novel, *Mockingjay* leaves many readers feeling frustrated and betrayed (Collins, "Q & A"; Sambell).

My primary texts for this article, then, are not just Suzanne Collins' *Mockingjay*, but all 153 of the one-star reviews of *Mockingjay* written and posted to the Amazon.com website. One star is the lowest rating a reader can give a book on Amazon.com. I analyze the reasons readers gave to explain their disappointment with the final installment of the series, tracing common patterns amongst these disillusioned reviewers.

Before proceeding to this analysis, here are a few statistics about reviewers of Suzanne Collins' three books on Amazon.com:

As of June 7, 2011, when the research for this article was originally conducted, 2,308 readers posted reviews of *The Hunger Games*, the first volume in Collins' trilogy. The vast majority of those readers (76 percent) gave the book five stars, the highest rating in Amazon.com's system. Exactly 15 percent gave the book four stars, with fewer than 7 percent rating the book at three stars or lower.

Only 910 readers reviewed *Catching Fire*, the second book of the trilogy, as of June 2011, compared the more than 2,000 who reviewed *The Hunger Games*. But the percentages of people responding positively to the second book mirrored those of the first: 72 percent gave *Catching Fire* five stars; 8 percent, four stars; and only 8.5 percent rated it three stars or lower.

In the first ten months after its publication, *Mockingjay* received reviews from 1,368 Amazon.com readers. This is not as many as had responded to *The Hunger Games*, but significantly more than had posted about *Catching Fire*. What is most striking about these postings, however, is not their raw numbers, but the difference in their percentages of positive reviews. Unlike *The Hunger Games* and *Catching Fire*, which garnered positives from more than three quarters of readers, only 42 percent of reviewers gave *Mockingjay* five stars. Exactly 18 percent more awarded the book four stars. But almost 40 percent of reviewers gave the books three stars or fewer. Just 11 percent, or more than one in ten readers, gave the book only one star, and readers in this last group wrote that they would give it zero stars if only Amazon.com allowed it. Many of these one-star reviewers wrote that they had loved the first two books in the series, so this phenomenon cannot be explained by a disproportionate number of people who had not posted about the first two books suddenly feeling moved to express their dismay at the third book.

Why, then, did so many readers with positive feelings about the first two books feel "disappointed" and "betrayed" by *Mockingjay*? In analyzing the responses of the 153 readers who gave *Mockingjay* only one star, five patterns emerged.

Pattern #1 (or lack of pattern): Tolkien was wrong, or, world building just doesn't matter

Many theorists of fantasy, drawing upon J. R. R. Tolkien's argument in "On Fairy-Stories," suggest that the key to engaging a fantasy reader is to create a convincing secondary world. As Tolkien describes it,

> the story-maker...makes a Secondary World which your mind can enter. Inside it, what he relates is "true": it accords with the laws of that world. You therefore believe it, while you are, as it were, inside. The moment disbelief arises, the spell is broken; the magic, or rather art, has failed. You are then out in the Primary World again, looking at the little abortive Secondary World from outside. (37)

Given Tolkien's theory, one might be forgiven for supposing that readers' disappointment in *Mockingjay* likely stems from some problem or contradiction in Collins' world-building. Intriguingly, though, only two readers who reviewed the book negatively commented upon discrepancies in the secondary world Collins constructs. As reader "K. Butler" notes, "The 'strategy' of the different warring factions here is scream-at-the-sky stupid. Huge chunks of technology established in previous books (stadium sized force fields for starters) are simply omitted." Reader "Brittany S." concurs:

> The main problem is that Collins wanted the war to resemble that of war how we know it. But in Panem, this doesn't fly. She wanted the soldiers to be in bloody combat to illustrate the effects it has on people. But are we suppose[d] to believe that in a world that can create mutts, programmed to kill, that the citizen would be engaging in the most dangerous aspects of the battle? Why sacrifice human life when you can crank out as many 'terminators' as you want?

Beyond these two comments, however, there appeared to be no criticisms of Collins' world-building in readers' negative reviews of *Mockingjay*, suggesting that literary critics may want to look in directions other than the power of world-building to account for how fantasy as a genre engages (or, in *Mockingjay's* case, fails to engage) its readers.

Pattern #2: "Bad. Writing. Period," or, who forgot to edit this manuscript?

While few readers found problems with Collins' world-building, almost all negative reviewers deemed *Mockingjay* badly written, particularly in comparison to the first two books of the trilogy. Very few reviewers, though, gave concrete examples to illustrate in what ways the writing itself differed from that in the previous two books. One reviewer noted the slow-down-then-hurry-up pacing; another commented that the writing felt choppy; and several felt that the book's ending felt rushed. One reader, "Joy Leppin," notes "Perhaps the tone was a metaphor to depict the way people are worn down by a long drawn out war ... that's the way it read ... sluggish, worn out ... barely able to move," but she viewed such a metaphoric deployment of tone as a negative quality, rather than an artful choice on Collins' part.

Such specific comments about Collins' writing though, were few and far between; the majority of reviewers who suggested that *Mockingjay* was badly written did not comment on Collins' writing itself. Rather, the description "bad writing" functioned as a synonym for plot or character construction that they disliked, or for an ideological stance that they found distasteful or unnerving. Thus, the final three patterns in this analysis will focus on problems reviewers had with the *content* of *Mockingjay*, even if they characterized such problems by using the catch-all phrase "bad writing."

Pattern #3: "What happened to the girl on fire?" or Katniss the unheroic

This pattern of negative reviews argues that Collins betrayed readers by being untrue to the characters she had created in the first two books, especially to the character of the books' heroine, Katniss Everdeen. A reader who signed him/herself as "A Kid's Review" describes the feelings of many readers:

> I started this series because I was intrigued by Katniss, by her courage, how she stood up for herself and the people she loved. She was gritty, almost an anti-hero but definitely strong.
>
> In [*Mockingjay*] she stumbles from scene to scene, always pushed by someone, just a pawn. I lost count how many times she woke up in the hospital while the story unfolded around her but always without her. Too many scenes end with her getting a shot in the arm that makes her black out. Too many times is she crying huddled in a corner. I'm not saying that she has no reason to be sad, but that is NOT the Katniss from the first two books.

"A Kid's Review" and many other readers disappointed with Mockingjay valued the Katniss of *The Hunger Games* and *Catching Fire* for her courage, for her ability to *act* in the face of oppression. As reader "October X" describes her, the Katniss of books one and two is "our firey, brash, ass-kicking, awesome, arrow wielding heroine"; in contrast, the Katniss of *Mockingjay* "turns into a whining, self-pitying, depressed emotional mess and spends much of the book wallowing in guilt over what she's doing to the two guys that like her. She turns into Bella, basically" (Bella being the less-than-kick-ass heroine of the *Twilight* series). Reader "Carrie Atlanta" concurs, noting that "Katniss really seems pathetic and a pawn in this book." For readers like "RobinLeanne," a heroine without agency can no longer be a heroine at all: "Katniss does not mature in this story, instead declines as a character. She has no true 'hero' moments with inspiring statements or thoughts and is mentally absent throughout this book."

Interestingly, several reviewers seem to recognize that their problems with Collins' construction of Katniss as a character are less about bad writing and more about their own frustrated desires. For example, the author of "A Kid's Review" writes, "I'm not saying that she has no reason to be sad, but that is NOT the Katniss from the first two books"; he or she then concludes, "This is fiction and I prefer people to ACT in my fiction, not be acted upon or do nothing for many, many pages." Reviewer "K. J. Troyer" articulates a similar philosophy about protagonists: "I want a strong, always on their game heroine. Not one who can't get a grip. I want someone who comes out stronger, a better person, not simply a survivor. A sucky survivor at that." A reviewer calling him/herself simply "a customer" goes so far as to rewrite the entire final book in a few sentences so that Katniss will better align with his or her expectations of an active heroine: "i think that [P]rim should have died during the middle of the book so that [K]atniss would escape district 13 with Gale and go to the capitol and kill a bunch of people and kick some ass. [S]he would kill [S]now and everyone would love her."

What all of these readers have in common is their interpretation of Collins' novels through the lens of high fantasy conventions, in particular the conventions of the active high fantasy hero, rather than through the conventions of dystopian fiction. Heroes, and, during the past thirty or so years, heroines, of high fantasy quest narratives *act*, and act with bravery. They succeed in restoring order to their lands, or in reinvigorating a troubled society. In contrast, heroes of dystopian literature for adults typically fail to change their worlds; as Kay Sambell argues, "the narrative closure of the protagonist's final defeat and failure is absolutely crucial to the admonitory impulse of the classic adult dystopia" (165). Far more familiar with the conventions of high fantasy in the wake of the Harry Potter phenomenon than they are with the conventions of the dystopian novel, readers bring their high fantasy expectations to a work of dystopian fiction and find themselves shockingly disappointed. As reviewer "T. Foster" notes, "If the world needs saving, give me Frodo or Harry Potter, please. Not Katniss, who fizzled out before the job was done." A passive, rather than an active, protagonist, a heroine who spends more time crying than kicking ass, is no heroine at all to readers comfortable with the conventions of high fantasy but unfamiliar with those of dystopia.

Pattern #4: "War is hell, but does reading have to be?" or, what's propaganda doing in my children's book?

Comments denigrating Collins as an anti-war propagandist abound in the negative reviews of *Mockingjay*. As "Letdownandout" writes, "Suzanne Collins ... shows you a dystopia where propaganda is spewed, recognized and bitterly swallowed by her characters. With this book she's the creator of equally distasteful propaganda that her readers had to do the same with. War is bad." The reviewer "Jaelyn Shilady" concurs: "This book was absolutely anti-war propaganda. The message I kept getting was that in war NOBODY WINS." Readers who criticize Collins for *Mockingjay*'s anti-war stance suggest that by infusing her story with ideology, she is no longer writing fiction: "War is an atrocity, life can be terrible—we know that. That's why fiction exists: to be different. To tell stories, not to send messages," argues reviewer "Emily C." Literary critic John Stephens has argued that the most difficult ideological message to find in a text is an ideology that coincides with one's own; perhaps the flip side of Stephens' argument may be that the easiest ideological message to tar with the label *propaganda* is one that differs most markedly from one's own.

Pattern #5: "Well-written but where's the hope?" or, can this really be a children's book?

The criticism that Collins is writing anti-war propaganda often comes hand in hand with another reproach: *Mockingjay* fails to provide "hope" to its young readers. As a reviewer called "What" writes, "Perhaps this is 'realistic' of war, but this is a book, not reality. We wanted a little bit of hope and received none. So, so disappointed.

I'm speechless." Amazon.com reviewer "Matthew Ackroyd" also points to hope as the missing ingredient in *Mockingjay*:

> As other reviewers have stated, this book is completely different from the previous two. They balanced the darkness and the light in humanity very well. One was never left bereft and hopeless. This book, however, has no balance...
> Good people lose, evil people win, nothing ever really changes. Wow. Way to ruin a great series. I am off to look for a little sunshine and hope now.

Significantly, the word "hope" appears in thirty-nine of the 153 one-star reviews of *Mockingjay* and is most often used to criticize Collins for its absence from the trilogy's final installment.

As theorists of children's literature well know, the belief that books intended for young people should give them hope is a central truism of the genre. A book for children that chooses to follow the rules of dystopian fiction for adults, which typically concludes without the hope of a triumphant overthrow of the repressive dystopian society, almost appear to readers as if they are not children's books at all.

But hope is also central to the promulgation of war, as demonstrated by two adult *Mockingjay* reviewers, who have ties to the military. "C. J. Mathews" writes, "This final novel was dark without reason and without realism. War is Dark. I get that and as a member of [the] military I see it everyday. However darkness in this novel wasn't real. There was no light. Hope is the thing that drives the soldiers of war." Reviewer "KMC," who is married to a military man, explains just what soldiers hope for:

> You can be anti-war. That's fine. War is a difficult thing to understand. It's not pretty. It's terrible. However, you can't deny that it's sometimes justified ... Nobody is saying war is a good thing. Nobody thinks that. However, some people view it as a necessary evil and want good in the world, but know it can't be achieved until the bullies are gone.

Hope that the war they are fighting is necessary and justified, is what drives the soldiers of war, these reviewers suggest; Collins' refusal to offer such hope, even to those who, like Katniss, fight for a cause that most would consider more than justified, feels like betrayal—not only to those whose lives are invested in maintaining the belief that some wars are good, but also to readers who wish to believe in good and evil in a larger sense. Collins argues that there are good and evil people on both sides of a rebellion, suggesting that war itself can lead good people to act in evil ways, no matter how justified their cause; this argument apparently proves unpalatable to a majority of readers who found *Mockingjay* inferior to its predecessors.

The research for this article was originally conducted in 2011, only ten months after *Mockingjay*'s release. In the years since, the popularity of the series as a whole has only increased, fueled in large part by the release of three of four planned feature film adaptations (*The Hunger Games*, 2012; *Catching Fire*, 2013; and *Mockingjay— Part 1*, 2014; and *Part 2*, 2015), as well as by the publication of myriad "companion" volumes, both official and unofficial, to both films and books. Have readers' opinions of any or all of The Hunger Games books changed since 2011?

For the first book, the answer is, not so much. As of July 8, 2015, the number of reviews of *The Hunger Games* on Amazon.com had risen nearly tenfold, from 2,308 to 23,844. But the breakdown of reader opinion in those reviews remained almost exactly the same: 77 percent, rather than 76 percent, now gave the book five-star ratings; 16 percent, up from 15 percent, gave it four stars; and 6 percent (down from 7 percent) gave it three stars or lower.

The release of The Hunger Games films has only increased *Catching Fire*'s popularity over the past four years. As of January 2016, the number of reviews posted to Amazon.com for the second book of the trilogy had risen even more dramatically than those for *The Hunger Games*, from 910 to 16,685. And its percentage of five-star reviews had risen to 76 percent (from 72 percent), while the percentage of four-star reviews increased to 18 percent (from 8 percent). In 2016, only 6 percent of readers, rather than 8.5 percent, grant the book three stars or fewer.

Mockingjay, too, has benefitted from the overall rise in popularity of the series and films. In its first year of publication, only 42 percent of reviewers gave *Mockingjay* five stars. But by January 2016, that percentage had increased markedly, to 62 percent. Four-star reviews remained fairly constant (19 percent in 2016, 18 percent in 2011). Thus, most of the shift has occurred due to a drop in the percentage of three-star or lower reviews. In 2011, almost 40 percent of reviewers gave the books three stars or fewer, with 11 percent, slightly more than one in ten readers, giving the book only one star. In 2016, three stars or fewer account for only 19 percent, a drop of slightly more than half.

Still, 831 reviewers, up from 153 in 2011, felt strongly enough to give *Mockingjay* one star and to write (often at length) about their reasons for so doing. Those reasons remain largely the same as those given by earlier negative reviewers. Reader "Hannah," one of the early Amazon.com reviewers to give *Mockingjay* only one star, provides a representative explanation: "The story was so bleak, the anti-war message so strong, that there was no enjoyment in the book. You couldn't root for the rebels. You couldn't root for Katniss. You couldn't root for Gale or Peeta. You couldn't root for the Capitol. So what was the point? Just to read something and think, 'my god, war is BAD BAD BAD!'"

Suzanne Collins herself provides "Hannah" and her fellow disillusioned readers a possible solution to their dilemma. When asked by an interviewer, "What do you hope readers will come away with when they read The Hunger Games trilogy?" Collins' answered, "Questions about how elements of the books might be relevant in their own lives. And, if they're disturbing, what they might do about them" (Collins, Q & A).

Collins' words here are remarkably similar those of critics who have written about the purpose of dystopian fiction. As Kay Sambell suggests, dystopian fiction for children functions as an admonition, to "caution young readers about the probable dire consequences of current human behaviors" and to "shock its readership into a realization of the urgent need for a radical revisioning of current human political and social organizations" (Sambell 163). Unfortunately for Collins, and for many of her readers, the first two books evoke desires associated with high fantasy: the desire to identify with, or root for, a heroine; the desire to participate vicariously in action and violence; and the desire for good to win out easily over evil. The evocation of these desires in *The Hunger Games* and *Catching Fire* has fooled readers like "Hannah," who either ignored hints that, in *Mockingjay*, Collins was simultaneously drawing upon another genre and its conventions, or who were simply unaware that such different conventions exist. Feeling as if they have been the victims of a dishonest bait and switch, readers such as "Hannah" refuse to take on the role of *Mockingjay*'s implied reader, a term coined by Wayne Booth and further developed by Wolfgang Iser that refers to "the author's image of the recipient that is fixed and objectified in the text by specific indexical signs" (Schmid, *Implied Reader*). In other words, the implied reader embraces, rather than ignores or rejects, the response-inviting structures embedded in any given text. Hannah wishes to be the inspired, uplifted reader of heroic high fantasy, so she rejects taking on the reader role that *Mockingjay* implies, a reader familiar with the trauma and disillusionment common to dystopian fiction.

The release of the film *Mockingjay—Part 2* in November of 2015 did not give rise to a significant increase in positive reviews of the book, at least not on Amazon.com. In large part, I would argue, this is because, like the second half of Suzanne Collins' book, *Mockingjay—Part 2* the film contains most of the material to which one-star reviewers object: the "emotionless" and "meaningless" deaths of Finnick and Prue; Katniss' passivity; the lack of emotional connection between Katniss and Peeta after his rescue; and Katniss' decision not to kill President Snow. The film's creators resisted the urge to erase the typically bleak, negative ending of dystopian fiction and replace it with the triumphalism of high fantasy, remaining true to Collins' message that war, even war motivated by a just cause, is dehumanizing and corrupting.

Likely much to the dismay of Amazon.com reviewers like "jdub," who thought Collins' central focus was "the work of amazing people bringing down a cruel empire, not [the notion that] war is bad."

Works Cited

Booth, Wayne C. *The Rhetoric of Fiction*. 1961. 2nd ed. Chicago: U of Chicago P, 1983. Print.

Collins, Suzanne. *Mockingjay*. New York: Scholastic, 2010. Print.

_____. "A Q&A with Suzanne Collins, Author of *Mockingjay (The Final Book of The Hunger Games)*." *Amazon.com*. Amazon.com, Inc., n.p. Web. 20 Jan. 2016. 11 Jan 2011.

Iser, Wolfgang. *The Implied Reader: Patterns of Communication in Prose Fiction from Bunyan to Beckett*. Baltimore: Johns Hopkins UP, 1974. Print.

Sambell, Kay. "Presenting the Case for Social Change: The Creative Dilemma of Dystopian Writing for Children." *Utopian and Dystopian Writing for Children and Young Adults*. Ed. Carrie Hintz and Elaine Ostry. New York: Routledge, 2002. Print.

Schmid, Wolf. "Implied Reader." *The Living Handbook of Narratology*. Interdisciplinary Center for Narratology, University of Hamburg, 27 Jan. 2013. Web. 22 Nov. 2015. Print.

Stephens, John. *Language and Ideology in Children's Fiction*. London: Longman 1992. Print.

Tolkien, J. R. R. "On Fairy-Stories." *Tree and Leaf*. 1964. London: HarperCollins, 2001, 3–81. Print.

His Fordship in the Capitol and Big Brother in the Districts: The Hunger Games and the Modern Dystopian Tradition

Amy H. Sturgis

What is the worst that could happen? Authors of dystopian literature seek to answer this question. Through their works, they provide detailed road maps to worlds gone wrong, vivid streets signs warning us not to follow crooked paths or slide down slippery slopes to tragic consequences. In so doing, writers of dystopian stories challenge us to solve contemporary problems while there is still time—before our reality grows to resemble their fiction.

The *Oxford English Dictionary* (third edition) quotes from the January 5, 1967, issue of the weekly magazine *Listener* in its extended definition of dystopia: "The modern classics Aldous Huxley's *Brave New World* and George Orwell's *Nineteen Eighty Four* are dystopias. They describe not a world we should like to live in, but one we must be sure to avoid." Indeed, Huxley's (1932) and Orwell's (1949) influential books—both of which followed the first great modern dystopian novel, Yevgeny Zamyatin's *We* (1924)—have defined the contemporary debate regarding how society might decline and degenerate into tragedy. Could we be persuaded to surrender our freedom willingly, trading liberty and self-determination for security and entertainment, until we are as helpless and dependent as children, as Huxley suggests? Or is it more likely that, as Orwell relates, our freedom will be torn from us by force, leaving us prisoners in our own homes, always watched, captive, and afraid?

One of the most innovative contributions of The Hunger Games trilogy is its answer to the often-posed question of which British author was more accurate and relevant in his warning, Huxley or Orwell. In telling her tale of the futuristic Panem, Suzanne Collins carefully balances a Huxleyan nightmare in the Capitol against an Orwellian horror in the districts. Thus she incorporates both classic dystopian visions into a new and highly successful one, demonstrating how each set of concerns—and the larger genre itself—resonates with readers today.

The Origin of Dystopia

Thomas More introduced the concept opposite to dystopia—not the worst-case scenario, but the best—in his 1516 novel of an idealized, imaginary society entitled *Utopia*, which gave us the word we still use today to denote a perfect world. Nearly 350 years later, another British philosopher, John Stuart Mill, in a speech on "The State of Ireland" before the House of Commons, identified those who supported a policy he opposed as "dys-topians or caco-topians," because "what they appear to favour is too bad to be practicable" (248). Dystopia eventually became the accepted term for the "What if?" dark destination we should strive to avoid.

By the end of the nineteenth and beginning of the twentieth century, authors like the British H. G. Wells (in works such as 1895's *The Time Machine* and *When the Sleeper Wakes*, which was serialized in 1898 and 1899 and later reworked as 1910's *The Sleeper Awakes*), the American Jack London (in 1908's *The Iron Heel*), and the British E. M. Forster (in 1909's "The Machine Stops") were articulating their concerns about the economic and social repercussions of industrialization, automation, and class segregation through novels and short stories about worlds gone wrong. The birth of a truly modern dystopian literary tradition, however, required one more ingredient: the rise of the totalitarian nation-state.

The bloody Russian Revolution and resulting Soviet communism led to Yevgeny Zamyatin's pioneering *We* (1924), a dystopian novel that would be banned in Zamyatin's home country of Russia for more than sixty years and earn its author permanent political exile. In his story, Zamyatin forecasts a dismal future extrapolated from the political trends he witnessed firsthand; he imagines a powerful One State that dictates all aspects of human life, down to the number of times every person chews each bite of food. That same One State also seeks to expand its rigid and relentless control throughout the universe.

Through *We*, Zamyatin provides many of the essential building blocks that appear repeatedly in other works of dystopian storytelling, including The Hunger Games trilogy. For example, Zamyatin conveys the dehumanization of the citizens of the One State by denying them names and designating them by numbers instead. Although the characters in *The Hunger Games* retain individual names, their home regions are not so fortunate; Katniss Everdeen hails not from the evocative Appalachia, but rather the sterile-sounding District 12. Moreover, once the Games begin, the identities of tributes, such as Katniss and Peeta Mellark, are directly tied to the number of the district they represent.

In another instance of trendsetting, Zamyatin depicts the constant surveillance conducted by the One State by describing the buildings of the future as constructed of transparent glass. Everyone quite literally is always watching everyone else, while the ruling Benefactor presumably watches all. Similarly, in The Hunger Games trilogy, Katniss learns from an early age that as an ordinary citizen of District 12, she may be observed at any time. Singing the wrong song in her home or wearing the wrong expression during a public announcement might be a costly mistake. After she volunteers as tribute, her life is transformed by the need to play to the ever-present cameras and the audience members behind them—most importantly, of course, President Snow—if she hopes to survive.

Hope appears in *We* in the form of the forest beyond the walls of the One State, where a few survivors of the Two-Hundred-Year War managed to elude capture. As the revolutionary I-330 explains, "a small group of them survived and stayed to live there, behind the walls. Naked, they went off into the woods. They learned from the trees, the beasts, the birds, the flowers, the sun" (Zamyatin 144). The forest likewise symbolizes freedom and escape to Katniss, thanks to her late father, who taught her to hunt game and gather food and find self-sufficiency in nature, skills that gave her a distinct advantage during the Hunger Games.

Echoes of *We* appear in later and equally classic works by authors who read Zamyatin, from "Anthem" (1938) by Russian-turned-America Ayn Rand to *Kallocain* (1940) by Swede Karin

Boye, from *Cat's Cradle* (1963) by American Kurt Vonnegut to *The Dispossessed* (1974) by American Ursula K. LeGuin. George Orwell made no secret of the tremendous debt that his own *1984* owed to *We.* He also asserted that "Aldous Huxley's *Brave New World* must be partly derived from it" (Orwell, "Review of *We*" 96), although the question of such direct inspiration remains open—and rather academic. Whether or not Huxley consciously drew from the novel, his work resonates with themes it shares in common with Zamyatin's work and represents a next step in the evolution of the genre.

His Fordship in the Capitol

In *Brave New World* (1923), Aldous Huxley paints a portrait of a futuristic Earth in which humanity is mass produced and custom designed for assigned tasks. The historical Henry Ford, the American industrialist who sponsored development of the assembly-line technique of production, is revered like a god. Ten World Controllers of the World State (each of whom is addressed as "His Fordship") reign over this highly stratified, tightly constrained, stagnant society.

Like *We* before it and *1984* and *The Hunger Games* after it, *Brave New World* suggests that a violent conflict—in this case the Nine Years' War—led to the dystopian society. As World Controller Mustapha Mond explains to the outsider protagonist, John,

> "*That* made them change their tune all right. What's the point of truth or beauty or knowledge when the anthrax bombs are popping all around you?... People were ready to have even their appetites controlled then. Anything for a quiet life. We've gone on controlling ever since. It hasn't been very good for truth, of course. But it's been very good for happiness." (Huxley 155)

In other words, the generation who lived through the war never wanted to experience its like again, and thus its members chose to trade personal independence for the promise of stability. Their descendants are not offered the same choice. From their artificial conceptions, the new generations are manipulated through genetic modification, programmed via subconscious suggestion, and conditioned by constant propaganda to want what they have.

As the oft-repeated slogan goes in this brave new world, "Everybody's happy nowadays." But what does this happiness entail? Huxley anticipates a shallow, hedonistic society in which citizens are entertained into mindlessness. They are the ultimate passive consumers, watching immersive multisensory films ("feelies"), playing ridiculous games (such as "centrifugal bumblepuppy"), engaging in meaningless recreational sex (and on frequent occasions the cathartic group "orgy porgy"), and disappearing into "holidays" in their own minds courtesy of the hallucinogenic drug *soma*. They are not challenged by their work or engaged in serious decision-making or focused on anything beyond their own short-term, self-centered pleasure. They are dependent and thus easily led and controlled.

Clearly, Suzanne Collins' citizens of the Capitol share much in common with Huxley's citizens of the World State. In *The Hunger Games*, the majority of those who live in the Capitol are consumed by the trivial. Fad and fashion rule, making stylists—described by Katniss as "so dyed, stenciled, and surgically altered they're grotesque"—celebrities in their own right (Collins, *Hunger Games* 63). Katniss comes to realize that the Capitol dwellers are little more than ignorant, gullible, and dependent youngsters, no more responsible for themselves or the society they inhabit than an infant would be. In *Mockingjay*, she defends the remaining members of her Capitol prep team from the leadership of District 13, saying, "They're not evil or cruel. They're not even smart. Hurting them, it's like hurting children. They don't see ... I mean, they don't know..." (53).

The protagonists of both tales are outsiders. In *Brave New World*, members of the public view John as wildly primitive because he grew up beyond their regulated society on a Reservation, where behavior occurs that they see as beastly (and which we as readers see as natural), such as the practice of sexual reproduction, the maintenance of family relationships, and the observance of cultural and religious rituals. The citizens of the World State deem John "the Savage" because of his perceived uncivilized origins.

Similarly, Katniss in *The Hunger Games* is viewed as something different and less sophisticated because she hails from the primitive District 12 and defies Capitol aesthetics; the "savage" idea comes across clearly when members of her prep team fuss over her natural (that is, rough and hairy) body. Once they have transformed her through waxing and plucking and scouring and scrubbing, Flavius announces, "You almost look like a human being now!" and they all laugh (Collins, *Hunger Games* 62). This Other-ing works both ways, of course. Standing naked before the stylists, Katniss knows she should feel embarrassed, "but they are so unlike people that I'm no more self-conscious than if a trio of oddly-colored birds were pecking around my feet" (62).

John and Katniss—reflections of natural humanity, neither artificial nor altered—represent something alien, and therefore the audiences from the World State and Capitol, respectively, view their lives, sufferings, and even deaths without empathy. Huxley describes how "Darwin Bonaparte, the Feely Corporation's most expert big game photographer," plants microphones and cameras around the home to which John has retreated to escape. It's telling that Bonaparte is known for filming animals and that his stalking of John is described like a hunt, with Bonaparte waiting in "his carefully constructed hide in the wood three hundred metres away" (Huxley 172). He congratulates himself on getting footage of "the Savage," "the greatest since his taking of the famous all-howling stereoscope feely of the gorillas' wedding" (172). John's private, personal anguish becomes the multisensory movie *The Savage of Surrey*, "seen, heard and felt in every first-class feely-palace in Western Europe" (173).

Likewise, in the Collins trilogy, the children of the districts are reaped for the Hunger Games so that their suffering can be broadcast—as a warning and reminder to the people of the districts, of course, but also as entertainment for the citizens of the Capitol, who place bets and follow the killings as if watching a sports competition. When Katniss mourns Rue and treats her corpse with love and respect, she takes a first step toward forcing the audience from the Capitol to recognize the tributes' inherent humanity. She makes Rue's life and death abruptly *real* for the Capitol viewers.

Individuals fare similarly—that is, poorly—in the dystopias of Huxley and Collins. For example, in *Brave New World,* the few independent minds who rise above the ranks of conformity are banished. The gifted Helmholtz Watson is one such character. A handsome and brilliant lecturer at the College of Emotional Engineering, he can't help but rebel at the stifling prospect of writing endless and artless propaganda for the World State. Instead, he tries to encourage others to think for themselves, reading his students forbidden work on the heretical virtues of solitude and helping John destroy rations of the brain-numbing *soma* drug, knowing that he's ensuring his own downfall in the process. Ultimately, His Fordship Mustapha Mond permanently banishes Watson but gives him the choice of which island will serve as his prison. Watson chooses the inhospitable climate of the Falkland Islands for the sake of his art: "I believe one would write better if the climate were bad. If there were a lot of wind and storms, for example…" (Huxley 156).

The World Controller obviously admires Watson's keen mind, artistic sensibility, and personal courage: "I like your spirit, Mr. Watson. I like it very much indeed. As much as I officially disapprove of it" (Huxley 156). His admiration does not stop Mond from giving Watson what amounts to a life sentence, however, for the sake of the One State's stability. In fact, as Mond muses about the fate of unconventional outliers such as Watson, he notes that the condemned should be thankful that the Earth holds so many islands for their containment. He says of the islands, "I don't know what we should do without them. Put you all in the lethal chamber, I suppose" (155–156).

Like Watson, the character of Cinna in Suzanne Collins' trilogy is a product of his vapid Capitol culture, and yet he rises above it. From the first moment Katniss meets him, she can see he is an independent soul because his appearance reflects his own aesthetic taste rather than the current popular fad. As they work together, Katniss realizes that his exquisite designs are also intentionally provocative and politically subversive. When Katniss' would-be wedding dress transforms into the defiant form of a mockingjay in *Catching Fire*, Caesar Flickerman asks Cinna to take a bow before the cameras in acknowledgement of his artistic achievement. Katniss thinks, "And suddenly I am so afraid for him. What has he done? Something terribly dangerous. An act of rebellion in itself" (Collins, *Catching Fire* 253). Unfortunately for Cinna, President Snow does not simply ban rebels to convenient islands. Cinna pays for his nonconformity with his life. Like Huxley's Watson, however, Cinna appreciates the danger he courts—in time to leave costume designs and encouraging words to help Katniss in her final fight against the Capitol.

The key to the Huxleyan nightmare Suzanne Collins presents in the Capitol is choice. Did the Capitol citizens choose to relinquish their autonomy in favor of becoming dependent children? Collins gives us her answer in the name of the dystopian nation itself: Panem. This refers to the ancient satirical poet Juvenal's critique of his fellow Romans. In his *Satire X*, Juvenal laments that the Roman citizens have traded their birthright of political engagement willingly for security and amusement. Plutarch Heavensbee explains this to Katniss in *Mockingjay*:

> "It's a saying from thousands of years ago, written in a language called Latin about a place called Rome ... *Panem et Circenses* translates into 'Bread and Circuses.' The writer was saying that in return for full bellies and entertainment, his people had given up their political responsibilities and therefore their power." (Collins, *Mockingjay* 223)

The citizens of the Capitol are mirror images of the decadent Romans. They have chosen to surrender both rights and responsibilities in favor of such Roman amusements as feasting (and purging and feasting again, as Peeta discovers in *Catching Fire*) and watching gladiators (or tributes) fight to the death in spectacular games. It's no surprise that in an interview with Rick Margolis of *School Library Journal*, Collins names Spartacus, the gladiator-turned-leader of the Third Servile War against Rome, as a key inspiration for Katniss (Collins, "The Last Battle").

In Collins' Panem, however, characters have the opportunity to change their minds and make new choices. When enough members of the Capitol wake up to their dependent plight and decide to challenge President Snow and his regime—Plutarch, for instance, and Cressida and her camera crew—they help to bring about permanent change. Alone, Huxley's "John the Savage" takes his own life in despair, but surrounded by allies, Katniss the Mockingjay survives.

Big Brother in the Districts

In *1984* (1949), George Orwell imagines that the Britain of the future has emerged from a devastating nuclear war to become Airstrip One, a claustrophobic society whose rulers are symbolized by the ever-present image of an ever-watching Big Brother. Members of the populace are never truly alone; they are monitored in their comfortless barracks by not only their family members and neighbors but also their two-way television sets to confirm that they are loyal and obedient. Citizens' knowledge is manipulated by a government that constantly rewrites both distant and recent history to serve the function of pro-state propaganda, and their ideas are constrained by Newspeak, a limited language designed to make traitorous (that is, independent) thoughts unspeakable—and therefore ultimately unthinkable.

Airstrip One does not represent the choice of the people. Instead, it represents the will of the powerful few imposed and maintained by fear and pain on the many. When the protagonist, Winston Smith, comes to appreciate the nightmare in which he's living and struggles to liberate himself, he is brutally tortured and twisted and finally broken. His tormentor articulates the primary warning of the novel eloquently when he says,

> always there will be the intoxication of power, constantly increasing and constantly growing subtler. Always, at every moment, there will be the thrill of victory, the sensation of trampling on an enemy who is helpless. If you want a picture of the future, imagine a boot stamping on a human face—forever. (Orwell, *1984* 267)

Orwell had seen firsthand what the consolidation of power in the hands of the few—a sophisticated, subtle, technologically savvy few—looked like thanks to the Stalinist Soviet Union, and he found the result to be deadly. The same warning about what the power-hungry will do to establish and enhance their authority appears in The Hunger Games trilogy. Thus President Coin in *Mockingjay* proves to be equally willing to sacrifice human lives in the cause of consolidating her power as President Snow is in all three novels.

Life in District 12 (and a majority of the rest of the districts) in Collins' novels shares many similarities with life in Orwell's Airstrip One. Buildings reflect shabby decay. The people exist in a perpetual state of want. They attend public rallies and view government-made propaganda films because they are required to do so. They labor in assigned industries to fill quotas dictated by the central government. The products of these industries are insufficient to fulfill needs; therefore, both Smith and Katniss turn to illegal black-market alternatives until those options are taken away from them.

Furthermore, in Orwell's dystopia, a person must not entertain any idea that contradicts or questions the state ("thoughtcrime") or even appear to do so ("facecrime"). In *The Hunger Games*, Katniss notes that the same is true in the districts:

> When I was young, I scared my mother to death, the things I would blurt out about District 12, about the people who rule our country, Panem, from the far-off city called the Capitol. Eventually I understood this would only lead us to more trouble. So I learned to hold my tongue and to turn my features into an indifferent mask so that no one could ever read my thoughts. (6)

In two important and related parts of her trilogy, Suzanne Collins draws readers' attention to parallels with *1984* only to give them an original twist at the end. First, Peeta's "hijacking" in *Mockingjay*—his physical torture and psychological reconditioning in the Capitol—clearly hearkens back to Winston Smith's physical and psychological torture in custody at what is presumed to be the Ministry of Love and, finally, in the dreaded Room 101. Smith is told, "We, the Party, control all records, and we control all memories" (Orwell 248). Peeta's memories are refashioned to fit President Snow's designs, until he doesn't know what is real and what is false. Smith is tormented so that he betrays his lover, Julia, and begs for her to be tortured in his place. Peeta is programmed so that he attacks his love, Katniss, and tries to strangle her. In both instances, the rulers release their victims in order to send a message about the ultimate power the government wields over its people, power enough to break and remake each citizen. Smith becomes a warning, Peeta, a weapon.

On a related (and musical) note, Collins employs the song "The Hanging Tree" in her tale, much as Orwell repeats the song "The Chestnut Tree" in *1984*. Orwell did not invent "The Chestnut Tree"—it was a popular Glenn Miller tune at the time Orwell was writing his novel—but he changed key words that his readers easily would recognize. Romantic love and emotional attachment are forbidden in Airstrip One because no other commitment should come before each person's loyalty to Big Brother. Therefore, the original and familiar "Under the spreading chestnut tree/I loved you and you loved me" becomes in Orwell's dystopia "Under the spreading chestnut tree/I sold you and you sold me" (Orwell 77). This "selling" speaks to how, in the end, Big Brother always wins. Smith and his lover each betray the other while in custody. That betrayal assists in the breaking of Smith, who goes from writing "DOWN WITH BIG BROTHER" at the story's start (18) to, in the final line of the novel, realizing "He loved Big Brother" (297). In *Brave New World* fashion, Smith has been remade to want what he has: his own subjugation in his dystopian world.

Collins nods to Orwell with Peeta's ordeal and "The Hanging Tree" song, but she ends these homages with a twist. Unlike Smith, Peeta is not fully broken by his physical and psychological torment. With the help of Katniss, he fights to restore and replace his memories and overcome his fear conditioning. Ultimately, he brings her not death, as the Capitol intended, but life—a life with him and the new life of the children they make together. Furthermore, "The Hanging Tree" is not, like Orwell's song "The Chestnut Tree," a reminder of how the state triumphs over everything, even love. Collins' song is quite the opposite. "The Hanging Tree" is a subversive song about a man, condemned to be hanged, who calls to his love to join him, so that the two can die together and be free.

Only in *Mockingjay*, when Katniss has "a couple of trips to the Hunger Games under my belt," does she comprehend why her mother had wanted her to forget the song her father taught her and never sing it again. Katniss lives in a place where "plenty of people were executed" by hanging, whether they were actually guilty of offenses or not. Of the character singing the song, she thinks, "Maybe his lover was already sentenced to death and he was trying to make it easier. To let her know he'd be waiting. Or maybe he thought the place he was leaving her was really worse than death. Didn't I want to kill Peeta with that syringe to save him from the Capitol?" (Collins, *Mockingjay* 126). "The Hanging Tree," then, is the exact opposite of "The Chestnut Tree." It's not about lovers selling each other out to the state: it's about love stronger than the power of the Capitol, stronger than even the survival instinct. It's about defiance and hope for something better. It becomes a valuable weapon in Katniss the Mockingjay's arsenal against President Snow.

Unlike *Brave New World* and the Capitol, the dystopias of *1984* and the districts do not represent a population's willing surrender of individual liberty. Both Orwell and Collins in her depiction of the districts in The Hunger Games trilogy describe a populace whose freedom has been taken and trampled by force. The government maintains its authority through fear and violence. In his final passages, Orwell leaves us with the individual destroyed. Collins, however, leaves us with individuals who are wounded and scarred, to be sure, but who have survived and prevailed against the powers that oppressed them.

The Innovation of *The Hunger Games*

The dystopian genre became a global and thriving one in the second half of the twentieth century and the first decades of the twenty-first. Huxley and Orwell continue to influence new generations of writers, and their novels remain voices that must be answered in some form or fashion by each new entry in the dystopian conversation. Or to put it another way, with each fresh dystopian work, readers discover whether the author identifies with Team Huxley or Team Orwell.

These works include young adult dystopian novels, some of which have helped to blaze the trail that Suzanne Collins followed, depicting young protagonists who were somehow "gamed" or "played" by the rulers of their worlds gone wrong. Numerous recent novels establish this theme: *Ender's Game* (1985) by American Orson Scott Card, *Invitation to the Game* (1990) by British-Canadian Monica Hughes, *Battle Royale* (1999) by Kōshun Takami of Japan, *Surviving Antarctica: Reality TV 2083* (2005) by American Andrea White, and the Bone World Trilogy by Peadar Ó Guilín of Ireland (the first book of which, *The Inferior*, was first published in 2007). These novels, in a way, set the stage for The Hunger Games trilogy. Others have followed *The Hunger Games*, also using the "gamed" or "played" theme, most notably *The Girl in the Arena* (2009) by American Lise Haines and *Red Rising* (2014), the first novel in American Pierce Brown's trilogy, which shares the novel's name.

A relatively recent development in publishing is known as the "*Hunger Games* effect;" adults are crossing publishers' categories to read dystopias (and other works) marketed as young adult fiction. Critics first noticed the phenomenon thanks to the remarkable sales of The Hunger Games trilogy in e-book as well as print editions (Sturgis 47–48). Indeed, *The Hunger Games* has been a leader in the unprecedented explosion of young adult dystopian fiction in the twenty-first century, which has yielded novels that are consumed by audiences of all ages. These include works that anticipated The Hunger Games series, such as Lois Lowry's The Giver trilogy (1993–2004, with *Son* making it a quartet in 2012), and others that followed The Hunger Games trilogy, such as the Divergent trilogy (2011–2013) by Veronica Roth.

Surely one reason for the tremendous success of the trilogy is its innovative answer to the question posed by Huxley and Orwell. Which author was more accurate in his warning? As American critic Neil Postman reminds us in 1985 book *Amusing Ourselves to Death*:

Orwell feared that the truth would be concealed from us. Huxley feared the truth would be drowned in a sea of irrelevance. Orwell feared we would become a captive culture. Huxley feared we would become a trivial culture, preoccupied with some equivalent of the feelies, the orgy porgy, and the centrifugal bumblepuppy. (vii)

In telling her tale of a heroine named Katniss, Collins identifies herself as representing both Team Huxley and Team Orwell, carefully balancing a Huxleyan nightmare in the Capitol against an Orwellian horror in the districts. Rather than choose between them, she incorporates both classic dystopian visions into a new and insightful one, demonstrating how both Huxley's and Orwell's concerns—and the dystopian genre they both championed—continues to speak to contemporary audiences.

In addition, Collins adds her own ending note. Orwell leaves readers with a broken wreck of a protagonist, a beaten-down and brainwashed servant of Big Brother. Huxley's hero takes his own life. Collins, however, creates a protagonist who appears more resilient, and, in so doing, presents hope. In this way, Collins brings us full circle, back to the first great modern dystopia, Zamyatin's *We*. While it is true that *We*'s protagonist finds no happy ending—D-503 endures a lobotomy-like brain surgery that restores him to passive obedience, while his love, I-330, is brutally executed—Zamyatin offers readers the promise of something more. The character O-90, pregnant with D-503's child, manages to escape the One State and find refuge beyond the wall in the forest. The next generation will be born free.

This is where Collins leaves us in *Mockingjay*, with the children of Katniss and Peeta playing freely and without fear in the Meadow. The little girl and her brother "don't know they play on a graveyard" (Collins, *Mockingjay* 390). Katniss and Peeta will never fully recover from all they have endured, but they will find joy in watching their children experience the kind of childhood they never had, and this brings hope. Their next generation can "take the words of the song for granted": "Here it's safe, here it's warm" (389).

Worlds can go wrong in both Huxleyan and Orwellian ways. They can also be saved.

Works Cited

Collins, Suzanne. *Catching Fire*. 2009. New York: Scholastic, 2009. Print.

_____. *The Hunger Games*. 2008. New York: Scholastic, 2008. Print.

_____. "The Last Battle: With 'Mockingjay' on Its Way, Suzanne Collins Weighs in on Katniss and the Capitol." Interview with Rick Margolis. *School Library Journal* Online. SLJ, 1 Aug. 2010. Web. 20 Jan. 2015.

_____. *Mockingjay*. 2010. New York: Scholastic, 2010. Print.

"dystopia, n." *OED Online*. Oxford UP, n.d. Web. 16 June 2015.

Huxley, Aldous. *Brave New World*. 1932. New York: Harper & Row, 1978. Print.

Mill, John Stuart, "The State of Ireland." 1868. *The Collected Works of John Stuart Mill, Volume XXVIII—Public and Parliamentary Speeches Part I November 1850—November 1868*. Ed. John M. Robson and Bruce L. Kinzer. Toronto: U of Toronto P, London: Routledge and Kegan Paul, 1988. 2 Aug. 2015. Web. 16 June 2015.

Orwell, George. *1984*. 1949. New York: New American Library, 1977. Print.

_____. "Review of *We* by E.I. Zamyatin." 1946. *The Collected Essays, Journalism and Letters of George Orwell*. Ed. Sonia Orwell and Ian Angus. Vol 4. *In Front of Your Nose, 1845–1950*. Hammondsworth: Penguin, 1970. 95–99.

Postman, Neil. *Amusing Ourselves to Death*. 1985. New York: Penguin, 1986. Print.

Sturgis, Amy H. "Not Your Parents' Dystopias: Millennial Fondness for Worlds Gone Wrong." *Reason* 46 (Oct. 2014): 46–51. Print.

Zamyatin, Yevgeny. *We*. 1924. Trans. Natasha Randall. New York: Random House, 2006. Print.

CRITICAL
READINGS

"You Love Me. Real": Gender in The Hunger Games Trilogy

Danielle Bienvenue Bray

Even the most casual reader of Suzanne Collins' Hunger Games trilogy cannot miss the books' political message: large national governments, no matter their political philosophies, are dangerous beasts. Different critical theories can help illuminate some nuances to that reading, however. For example, a feminist reading of the series reveals a complex and interesting gender dynamic underpinning the books' politics. Those characters in the books we seem most disposed to root for, especially Katniss and Peeta but also more minor characters, are motivated largely by their relationships with others. Characters who are less sympathetic, Gale and President Coin in particular, are motivated primarily by the hope of public-sphere success, especially in politics or on the battlefield. In her Hunger Games trilogy, Collins invokes the gender associations of the public and domestic spheres to create a hierarchy in which the traditionally feminine domestic sphere, associated in the books with off-the-grid living in the outer districts, is superior to the traditionally masculine public sphere, associated with the governments of both the Capitol and the rebels led by District 13.

Feminism Primer: The Three Waves

While feminist critical theory is complex and varied, the popular perception of feminism is much narrower in its scope. That mainstream, popular understanding of feminism connects primarily to the second of what scholars tend to regard as three distinct "waves" of feminist thought and activism. As the "first" suggests, first-wave feminism, placed broadly in the nineteenth and early twentieth centuries, is the beginning of feminist political thought, including movements such as the campaign for women's suffrage. Feminism's second wave is the feminist ideology of the mid-twentieth century, the "women's liberation" movement associated with activists like

Betty Friedan and Gloria Steinem. By the 1980s, though, it had become clear to many feminists that the second-wave brand of thinking was problematically narrow in its definition of who women were and what they wanted. In response, the third wave was born: a wide variety of feminist ideologies, speaking to the concerns of diverse groups of women.

In children's literature criticism as in popular culture, the most common understanding of the meaning and goals of feminism is still second wave. That is, it is concerned primarily with the access of women to the ideal of success traditionally pursued by men, symbolized by a high-paying, high-status job in the public sphere. In keeping with this singular focus of second-wave, or liberal, feminism, the typical yardstick for "nonsexist" children's books tends to be the extent to which they represent girl characters performing roles that are generally perceived as male-dominated. This metric can be identified as early as 1972, when Lenore Weitzman and her colleagues did the content analysis that became the model for decades of later studies (Clark, Kulkin, and Clancy 71–4, 78–80). While the representation of female characters making inroads in traditionally masculine areas is certainly one area of feminist interest, it should not be the only one, and this is where the "liberal bias" identified by Clark, Kulkin, and Clancy becomes problematic.

One drawback of this second-wave feminist approach to children's literature is that like the second-wave feminist movement more broadly, it is concerned almost exclusively with women's success in traditionally male-dominated arenas, marginalizing just as much as traditional "patriarchal" thinking those traits and activities traditionally connected to womanhood. Amanda B. Diekman and Sara K. Murnen conclude from their 2004 study that "nonsexist books were more egalitarian than sexist books only in their representation of masculine personality characteristics" (380); that is, while books called "nonsexist" portray female characters engaging in activities traditionally considered to be for males only, they are no more likely than "sexist" books to celebrate boys or girls taking up traditionally feminine pursuits. Nancy Taber, Vera Woloshyn, and Laura Lane note this prejudice in responses to *The Hunger Games*; preteen girl participants in a book club they studied disliked the character of Peeta, whom they found "a little bit girly" and criticized for not playing the traditionally masculine role of protector to Katniss (1030-1). Thus, while female characters are seen to be improving their circumstances by pursuing traditionally masculine goals, the goals and interests themselves that are traditionally associated with femininity are being trampled in the process.

Cultural feminism, associated with theorists like Carol Gilligan, is one school of third-wave feminist thought concerned particularly with the celebration of interests and behaviors traditionally regarded as feminine. In *The Feminist Spectator as Critic*, theatre scholar Jill Dolan identifies as the goal of cultural feminist art the generation of a "feminine aesthetic" that celebrates traditionally feminine values in the same way that existing aesthetic systems celebrate traditionally masculine values (83–4). In The Hunger Games trilogy, Suzanne Collins creates such a feminine aesthetic through the way she represents characters who—regardless of their biologically assigned sex—celebrate values traditionally perceived as feminine.

The Domestic Made Public: District 12

In Katniss Everdeen's home district, femininity is a luxury not available to most of the characters. With the Capitol in power, the harshness of life in the outer districts forces the characters into mostly-masculine gender identities, even in circumstances where these identities would not typically be expected to manifest. Many of the traditional trappings of femininity, the economic freedom to choose homemaking as a primary occupation, for example, are not available to those living in the Seam. Many families are headed by single mothers whose husbands have died in coal mining accidents, forcing these women to function in the traditionally masculine role of breadwinner. Masculine behaviors and pursuits, like hunting and working outside the home to earn a living, are dominant throughout the district.

The Hunger Games begins in District 12, with Katniss and Gale Hawthorne out hunting together. Procuring food is their primary occupation, and while the feeding of others might traditionally be regarded as a feminine pursuit, the way Katniss and Gale do it is distinctly masculinized. For them, hunting is a form of commerce; they barter much of the game they catch for other goods (Collins, *Hunger Games* 7, 11). They even barter their own lives for food by accepting tesserae, meager rations of grain and oil granted to youths in exchange for their names being entered extra times into the reaping bowl for the annual Games (13–14). Even when Gale offers Katniss a more traditional gesture of food sharing, a loaf of fresh "bakery bread," he fires an arrow into it first, presenting it to her as something he "shot" (7). Similarly, Katniss masculinizes her relationship with Buttercup, her sister Prim's cat. Buttercup "hates" Katniss, and she makes peace with him by feeding him "entrails" whenever she cleans a "kill" from her hunting (3–4); as with Gale's bread, a traditionally feminine act of food-sharing is made more masculine by its association with hunting and with Collins' blunt, visceral word choice (4). Indeed, in a text that turns on "gender deviation," Katniss is, as Jennifer Mitchell notes, "the prime site of constantly shifting gender variance" (128-9).

Both Katniss and Gale also regard themselves as father-figures within their households, responsible for their younger siblings and even their mothers as if they were all children (Collins, *Hunger Games* 9). Katniss receives the "medal of valor" after her father's death in a mine explosion because of her role as "oldest child" in her family (23), but this also positions her as the "man" of her household, acting on her father's behalf in a public ceremony. Katniss claims this title openly a short time later: "At eleven years old, with Prim just seven, I took over as head of the family" (27). Even Katniss' farewell to her family when she is to depart for the Games focuses primarily on their financial security while she is away, a traditionally masculine concern (34–5).

Her adoption of the role of surrogate father to her own mother and sister also frees Katniss from a traditionally feminine occupation that is rendered unthinkable by the Capitol's treatment of the districts: motherhood. Katniss tells Gale very early in *The Hunger Games* that she does not want to bring children into her life in District 12 (Collins, *Hunger Games* 9). She reflects again on her determination not to get married at the book's end, when Peeta finds out that her share of their romance was feigned for the Capitol's TV cameras (373). Katniss maintains throughout the series her position that marriage and motherhood are hopeless in the world in which she lives, thereby avoiding a relationship discussion with Gale after the announcement of the Quarter Quell (Collins, *Catching Fire* 185). One of her moments of strongest connection to Peeta occurs during the Quarter Quell interviews, when he has announced their fictitious pregnancy and the look on his face tells her that he shares her fear of "the loss of my children to the Games" (257). Katniss resists motherhood even in her interactions with other adults, quipping to Haymitch after she pours water over him to wake him for the Victory Tour, "if you wanted to be babied, you should have asked Peeta [to wake you]" (14). The only times Katniss does act in a motherly way are when she's rebelling against the Capitol, as when she forms her alliance with Rue in the first Games, feeding her and then sharing a sleeping bag with her as her own mother sleeps with Prim (Collins, *Hunger Games* 202–8; *Catching Fire* 3). Katniss also feeds bread to Bonnie, a starving refugee from District 8, whom she associates with Rue in her mind (Collins, *Catching Fire* 142–3).

By taking on the father-role in her household, Katniss also enables her mother and sister to retain some of their femininity. This, too, is tinged with the need to address more traditionally masculine, public-sphere concerns, however. An "apothecary" or "healer," Katniss' mother is employed in a feminized version of a traditionally masculine occupation, doctor (Collins, *Hunger Games* 8). Prim, lovable to everyone and herself a lover of animals, turns these gifts toward traditionally masculine pursuits as well, raising a goat in order to earn an income from its milk and cheese, and becoming a breadwinner like her older sister (4, 7, 34–5, 268–73). Like her mother, Prim is also a superior healer (256). In *Catching Fire*, Katniss, too, finds her feminine gender expressions masculinized in District 12. After her first kiss with Gale, a classic girls' book moment, Katniss' response is not a traditionally feminine emotional one, but rather is analytical. She tries to decide "how I felt about the kiss, if I had liked it or resented it," but is only able to remember the physical sensation of it without any emotionality attached (27). Katniss likewise is unable to develop an interest in the "suitable" feminine hobbies Effie Trinket and her mother suggest for her after the first Games, finally taking up fashion design when Cinna, a man, suggests it (39).

Because of the role of the Capitol in skewing gender expression in the outer districts, many of these masculine acts are furthermore intrinsically political. When Gale thinks of the tesserae he has taken to feed his mother and siblings, he acknowledges this as a political strategy to keep those in the districts too weak and frightened to rebel (Collins, *Hunger Games* 13–4). The line between family and political life blurs again when Gale says goodbye to Katniss before she departs for the Games, hugging her and also talking "grimly" about how similar the acts of hunting animals and killing people in the arena probably are in practice (38–40). Haymitch's initial liking for Katniss is likewise political. When she volunteers for Prim, he declares she has "Spunk!," shouting directly into the television camera and thus at the Capitol, "More than you!" (24).

After the first Games, political and military strategy become a primary occupation for both Katniss and Gale. Katniss' first instinct is to protect those she cares about by fleeing with them all into the woods outside District 12, though she is miffed when Gale's declaration of love for her disrupts the flow of her pragmatism (Collins, *Catching Fire* 96–8). Again, her traditionally feminine concern for the well-being of her loved ones is rendered masculine by the need to strategize their care. Gale's plotting, however, operates on a larger scale. Once Katniss has told him that uprisings have begun in the outer districts, Gale wants to stay and participate (99–100). At first, this appears to make Gale the more other-centered of the two; he challenges Katniss' concern for their families by asking, "What about the other families, Katniss?" (100). As the story proceeds, though, Gale's interest in the rebellion becomes increasingly focused on public-sector victory and the annihilation of his enemies; in *Mockingjay*, he tells Katniss, "'If I could hit a button and kill every living soul working for the Capitol, I would do it. Without hesitation'" (31).

In some ways, District 12 is a place dominated by families' desire to care for one another, on its surface a domestic, and thus feminine, virtue. The Capitol's exertion of its power over the families of 12, particularly those living in the Seam, renders this desire public. To truly care for these families means to keep their children out of the Games and to ensure basic food security and physical safety for the people of the district. Bringing about this kind of change in a place like District 12 is a political act and, therefore, a public and masculine one.

The Mask of Strategy: The Games and the Capitol

Much as even the simplest acts are rendered public in the outer districts by the politicized nature of the characters' lives, the Capitol, including the Tribute Center and various Hunger Games arenas, are by definition public because of President Snow's surveillance state. From the moment they arrive, the lives of the tributes are, as Amy L. Montz notes, rendered "as public spectacle" (141). Everything that happens in the Capitol is recorded on camera, and thus every act is public. This degree of surveillance forces those in the Capitol and the arena to strategize their every move, employing what Simon Baron-Cohen calls the "male brain," which he argues is "predominantly hard-wired for understanding and building systems" (qtd. in Fine xix).

During the first Games, from the moment she boards the train to the Capitol, Katniss begins using her "male, systemizing" brain to strategize her safe return to her family (Fine xix). Furthermore, she assumes that everyone around her is thinking in the same way, perceiving everything Peeta does and says to be part of his own secret plan to win the Games and thus, of course, to kill her (Collins, *Hunger Games* 40–1, 48, 60, 72, 84, 91–2, 161). Katniss continues to project her strategizing onto others in the Quarter Quell, in which she elects not to try to save Beetee and Wiress right away because she expects her ally, Finnick Odair, to turn on her (Collins, *Catching Fire* 274).

Despite Katniss' attempts to rely on her systemizing, strategizing male brain, she does allow herself to form an emotional attachment to Peeta during their training for the first Games. When she learns that he has asked to be trained separately on the day before the pre-game interviews, she surprises herself by feeling betrayed, only then realizing how much she had allowed herself to be disarmed by Peeta (Collins, *Hunger Games* 113–4). Katniss likewise develops a camaraderie with Finnick when they are allies in the Quarter Quell (Collins, *Catching Fire* 316–7). Under the watchful eye of the Capitol, however, even romance must be made part of a system: Katniss is only able to comprehend the idea of returning Peeta's romantic feelings for her when she understands them as a strategy (Collins, *Hunger Games* 136–7). Even when Katniss does experience a personal betrayal, she frames it as a political one. When Peeta has joined the Career Pack in the first Games, Katniss regards him as a traitor not to any friendship they may have had outside the arena but to all of District 12 for allying himself with the tributes from the districts better cared for by the Capitol (161–2).

Although Peeta is employing a strategy in the Games, Katniss misreads it, which also masculinizes her because it indicates a failure of emotional intelligence, a trait Baron-Cohen associates with the "female brain" (Fine xix). Katniss' difficulty tapping into her "female, empathizing brain" is perhaps especially interesting in that Peeta's strategy relies heavily on his. Peeta makes his romantic feelings for Katniss his angle for the interview, a move that ameliorates Katniss' own difficulty making herself likeable in front of the cameras (Collins, *Hunger Games* 130–7). Since he has no expectation of winning the Games himself, he can only have done this to help her win (141). It eventually becomes clear to Katniss that Peeta has maintained this angle throughout the Games, at great personal risk (244–8). Much like the particular strategy he chooses for the Games, Peeta's gender expression also skews towards the feminine in other ways. His self-described special skill, for example, is "baking bread" (89).

Peeta is not the only caregiver tribute from District 12, however. Katniss' experience in the arena during her first Games is largely characterized by her caring for weaker tributes. From the first night in the arena, Katniss is concerned for Rue, the twelve-year-old tribute from District 11 (Collins, *Hunger Games* 157). She forms an alliance with Rue shortly thereafter (184–5, 200–1), and they strategize together, concocting a military-style maneuver to destroy the Careers' food stores (206–7). They hug before parting for the mission (213), and on the way back, when she knows Rue is in danger, Katniss exposes her own position to draw Rue's attackers away (232), much as a mother bird will draw predators away from her nest. Katniss then comforts Rue and sings to her as she dies (233–7), later describing the moment to Thresh, the other tribute from 11, as though she had been singing Rue a lullabye (288).

Katniss also serves as a caregiver to Peeta during their first Games. When the "rule change" permitting them to be co-victors is announced, she impulsively calls out for Peeta before realizing this exposes her position and then tracking him more quietly (Collins, *Hunger Games* 244–8). Once they are reconnected, Katniss recalls her mother's healing wisdom in order to treat Peeta's wounded leg (253–65), and when the injury proves too much for her alone, she risks her life in order to get Capitol medicine for him from the Cornucopia (274–89). In *Catching Fire*, Peeta recalls this, dubbing Katniss "the healer" when Finnick is injured (306).

During their time in hiding together, Katniss at first keeps up only the pretense of a romance with Peeta in order to benefit from gifts from the audience (*Hunger Games* 247–8, 253, 257, 260–1). Eventually, Katniss discovers she has actual feelings for Peeta (297, 342–5). It is impossible for her to disentangle those feelings from her drive to win the Games, her political life, and her basic humanity, though (348–9). Their first Games come to a head when the rules are changed back and Katniss suggests a suicide pact that is emotional in that it means neither of them has to live without the other, but also strategic in that it hurts the Capitol by leaving it without a victor for this year's Games (318–9, 342–5).

Katniss' use of her onscreen romance with Peeta to win over the Capitol viewers transposes her and Peeta's gender expressions in some ways. By becoming the calculating planner in the relationship, Katniss pushes Peeta into the more traditionally feminine, emotional position. Peeta owns as much at the start of the Victory Tour when he apologizes to Katniss for acting "wounded" that she is performing their romance for the cameras (Collins, *Catching Fire* 51). In a different research project, Woloshyn, Taber, and Lane note that this "marginalized masculinity" is noble but renders Peeta "*less than* Gale in context of the [G]ames" (153); however, Peeta uses his feminized position to augment his and Katniss' strategies as competitors. For example, Peeta continues to take the feminine role in their fictional romance when he fabricates and announces at the Quarter Quell interviews his and Katniss' secret marriage and pregnancy (255–7), news one might typically expect to hear from the bride. It is perhaps unsurprising then that when Peeta tries to persuade Katniss to let him be killed in the Games to save her life, he appeals to her feminine other-centeredness, reminding her that even if he dies, "there are other people who'd make your life worth living" (351). While he is held hostage in the Capitol in *Mockingjay*, Peeta mirrors this other-centeredness, fighting through a brainwashing technique the Capitol calls "hijacking" to warn Katniss and the rest of the people of District 13 that an air raid is on the way (133–4).

While Peeta's gender performance is tinged with femininity in the Capitol, Haymitch continues in the masculine role of military strategist. On the train to their first Games, he begins to take an interest in Peeta and Katniss when they start a physical fight with him over his drinking, and he immediately begins to give them the kind of advice he laughingly denied them a moment before (Collins, *Hunger Games* 56–8). Once Katniss is in the arena, Haymitch's provision and withholding of sponsor gifts is also strategic, a form of communication. When Katniss is dehydrated and Haymitch does not send her any water, she understands this to mean that she must be near a natural supply (168–71). Likewise, Katniss understands the success of her performed romance with Peeta from the quality of the gifts of food he sends (261, 302). This strategizing is never callous, however; when Katniss and Peeta need medical attention, Haymitch gives them what they need to get it (188, 274–7). Haymitch is able to capitalize further on this strategy in the Quarter Quell, using gifts of bread to tell the rebels in the arena when and where their rescue will take place (Collins, *Catching Fire* 385).

Haymitch also collaborates with Cinna in strategizing to keep Katniss safe. Cinna's idea that she and Peeta hold hands at the opening ceremonies and dress alike for training sends them into the first Games as a pair rather than as enemies, and Haymitch latches onto this strategy (Collins, *Hunger Games* 69, 79, 87–8, 92). Cinna is also able to turn Katniss visually into the love-struck young girl Haymitch wants her to be for the post-arena interview, when the Capitol is angry at her for making it look bad with her threatened suicide pact (355). Once Katniss is removed from the arena after the first Games, Haymitch even becomes fatherly in his attentions toward her, preventing the Capitol surgeons from giving her breast implants while she is unconscious (354). Cinna joins Haymitch in this fatherly act, too, during the Victory Tour when he prevents "alterations" to Katniss' body by the prep team (Collins, *Catching Fire* 48–9).

Haymitch's strategizing becomes more overtly political in the second and final books of the trilogy. He helps Katniss to realize during the Victory Tour that no tribute truly leaves the arena; the victor may live, but he or she remains in the Games through trauma and governmental control. For Katniss, this means that she will eventually "have to marry Peeta" (Collins, *Catching Fire* 44); this realization is difficult for Katniss, who has grown up in a place where the choice of whom and whether to marry is "[o]ne of the few freedoms we have" (45), but the knowledge enables her to view her eventual marriage as President Snow does: as a piece of political currency (73). During the training period for the Quarter Quell, Haymitch offers Katniss guidance, but also demonstrates empathy for her in his nuanced understanding of her character. He encourages Katniss and Peeta to form alliances with tributes "who might be of some use" in the arena and scoffs when Katniss asks for Beetee and Wiress, perceived by the others as oddballs (223–4); nonetheless, he understands enough of Katniss' character to ensure that her alliance in the arena includes them (320–4).

One ally who is more useful in Haymitch's terms is Finnick, a younger man from District 4. A primary strategy of Finnick's is to project a traditionally masculine, calculating exterior to mask the depth of his emotional attachments. Although on his first introduction, Katniss perceives Finnick to have been taken in by the "Capitol ways" (208–11), she later learns that this is a defense strategy for dealing with the Capitol's mental abuse (Collins, *Catching Fire* 388–9; *Mockingjay* 170). Finnick also demonstrates traditionally feminine behaviors in the arena in his healing gifts (Collins, *Mockingjay* 280–1) and in the depth of his grief over the loss of Mags, the elderly woman tribute from his district who walks into her death to prevent herself from becoming a burden on the others (301, 315).

Emotionality such as Finnick's is the currency that enables President Snow to control the people of the districts. Snow's primary tool of power is to twist and disrupt relationships. In *Catching Fire*, when he is angry with Katniss for undermining the power of the Capitol by threatening her joint suicide with Peeta, he pushes her into an onscreen romance with Peeta by threatening to kill Gale, whom he believes she truly loves (21–4, 29). By forcing this relationship with Peeta, which Katniss realizes will have to culminate in a marriage, Snow takes from Katniss "the right to marry who we want or not marry at all" (Collins, *Catching Fire* 44–5). Snow further allows Peeta and Katniss to believe a demonstration in District 11 that ends with Peacekeepers executing civilians is their fault (58–62). When the Victory Tour arrives at the Capitol, Snow immediately lets Katniss know he believes she has failed to convince the districts she loves Peeta, but then drags out their talk of her engagement and wedding plans throughout the visit (74–6).

Snow's psychological attacks on Katniss continue into the Quarter Quell. Before the Games, Snow has Katniss' stylist, Cinna, beaten to death in front of her to throw her off balance as she enters the arena (Collins, *Catching Fire* 261–3). During the Games, Katniss and Finnick encounter jabberjays that repeat the tortured screams of their loved ones (339–47). When the District 13 hovercraft rescues Katniss from the arena, Snow firebombs her entire district in retaliation, knowing that she will blame herself for the loss of life (390–1). The attacks follow her to District 13, too, where Snow drops a dozen of his trademark white roses to accompany an air raid on the district (Collins, *Mockingjay* 161). In all of these tactics,

Snow is employing emotional abuse, playing on the traditionally feminine emotionality of the people of the districts to cement his own power. Thus, at the same time that Snow robs the districts of much of their femininity, he forces it back onto them in a abject form to shore up his own political power.

Over the course of their feigned relationship, Katniss does permit herself to develop strong feelings for Peeta, which Snow then uses to torture her (Collins, *Mockingjay* 156). During the Victory Tour, Peeta begins spending the night in Katniss' train compartment in part because they hope rumors about the visits will add credibility to their love story for Snow (Collins, *Catching Fire* 72–4). During their night-time visits, though, Katniss and Peeta bond over their shared trauma from the first Games and develop an affection for each other that then enables Snow to use Peeta as a weapon against Katniss. When a team from District 13 rescues Peeta from his cell in the Capitol, they discover that he has been "hijacked": through the use of hallucinogens, the Capitol has warped Peeta's memories of Katniss until he believes that she is inhuman and dangerous (Collins, *Mockingjay* 180–1).

Finnick's apology to Katniss for being unable to rescue Peeta during the Quarter Quell perhaps best summarizes the nature of Snow's tactics: "I wish they were all dead and we were, too. It would be best" (Collins, *Catching Fire* 389). Snow is able to exploit empathy in a way that makes people wish those they love most were dead so that they were safe from being used as tools in his torture campaigns. He so twists feminine emotionality that the only way to remain safe from him is to reject that femininity as Finnick does so successfully in the Capitol before the Quarter Quell, when he is able to convince Katniss that he is without emotionality or personal attachment.

A World without Emotions: District 13

While Snow uses emotionality as such an effective weapon that his victims turn toward more masculine gender expressions for escape, President Coin, the leader of District 13, at first appears to squash emotionality in her people because it is inefficient. She has Katniss rescued from the Quarter Quell not out of regard for human life but because the Mockingjay is a symbol important to her cause (Collins, *Catching Fire* 386–7). Likewise, while the refugees from District 12 perceive their welcome into 13 to be an act of benevolence, it, too, is pragmatic. The district is literally sterile due to an "epidemic that killed a bunch of them and left a lot more infertile" (Collins, *Mockingjay* 8). This sterility is also evident in the meals provided by Coin's mess hall, which have been stripped of their ability to comfort: "They have nutrition down to a science. You leave with enough calories to take you to the next meal, no more no less" (35).

Like nutrition, the healing arts in District 13 are removed from the domestic sphere and made clinical. Katniss' mother, a sought-after healer in District 12 who treated patients in her own kitchen (Collins, *Catching Fire* 111–2), is perceived as "more of a nurse than a doctor" in District 13 (Collins, *Mockingjay* 49–50). Prim, however, seems to have a softening effect on Coin's policies. Her aptitude for healing has gotten her tapped for medical training (149). And although, initially, the keeping of pets is considered to pose "extreme difficulties" (38), Coin even begins to see the positive impact Buttercup has on morale; she allocates "a special set of batteries" to power a flashlight so that he can play Crazy Cat to entertain the district children (153). With time, he is even allotted a "daily food allowance," a sign that he has been accepted as a member of the district (183).

The more Katniss learns about her, though, the more Coin's tactics begin to resemble Snow's. Ellyn Lem and Holly Hassel apply to the books a definition of "patriarchy" derived from the work of Allan Johnson, focusing on systems which privilege "male identification" over identification with the feminine and noting that such identification is "to some degree disconnected with the physiological realities of sex" (121-2); by this standard, Coin's government, which employs many of Snow's anti-feminine tactics of control, is as patriarchal as his. Coin abducts Katniss' prep team from the Capitol and keeps them in deplorable conditions, an act Katniss interprets as "a warning" not to cross Coin (Collins, *Mockingjay* 48–51). Shortly after this incident, Katniss overtly compares Coin to Snow, calling her "[a]nother power player who has decided to use me as a piece in her games" (59). Once all of the districts have joined the rebellion, Coin slowly downgrades

Katniss' role in their propaganda films, making her one member of a Star Squad instead of the singular Mockingjay, preparing to have Katniss assassinated if she becomes more threatening than beneficial to Coin's leadership (260–6). The maneuver that finally ends the war in Coin's favor capitalizes on a despicable tactic of Snow's, keeping a barricade filled with Capitol children around his presidential palace as a human shield; by the book's end, it is clear that District 13 soldiers operated the Capitol hovercraft that dropped bombs disguised as provisions onto the children (345–6). After the first of the bombs explodes, District 13 medics, Prim among them, rush in to treat the wounded just as the rest of the packages go off, killing the medics and even more children (346–7). While Coin tries to frame Snow for this atrocity, he has no clear motive for the act and she does; it ends the war quickly in her favor, and because Prim is killed, it pushes Katniss more deeply into an alliance with Coin as long as she believes the Capitol responsible (359–61).

Perhaps the most disturbing aspect for Katniss of Coin's final volley is Gale's apparent involvement in it. Under the sterilizing influence of the Capitol, Gale has become increasingly vengeful, without any regard for human life connected with the Capitol (31, 53–5). Gale spends most of his time in District 13 working with Beetee to develop high-tech weapons that exploit the psychological reactions of their victims, a strategy Katniss finds too similar to the tactics of the Capitol (Collins, *Mockingjay* 68, 185–6, 221–2). Eventually, Gale becomes a respected weapons designer, devising the attack that finally wins District 2 to the rebellion—by trapping a large group of civilian workers inside a fortification with no way out and no fresh air (202–4). When Katniss witnesses the "double-exploding" bomb attack that kills Prim and the Capitol children, she recognizes it as Gale's handiwork (360). While Gale seems to be happy with the person he becomes under District 13's influence, that person is as calculating and emotionless as Coin herself.

The Return of Domesticity: After the Assassination

Having learned all she has about the war and been given a weapon to execute President Snow, Katniss makes the only decision that makes any sense: she puts her arrow into Coin and leaves Snow to die of the disease that has been killing him slowly for years (Collins, *Mockingjay* 372–3). She is then sentenced to return to District 12, where Haymitch continues as her mentor (379). While this means separation from her mother, who cannot bring herself to return to the house where she lived with Prim (380), it is otherwise hardly a punishment. Katniss is essentially granted her wish from the beginning of *Catching Fire*: the chance to gather her loved ones out of the Capitol's reach.

When Peeta returns voluntarily, planting primroses to memorialize Prim (Collins, *Mockingjay* 382–3), Katniss' circle of loved ones grows a little. It grows further when Buttercup returns (386). While their gender roles remain crossed—"Peeta bakes. I hunt"—Katniss and Peeta establish a household pattern together and begin a memorial book for those they have lost (387). Without interference from the Capitol or District 13, Katniss and Peeta fall genuinely in love, and eventually, Katniss is able to accept her own femininity and even become a mother (388–9).

Although Katniss observes grimly that "No decent person ever" wins the Hunger Games (*Catching Fire* 117), it is the hypermasculine, strategizing influence of government that robs people of their decency in the books. Though Katniss is a successful breadwinner and soldier both in the Games and afterward, she is most interested in honoring alliances with other people, and it is by refusing to accept the male-dominated values thrust at them and instead using their traditionally feminine, empathizing traits to build a better world for themselves and their loved ones that she and Peeta truly win in the end. By using Katniss' empathy as a tool that helps her succeed in traditionally masculine ventures, Collins presents a subtle challenge to our existing concept of what is nonsexist and offers a new set of rules by which to crown our winners.

Works Cited

Clark, Roger, Heidi Kulkin, and Liam Clancy. "The Liberal Bias in Feminist Social Science Research on Children's Books." *Girls Boys Books Toys: Gender in Children's Literature and Culture*. Ed. Beverly Lyon

Clark and Margaret R. Higonnet. Baltimore, MD: Johns Hopkins UP, 1999. 71–82. Print.

Collins, Suzanne. *Catching Fire*. New York: Scholastic, 2009. Print.

_____. *The Hunger Games*. New York: Scholastic, 2008. Print.

_____. *Mockingjay*. New York: Scholastic, 2010. Print.

Diekman, Amanda B., and Sara K. Murnen. "Learning to Be Little Women and Little Men: The Inequitable Gender Equality of Nonsexist Children's Literature." *Sex Roles* 50.5/6 (2004): 373–85. *Project Muse*. Web. 3 Nov. 2014.

Dolan, Jill. *The Feminist Spectator as Critic*. Ann Arbor, MI: U of Michigan P, 1991. Print.

Fine, Cordelia. *Delusions of Gender*. New York: W. W. Norton, 2010.

Lem, Ellyn, and Holly Hassel. "'Killer' Katniss and 'Lover Boy' Peeta: Suzanne Collins' Defiance of Gender-Genred Reading." Pharr and Clark 118-27.

McCabe, Janice, Emily Fairchild, Liz Grauerholz, Bernice A. Pescosolido, and Daniel Tope. "Gender in Twentieth-Century Children's Books: Patterns of Disparity in Titles and Central Characters." *Gender & Society* 25.2 (2011): 197–226. *JSTOR*. Web. 11 May 2015.

Mitchell, Jennifer. "Of Queer Necessity: Panem's Hunger Games as Gender Games." *Of Bread, Blood and The Hunger Games: Critical Essays on the Suzanne Collins Trilogy*. Pharr and Clark 128-37.

Montz, Amy L. "Costuming the Resistance: The Female Spectacle of Rebellion." *Of Bread, Blood and The Hunger Games: Critical Essays on the Suzanne Collins Trilogy*. Pharr and Clark 139-47.

Pharr, Mary F., and Leisa A. Clark, eds. *Of Bread, Blood and The Hunger Games: Critical Essays on the Suzanne Collins Trilogy*. Jefferson, NC: MacFarland & Co., 2012. Print.

Taber, Nancy, Vera Woloshyn, and Laura Lane. "'She's More Like a Guy' and 'He's More Like a Teddy Bear': Girls' Perception of Violence and Gender in *The Hunger Games*." *Journal of Youth Studies* 16.8 (2013): 1022-37. *EBSCOhost*. Web. 28 Jan. 2016.

Woloshyn, Vera, Nancy Taber, and Laura Lane. "Discourses of Masculinity and Femininity in *The Hunger Games*: 'Scarred,' 'Bloody,' and 'Stunning.'" *International Journal of Social Science Studies* 1.1 (2013): 150-60. *Google Scholar*. Web. 28 Jan. 2016.

Game Macabre: Fear as an Essential Element in The Hunger Games_____

Rebecca Sutherland Borah

When the film version of Suzanne Collins' novel *The Hunger Games* arrived in theaters in March of 2012, like many fans of the trilogy, I wanted to see how this complex and exciting work would translate to the big screen. In particular, I was looking forward to seeing the most terrifying moment in the novel: the climactic cornucopia scene, when Katniss realizes the werewolf-like "muttations" chasing Cato, Peeta, and her are, in fact, the dead tributes transformed into horrific nightmares. Imagine my (and a lot of other people's) frustration when the only beasts that showed up were bear-sized, CGI Rottweilers with no distinguishable individual features to connect them with the deceased tributes. Aside from this specific disappointment, I left the theater with the feeling that something was missing from the film; something that made the books special just wasn't there. Then it hit me: there were scary moments; there were tense and exciting scenes; there was spectacle, and Jennifer Lawrence portrayed Katniss perfectly. However, where was the all-consuming fear that's a dark undercurrent in the books? When did the audience get to experience the intense feeling of terror necessary to realize just how insidiously awful a regime like the Capitol is? What we had was a sad story, a fashion show, and an athletic contest, in which deaths were downplayed while we rooted for a strong female protagonist. The film never required viewers to think more deeply about the significance of these narrative elements. As film critic David Edelstein concludes in his review of the film, "*The Hunger Games* (2012) leaves you content—but not, as with the novel, devastated by the senseless carnage. It is, I'm sorry to say, the work of moral cowards." Children being forced to kill children should not be an ethical gray area. The film's muddling of these moral issues—perhaps to earn a lucrative PG-13 rating—doesn't just neuter the violence; it also robs the audience of opportunities for insight and intellectual growth. In fact, when the element of fear is diluted in the story—as happened in the first film—the series' moral compass loses its bearings and creates an uncomfortable ethical paradox. We know we should root for Katniss, but we should also understand how much it costs her to kill and to wear a false mask to survive, but more importantly, we must recognize who is forcing her to take these desperate, soul-killing actions. We must be able to name the real monsters, even when that list includes us.

When it comes to classifying Suzanne Collins' Hunger Games trilogy, few would argue against describing the series as primarily a dystopia; however, that does not preclude the author's borrowing from other genres. Collins' future world is one that incorporates fear as a pervasive core element throughout the series. From the opening premise—twenty-four teens enter the arena and only one comes out alive—readers know we are in for a gruesome ride, which will be a brutal and damaging experience for the characters as well. No one can survive this experience and not be changed, and this includes not just the characters, but the readers of the book as well. Collins does not use elements of horror and terror as a gratuitous end in itself, but as a means to illuminate her themes throughout the series. The use of horror and terror creates an emotional resonance, which elucidates Collins' philosophical points about the oppressive and debauched regime of the Capitol and the overarching monstrosity of war.

Horror and terror are terms that can often be used interchangeably, but they can mean different things depending upon the context. They can be viewed as a genre, used as a marketing tool, or enjoyed as extreme emotions that reconnect us to our primal fight-or-flight response. Therefore, it's important to work through what exactly horror and terror are as a theoretical lens and how Collins evokes these emotions as a means to her end and not as an end in itself. Stephen King, in his book-length treatise on the horror genre—*Danse Macabre*—describes the literature of fear as working on three levels: At the bottom is *revulsion*, which operates on the basest, gross-out level of spectacle, such as when Tom Skerritt's chest explodes in *Alien* or the Nazi's face melts in *Raiders of the*

Lost Ark. In the middle is *horror*, which is physical and evokes a visceral response, such as when Michael Myers is blindly slashing around the operating room with a scalpel trying to get Jamie Lee Curtis in *Halloween* or when Black Widow struggles to stay ahead of the enraged "Savage" Hulk, who seems to have every intention of killing her in the first Avengers film. At the top level is *terror*, which shows nothing and preys on the reader's imagination, such as in Edgar Allan Poe's intense story of guilt-ridden murder and insanity, "The Tell Tale Heart," or W. W. Jacobs' "The Monkey's Paw," involving a mother's ill-advised wish for the return of her dead son (King 22–25). These three levels of fear can be reached independently or built one upon another. Their use is pervasive in a variety of styles by authors such as George R. R. Martin, Joyce Carol Oats, or Toni Morrison, who also use them to heighten or emphasize their points. Theorist James B. Twitchell in *Dreadful Pleasures: An Anatomy of Modern Horror* postulates, "It is the nature of the medium that the novel and the movie become prime habitations for horror images, not in the fact that print or film were somehow corrupted by their presence" (27).

Thus, it comes as no surprise that Collins uses terror, horror, and even revulsion (to a lesser extent) throughout the trilogy to build emotional significance, which in turn illuminates her philosophical points about not only the brutal Capitol, but also the atrocities of war and violence. Collins' main character, Katniss Everdeen, is fighting for her life, her integrity, and some semblance of her sanity throughout the series. By the second book, she has developed her own mantra: "My name is Katniss Everdeen. I am seventeen years old. My home is District 12. I was in the Hunger Games. I escaped. The Capitol hates me" (Collins, *Mockingjay* 4). As the first novel opens, we follow Katniss through Reaping Day and discover a scene reminiscent of Shirley Jackson's notorious short story, "The Lottery." Two "tributes" are to be selected by lot, not as a fertility sacrifice (as in Jackson's story), but as a reminder of a war fought and, in the case of the thirteen districts, lost seventy-four years before in the aftermath of some sort of far-reaching disaster that destroyed their civilization. Collins uses this day-in-the-life approach to introduce readers to a character and a society, which have been damaged and warped by political oppression, occupation, forced labor, poverty, and starvation. As Katniss reveals her past—the death of her beloved father in the coal mines when she was eleven, her mother's depression and mental absence, and Katniss' struggle to provide food for her family—the reader comes to understand what a tough and determined, but damaged, individual she is to have beaten the odds. When her younger sister Prim's name is called at the reaping, there is no doubt that Katniss will step in and take her place. As Prim clings desperately to her older sister, Katniss knows she already has to put on her game face. "'Prim, let go,' I say harshly, because this is upsetting me and I don't want to cry. When they televise the replay of the reapings tonight, everyone will make note of my tears, and I'll be marked as an easy target. A weakling. I will give no one that satisfaction. 'Let go!'" (Collins, *Hunger Games* 23). At the same time, the reader comes to realize the sadistic nature of the Capitol's oppression. Despite handler Effie Trinket's grotesquely bright and perky voice and appearance, she represents a government that knows how to beat down its citizens through psychological terror as well as physical force and warfare, while expecting the people not to express any emotional reaction to that terror. The message is clear: *No one is safe, especially not your children.*

Unlike King, who freely admits that he will use revulsion to gross readers out if he cannot manage to induce horror or terror (*Danse Macabre* 26), Collins only uses this lowest level on a few occasions, mostly when shifting up or down from horror or terror. Perhaps the best example is from the first book, when Katniss finally takes possession of the bow and arrows in the game after she drops the tracker jacker nest on the Career tributes.

I reach Glimmer as the cannon fires. The tracker jackers have vanished. This girl, so breathtakingly beautiful in her gold dress the night of the interviews, is unrecognizable. Her features eradicated, her limbs three times their normal size. The stinger lumps have begun to explode, spewing putrid green liquid around her. I have to break several of what used to be her fingers with a stone to free the bow. The sheath of arrows is pinned under her back. I try to roll over her body by pulling on one arm, but the flesh disintegrates in my hands and I fall back on the ground. (Collins, *Hunger Games* 192)

It's not clear if the grotesque carnage is real or if Katniss is already suffering from venom-induced hallucinations, but either way, the experience proves excruciating for Katniss and sadistically entertaining for the audience and the Gamemakers as she continues to struggle. She quickly progresses from the revulsion of physically recovering the quiver of arrows from Glimmer's decomposing body to the horror of escaping pursuit in the woods and the psychological terror of the poison's incapacitation and hallucinogenic effects.

I enter a nightmare from which I wake repeatedly only to find a greater terror awaiting me. All the things I dread most, all the things I dread for others manifest in such vivid detail I can't help but believe they're real. Each time I wake, I think, *At last, this is over*, but it isn't. It's only the beginning of a new chapter of torture. How many ways do I watch Prim die? Relive my father's last moments? Feel my own body ripped apart? This is the nature of the tracker jacker venom, so carefully created to target the place where fear lives in your brain. (Collins, *Hunger Games* 195)

Her recovery takes days, and all the while, the audience continues to see her struggle played out large on live television. The more we find out about the Capitol's machinations and the Games themselves as we follow Katniss on her journey, the more deeply disturbing and unsettling the story becomes. The regime encourages the citizens of Panem to indulge in this voyeurism as a national guilty pleasure, and much of the citizenry, especially those in the Capitol, comply.

As previously mentioned, perhaps the most disturbing scene in the first book, if not the entire series, involves the final three tributes' encounter with the pack of werewolf-like "muttations" that may actually be the other murdered tributes whose corpses have been recycled by the Capitol to create monsters who can walk on two legs and resemble each of the twenty-one eliminated competitors reborn with fur, four-inch razor claws, and familiar, hate-filled human eyes. From the top of the cornucopia, Katniss observes them:

The mutts are beginning to assemble. As they join together, they raise up again to stand easily on their back legs giving them an eerily human quality. Each has a thick coat, some with fur that is straight and sleek, others curly, and the colors vary from jet black to what I can only describe as blond. There's something else about them, something that makes the hair rise up on the back of my neck, but I can't put my finger on it....

The green eyes glowering at me are unlike any dog or wolf, any canine I've ever seen. They are unmistakably human. And that revelation has barely registered when I notice the collar with the number *1* inlaid with jewels and the whole horrible thing hits me. The blonde hair, the green eyes, the number ... it's Glimmer.

A shriek escapes my lips and I'm having trouble holding the arrow in place....

My head snaps from side to side as I examine the pack taking in the various sizes and colors. The small one with the red coat and amber eyes ... Foxface! And there, the ashen hair and hazel eyes of the boy from District 9 who died as we struggled for the backpack! And worst of all, the smallest mutt, with dark glossy fur, huge brown eyes and a collar that reads 11 in woven straw. Teeth bared in hatred. Rue.... (Collins, *Hunger Games* 332–34)

The uncanniness of the creatures evokes horror, and, as their possible origins dawn upon the surviving tributes and us as readers, the fear level steadily rises to terror. We now know the sadistic depths to which the regime will sink to provide entertainment for its own citizens and to terrorize the other subjugated districts. *Not only are your children not safe; we can turn them into monsters inside and out.*

Creatures as monsters are a staple of the horror genre, and Collins employs them primarily in the form of genetic mutations, which she calls "muttations" or mutts, that were first created by the Capitol during the war with the districts. Unfortunately, just as with conventional weapons, the Gamemakers have full access to the mutt arsenal and the technology to employ, without restrictions, whatever their twisted brains can imagine in the arena. Once the rebellion starts, the Capitol regime doesn't hesitate to unleash its enhanced creations on the rebels, collateral damage to its troops or innocent citizens be damned. In *Mockingjay*, as Katniss' team infiltrates the Capitol and is attacked by the lizard mutts in the sewers, she realizes:

> No mutt is good. All are meant to damage you. Some take your life, like the monkeys. Others your reason, like the tracker jackers. However, the true atrocities, the most frightening, incorporate a perverse psychological twist designed to terrify the victim. The sight of the wolf mutts with the dead tributes' eyes. The sound of the jabberjays replicating Prim's tortured screams. (Collins, *Mockingjay* 311)

Those are the truly nasty pieces of work because they are so personal and operate on such a deep psychological level. Twitchell divides monsters in "horror arts" into three classical molds: created monsters (Frankenstein's monster), shape shifters/changing monsters (the werewolf), and vampires (10). Collins' mutts are weaponized versions of created monsters. Despite some resembling werewolves, there is no going back for the wolf mutts if they are mutated versions of the dead tributes. Collins leaves their exact origins a mystery, which only increases the terror factor when the question remains unanswered by the series' end. Because they and the other seemingly mindless mutts are weapons, they differ from Mary Shelley's Adam (who is known in popular culture as "Frankenstein's monster" or just Frankenstein) in that these mutations desire no connection to humans aside from wreaking havoc and destruction. As David A. Hedrich Hirsch notes in "Liberty, Equality, Monstrosity: Revolutionizing the Family in Mary Shelley's *Frankenstein*," central to Shelley's novel is the "conflict of interests between blood relatives and monstrous others" who dare to question the established order by attempting to assert their humanity (118).

Collins' hybrids lack Adam's degree of self-awareness; however, over the course of the series, both Peeta and Katniss begin to identify with the monsters. In the first novel, on the night before the Games begin, neither Peeta nor Katniss can sleep. She retreats to the training center's roof and finds him there watching the Capitol's citizens celebrating in the streets and trying to come to terms with his likely death in the arena. "'I don't know how to say it exactly.

Only … I want to die as myself. Does that make any sense?' [Peeta] asks. I shake my head. How could he die as anyone but himself? 'I don't want them to change me in there. Turn me into some kind of monster that I'm not'" (Collins, *Hunger Games* 141). For Peeta, it's the loss of agency and identity that he fears will make him a monster. It is not until Rue's death that Katniss fully understands what he means.

> I can't stop looking at Rue, smaller than ever, a baby animal curled up in a nest of netting. I can't bring myself to leave her like this. Past harm, but seeming utterly defenseless. To hate the boy from District 1, who also appears so vulnerable in death, seems inadequate. It's the Capitol I hate, for doing this to all of us....
>
> Rue's death has forced me to confront my own fury against the cruelty, the injustice they inflict upon us....
>
> Then I remember Peeta's words on the roof. "Only I keep wishing I could think of a way to … to show the Capitol they don't own me. That I'm more than just a piece in their Games." And for the first time, I understand what he means. (Collins, *Hunger Games* 236)

Katniss, who understands killing and has just taken her first human life, leaves out the monster reference, but she now fully comprehends Peeta's point about having the ability to make his own choices and be true to his own sense of self. He sees this statement as a description of how he wants to die as himself, but Katniss uses the insight to channel her rage into an act of defiance. She has chosen to "weaponize" on her terms, while he wants to die on his.

Ironically, after Peeta is captured in *Catching Fire*, he is the one who goes through drastic physical and mental changes, which shock Katniss as she watches Caesar Flickerman interview him on television: "The healthy, clear-eyed boy I saw a few days ago has lost at least fifteen pounds and developed a nervous tremor in his hands. They've still got him groomed. But underneath the paint that cannot cover the bags under his eyes, and the fine clothes that cannot conceal the pain he feels when he moves, is a person badly damaged" (Collins, *Mockingjay* 112). Before long, we learn he has been starved, beaten, and subjected to a form of torture known as hijacking, which in his case involves altering memories using tracker jacker venom so that Katniss becomes associated with fear and hatred in his mind. Once Peeta is rescued from the Capitol and taken to refuge in District 13, he tries to strangle Katniss as she rushes to embrace him. The doctors attempt to deprogram him by introducing Delly, a childhood friend to talk to him, but he soon latches onto altered memories of Katniss:

> "Because [Katniss is] lying! She's a liar! You can't believe anything she says! She's some kind of mutt the Capitol created to use against the rest of us!" Peeta shouts.
> "No, Peeta. She's not a—" Delly tries again.
> "Don't trust her, Delly," says Peeta in a frantic voice. "I did, and she tried to kill me. She killed my friends. My family. Don't even go near her! She's a mutt!" (Collins, *Mockingjay* 198)

Delly is quickly pulled out of the room as Peeta struggles against his restraints in a mad frenzy. Although the Capitol has engineered Peeta's false memories of Katniss being less than human and guilty of monstrous acts, during his recovery he begins to associate himself with mutts and monsters. Applying Twitchell's theory, Peeta has become a version of the changing monster. Similar to Stevenson's Dr. Jekyll or Lee and Kirby's Bruce Banner, he now harbors a monster ready to transform him into the Capitol's weapon. As Katniss noted, the most effective mutts are designed with an extra twist, and Peeta's torture and transformation is one of the nastiest twists of all. Not only does it remove his autonomy and sense of who he is; even worse, his pure and selfless love for Katniss has been corrupted into hatred. "Not only does he hate me and want to kill me, he no longer believes I'm human. It was less painful being strangled" (Collins, *Mockingjay* 199). Not only does Katniss recognize the extent of his damage, she is heartbroken and wonders if it might be a mercy to kill him.

As shocking and cruel as Peeta's torture and transformation are, there is one even more diabolical twist involving muttations and psychological warfare waged on Katniss. At the beginning of *Catching Fire*, Katniss is paid a surprise visit by none other than

President Snow himself. Katniss often compares him to a venomous snake, especially his eyes. This seems appropriate because we later find out he voluntarily imbibes a cocktail of poisons to give him some immunity in case his rivals try to poison him. She then notes, "his lips are overly full, the skin stretched too tight" (Collins, *Catching Fire* 19). Soon, the degree of his displeasure with Katniss' perceived acts of rebellion becomes transparent as he confronts her about the suicidal ploy with the poisonous berries and her conflicted feelings about the love story narrative with Peeta. In less than the time it takes to eat cookies and drink a cup of tea, Snow manages to threaten everything near and dear to Katniss and blame her for any seditious acts that might threaten the regime. Shocked, Katniss offers to do anything necessary to keep the peace, even if it means her death; despite her submission, Snow dismisses her suggestions because she will be seen as a martyr for the rebel cause. As the exchange goes on, Katniss notices "The smell of roses and blood has grown stronger now that only the desk separates us. There's a rose in President Snow's lapel, which at least suggests a source of the flower perfume, but it must be genetically enhanced, because no real rose reeks like that. As for the blood ... I don't know" (Collins, *Catching Fire* 20–21). Katniss may not be aware of it, but the bloated lips, snake-like eyes and demeanor, and the smell of blood all point toward Twitchell's third type of monster, the vampire. One could even argue that the genetically enhanced roses used to cover the smell of Snow's poison-ulcerated mouth correspond to funereal floral arrangements or the custom of planting thorny rose bushes on graves to entrap any restless revenants that might try to wander from a grave. Even his preferred white variety symbolizes the memory of a deceased relative. Furthermore, the act of his crossing Katniss' family threshold without permission and threatening her in her own home is a violation of the ancient guest-host relationship and breaks a taboo that runs across most cultures. Although a practical character such as Katniss might not equate Snow with Count Dracula, he personifies a government every bit as cruel as the historical tyrant Vlad Tepes. The Capitol has ravaged and exploited the other districts and annually robbed them of their children, who are sacrificed to keep the citizens cowed and the Capitol entertained. Someone who dines among the impaled bodies of his enemies would probably give a thumbs up to Panem's Draconian practices and sip tea quite chummily with President Snow.

Collins, however, goes beyond implying that Snow is a reimagining of a classical monster-type by building upon the trope's essential elements with her own mutated, psychological twists tailored to play upon Katniss' fears. Snow's association with his obnoxiously-scented roses gives him the opportunity to use them as calling cards to send Katniss an unpleasant and unmistakable message throughout the series. For example, when she revisits the Victors' Village in the otherwise destroyed District 12 at the beginning of the third book, Katniss gets a subtle, but disturbingly unpleasant surprise in her bedroom as she retrieves her father's hunting jacket.

> The soft leather feels soothing and for a moment I'm calmed by the memories of the hours spent wrapped in it. Then, inexplicably, my palms begin to sweat. A strange sensation creeps up the back of my neck. I whip around to face the room and find it empty. Tidy. Everything in its place. There was no sound to alarm me. What, then?
>
> My nose twitches. It's the smell. Cloying and artificial. A dab of white peeks out of a vase of dried flowers on my dresser. I approach it with cautious steps. There, all but obscured by its preserved cousins, is a fresh white rose. Perfect. Down to the last thorn and silken petal.
>
> And I know immediately who's sent it to me.
>
> President Snow.
>
> When I begin to gag at the stench, I back away and clear out. How long has it been here? A day? An hour?... (Collins, *Mockingjay* 14)

Even more so than the face-to-face meeting in the study, the implication that Snow has invaded the private space of Katniss' bedroom is a personal defilement of her space and privacy. Not to mention that it is downright obsessive and creepy. The message is clear: *You have no safe or private places, and I will violate them any time I so choose.* When these private attacks do not prove enough, Snow picks a much more public venue. After the bombing attack on District 13, Katniss and her camera team make their way to the surface to film a defiant propaganda response.

> As we approach what used to be the grand entrance, Gale points out something and the whole party slows down. I don't know what the problem is at first and then I see the ground strewn with fresh pink and red roses. "Don't touch them!" I yell. "They're for me!"
>
> The sickeningly sweet smell hits my nose, and my heart begins to hammer against my chest. So I didn't imagine it. The rose on my dresser. Before me lies Snow's second delivery. Long-stemmed pink and red beauties, the very flowers that decorated the set where Peeta and I performed our post-victory interview. Flowers not meant for me, but for a pair of lovers … Snow knows exactly what he's doing to me. It's like having Cinna beaten to a pulp while I watch from my tribute tube. Designed to unhinge me. (Collins, *Mockingjay* 160–61)

This proves to be the final straw for Katniss because she gets Snow's message loud and clear. Peeta is still in his clutches, and Snow will take his pound of flesh from Peeta and make him suffer for anything Katniss does to oppose the Capitol. At least for the moment, Snow silences the Mockingjay because Katniss cannot manage to perform in front of the camera until Peeta is rescued.

Collins saves the most incongruous use of Snow's signature roses for Katniss' fight and flight through the Capitol's sewers, where many of her team members die and Peeta is kept in manacles because he is in real danger of "Hulking out" and attacking Katniss. As the group makes its way around deadly obstacles and engages Capitol forces, they encounter a new muttation-horror tearing the helmeted heads off a group of Peacekeepers in order to reach Katniss:

> For the first time, I get a good look at them. A mix of human and lizard and who knows what else. White, tight reptilian skin smeared with gore, clawed hands and feet, their faces a mess of conflicting features. Hissing, shrieking my name now, as their bodies contort in rage. Lashing out with tails and claws, taking huge chunks of one

---

another or their own bodies with wide, lathered mouths, driven mad by their need to destroy me. My scent must be as evocative to them as theirs is to me. More so, because despite its toxicity, the mutts begin to throw themselves into the foul sewer....

The smell of Snow's roses mixed with the victims' blood. Carried across the sewer. Cutting through even this foulness. Making my heart run wild, my skin turn to ice, my lungs unable to suck air. It's as if Snow's breathing right in my face, telling me it's time to die. (Collins, *Mockingjay* 311–12)

Just the visual horror of the lizard-men beasts is enough to induce panic, but the viciousness of engineering these created monsters with Snow's signature scent inspires a new level of terror, at least for Katniss. The idea that Snow's foul, perfumed breath would be her last overwhelming sensory impression just before her head is torn from her shoulders takes this beyond a political vendetta to an intimately personal fight. Snow admits later that his obsession with destroying Katniss led to his undoing when she finds him confined in his greenhouse sanctum, coughing blood and surrounded by his perfect roses during the third book's final chapters. "'My failure,' says Snow, 'was being so slow to grasp Coin's plan ... I was watching you, Mockingjay. And you were watching me. I'm afraid we have both been played for fools'" (Collins, *Mockingjay* 355). Like a dying dragon or basilisk, he imparts his last bit of toxic truth to Katniss and leaves her to process the information and let that knowledge inform her actions.

In the end, the bad actors such as President Snow and his would-be successor President Coin are exposed as the megalomaniacal monsters orchestrating the war and its atrocities. They serve their traditional, premodern purpose in the story: "monsters are there to be removed by the hero, thereby illustrating his [or her] superiority, as well as our need to follow him [or her]" (Twitchell 25). Interestingly, in modern horror tales, it is the monster who stays at the forefront of our memories and imagination as opposed to the hero, which is what separates Collins' trilogy from the horror genre. Katniss is far more complex and shaded than a bland protagonist fleeing and screaming steps ahead of the creature or maniac. In fact, when we are looking for monsters in the trilogy, both Peeta and Katniss identify themselves as mutts, while Gale, Beetee, and Plutarch are guilty of possible war crimes with their tit-for-tat back bombing, which in turn leads to Prim's fiery death and Katniss and Peeta's further suffering and disfigurement. One might even uncharitably argue that Katniss and Prim's depressive, grieving, and nameless mother functions as a representation of broken and ineffective motherhood just short of being monstrous.

However, we are leaving one very important monstrous entity out if we forget to look at ourselves in the mirror. Although we are in Katniss' head because she is our first-person narrator and the story is told from her limited, but informed and compelling point of view, she is on display from Reaping Day forward for the entire country, and we are honorary citizens of Panem, rooting for her from the audience's perspective. Noël Carroll in *The Philosophy of Horror, or Paradoxes of the Heart* notes,

> In horror fictions, the emotions of the audience are supposed to mirror those of the positive human character in certain, but not all, respects.... Our responses are supposed to converge (but not exactly duplicate) those of the characters; like the characters we assess the monster as a horrifying sort of being (though unlike the characters, we do not believe in its existence). This mirroring effect, moreover, is a key feature of the horror genre. For it is not the case for every genre that the audience response is supposed to repeat certain of the elements of the emotional state of the characters. (18)

I would argue that Collins places us as readers in the uncomfortable position of not just empathizing with Katniss, but also pulling back a step to objectify her and become part of the Hunger Games' audience. In and outside the novels, we are her fans. Because Collins is taking on the trappings and spectacle of beauty pageants, sporting events, newscasts, and reality television shows—viewing experiences with which most readers are all too familiar—we very comfortably settle into our mental armchairs and couches to take it all in, just like a

Capitol citizen. We may hope Katniss will triumph; we may ooh and ah over her costumes; we may cheer internally when she takes out her competitors in the arena (if you fist pumped, go sit in the penalty box with Plutarch); we may hope that she connects and finds comfort with Peeta (or Gale), but this only puts us more strongly on "Team Katniss," seated right beside the trilogy's television or studio audience.

Whether or not we thought about this while reading the books, it's clear from the films' marketing campaigns and the availability of mass-produced and fan-made merchandise that we may not have all wanted to look like Effie Trinket (butterfly-stencil eyelashes, flossy wigs, and all); however, lots and lots of us wanted Mockingjay jewelry, fashion (from leather hunting jackets to t-shirts to "I love the boy with the bread" underwear), and images (mugs, posters, dolls, action figures, and Lego sets). As fans of the books and the films, making and/or purchasing our own "artifacts" is part of the participatory process, but unlike *The Rocky Horror Picture Show* or other young-adult-novel-based fandoms, such as Harry Potter or the Twilight saga, The Hunger Games trilogy forces us as readers and viewers into the unusual position of identifying with the narrative's internal audience and fandom. If we leave this unexamined, the story has the same surface appeal as an amusement park ride: a few short adrenalin-fueled moments and that is all. However, if we make an effort to go deeper, as Collins invites us to do via example, if we've bothered to understand what Katniss does and how Panem works, we see some of our ugliest moments of consumer and fan culture reflected back at us in painful detail. From Effie and the makeup team's shallow artificiality to the love-story-wedding-baby story arc forced on Katniss and Peeta to the fashion parade and celebrity interviews with Caesar Flickerman, the picture of consumerism isn't pretty. To the odds-making and sponsor-wrangling to intrusive reality cameras to youth-centered image making to Avox slavery and the selling of tributes, none of this is humanity at its best. In fact, allowing these injustices and horrors to exist is monstrous. We cheer Katniss for taking the evil Capitol down. Stop. All we have to do is look up from the page, and it is all present right here in our pre-Panem world. Our culture does all this and tolerates more. Well, who are the monsters now? Who bears the responsibility for preventing the Dark Days? Ouch! It has to be that monster in the mirror.

The Hunger Games trilogy is not a simple tale of terror or a monster epic. Nevertheless, it owes a thank-you note and maybe a bouquet of President Snow's best blooms to the horror genre. Collins speaks the language of our culture and does not hesitate to use the tropes and trappings of horror to get her points across. She hits us both high and low by appealing to our better angel, while feeding our gators in the sewer. The horror elements are not there purely for an adolescent thrill or to add shock value. They are an essential element that connects readers to our shared, visceral instincts, and they make the higher-level concepts take hold more deeply and shine brighter by contrast. Without fear, we would not be able to measure the regime's capacity for committing heinous acts to provide entertainment for mass consumption and to terrorize the oppressed districts. The overall effect may not be cathartic, but Collins is instructive. Fear is the fire Collins applies to refine and elevate Katniss' story beyond simple young adult and genre fiction and to help create the catalyst for the trilogy's commercial and critical success.

Works Cited

Carroll, Noël. *The Philosophy of Horror, or Paradoxes of the Heart*. New York: Routledge, 1990. Print.

Collins, Suzanne. *Catching Fire*. New York: Scholastic, 2009. Print.

_____. *The Hunger Games*. New York: Scholastic, 2008. Print.

_____. *Mockingjay*. New York: Scholastic, 2010. Print.

Edelstein, David. "Acting Trumps Action in a 'Games' without Horror." *NPR.org*. National Public Radio, 22 Mar. 2012. Web. 10 May 2015.

Hirsch, David A. Hedrich. "Liberty, Equality, Monstrosity: Revolutionizing the Family in Mary Shelley's *Frankenstein*." *Monster Theory: Reading Culture*. Ed. Jeffrey Jerome Cohen. Minneapolis: U of Minnesota P, 1996. 115–140. Print.

King, Stephen. *Danse Macabre*. New York: Gallery Books, 1981. Print.

Twitchell, James B. *Dreadful Pleasures: An Anatomy of Modern Horror*. New York: Oxford UP, 1985. Print.

"Where You Can Starve to Death in Safety": Appalachia and The Hunger Games_____

Elizabeth Baird Hardy

I shall not leave these prisoning hills. (James Still, "Heritage" 1)

Finding District 12: A Real Landscape for a Fictional Place

In the third chapter of *The Hunger Games*, Katniss Everdeen reveals what may seem an obvious truth about her world: benighted, backwater District 12 is the region once known as Appalachia. In saving this overt revelation for the third chapter, Suzanne Collins is enforcing the importance of the novel's Appalachian underpinnings, as the number three is one of the trilogy's most vital touchstones, rarely used lightly or without meaning. She has also allowed the readers to independently form their own conclusions about the fenced-in coal district with its weary citizens and its dusty, dirty town in the midst of a lush landscape rich with resources forbidden to most inhabitants. At the same time, these inhabitants are subjected to vile stereotypes that have been created, enforced, and often made real by the media-savvy larger culture. For those familiar with the actual Appalachia, the fictional District 12 is hauntingly familiar. Unlike the futuristic or alien settings of so many speculative fictions, or even the settings elsewhere in the trilogy, District 12 is not the fanciful invention of an author's fertile imagination; rather, it is a painfully accurate re-envisioning of a possible Appalachia, mirroring the real region in its geography, flora, and fauna, as well as in the ways in which it has been stereotyped and labeled as a land of violent, inbred alcoholics and barbarians. Ironically, both District 12 and Appalachia suffer from stereotypes largely created by the very mainstream culture that looks down upon them, while both regions actually possess a rich and complex culture with a distinct worldview, sense of humor, musical and oral traditions, and unique perspective.

There is a distinct lack of consensus in the definition of Appalachia's actual location. Maps that specifically pinpoint the region often vary from one another. Though the Appalachian Mountain chain stretches from northern Alabama to Nova Scotia, where it drops into the sea to reappear, geologically, in the British Isles, definitions of the area known as Appalachia differ in their inclusion or exclusion of some counties or areas. There is also diversity in the maps that specify different regions of Appalachia, although those that designate the geographical differences within the region generally divide the entirety into several sections, such as the coal-rich Ridge-and-Valley and Cumberland Plateau regions, either of which would be the original location of 12; yet there is no clear border to Appalachia, no fence or barbed wire, at least not yet.

There is likewise ambiguity about the actual location of District 12 within this vast region. While some readers want to place Katniss' home as far west and north as Pennsylvania, the majority locate the district in the coalfields at the intersection of eastern Kentucky, West Virginia, and southwest Virginia, a placement supported by the cultural practices and foodways of 12, as well as by the accent Suzanne Collins herself employs when reading in Katniss' voice ("Suzanne Collins Reads"). However, Appalachian culture is vertical, not horizontal, in its coverage of the region, meaning that state lines and distances are less relevant than altitude in determining the cultural connections of the region. Thus, eastern Kentucky and southwestern Virginia have far more in common with each other, geographically and culturally, than they do with the other sections of their respective states.

There is even a lack of consensus on how to say the label *Appalachia*, a word created from a corrupt pronunciation of the name of a native tribe that actually inhabited modern-day Florida (Walls 56). Most central and southern Appalachian people cringe at the version of the word employed by mainstream media. The preferred pronunciation, as in the motto "I'll throw an 'Apple-at-cha,' if you say 'A-pa-lay-chee-uh' instead of 'Appalachia,'" carries substantial weight; as best-selling author and Appalachian scholar Sharyn McCrumb often notes, choosing a pronunciation is a political decision that indicates whether the speaker is an ally or an outsider (*Appalachia: A History of Mountains and People*). Despite confusion and mispronunciations, the region retains a unique character that echoes in District 12.

"You'll never starve if you can find yourself"

As the place where Suzanne Collins' circular trilogy both begins and ends, Appalachia is central to the story, imbuing the characters and the plot with specific features. Some of Katniss' most memorable characteristics, including her extraordinary skills at hunting and gathering, are directly connected to the remarkable diversity of plant and animal life to be found outside the District 12 fence. Her remarkable success in the seventy-fourth Hunger Games is due, in no small part, to the similarity of the arena's ecosystem to that of District 12. Just as Annie Cressida's District 4 swimming skills propel her to victory in a Games featuring a flood, Katniss' skill set, so well suited to her Appalachian homeland and its resources, is her salvation in an arena that replicates so many of the plants and animals she knows from home.

In fact, the mountains of Appalachia produce a tremendous variety of life, with a series of micro-climates ranging from the subtropical to the alpine. "In the coves of southern Appalachia are fifteen hundred species of flowering plants, including more kinds of trees than in all of northern Europe. Here are bewildering nuances of biodiversity, with mosses, fungi, spiders, salamanders, mussels, fish, [and] birds like none other on earth" (Bolgiano 5). Though the future world of Panem has certainly experienced environmental damage, the variety of flora and fauna retains the complexity known in Appalachia: "There are an estimated sixty-five species of mammals, eighty species of amphibians and reptiles, and 175 species of terrestrial birds in central and southern Appalachia" (Bolgiano 244). This diversity produces a copious amount of food for those skilled enough to harvest it and provided sustenance for the earliest human inhabitants of the region, Native Americans who lived in or merely hunted through the mountains, often employing the same methods as those Katniss has learned from her father and Gale Hawthorne.

When European explorers and settlers arrived, they frequently noted the abundance of wildlife and edible plants.

Ironically, many of the resources that these early visitors described, and upon which Katniss relies, have been reintroduced after some species were nearly hunted into extinction in the early twentieth century. Both the wild turkey and whitetail deer teetered on the brink of disappearance in the southern Appalachian region before successful reintroduction programs bolstered their populations, making controlled hunting feasible. The chestnut trees Katniss mentions would also be the products of reintroduction programs, as the American chestnut trees were decimated by the cataclysmic early twentieth-century chestnut blight, a plague that radically altered the composition and appearance of the Appalachian forest. Before their destruction, the chestnuts were the backbone of the Appalachian biosphere, providing excellent construction materials as well as nutrition, both for humans and for the free-range hogs that provided the vast majority of meat for early Appalachian families. Like the Mellarks, nearly every Appalachian family who could afford to do so raised at least one hog, routinely eating pork at every meal, particularly during the colder months when they were unable to rely upon the bounty of the landscape.

In addition to the chestnut, the other trees of the Appalachian forest provide a wealth of resources, ranging from their defensive and strategic uses for excellent climbers like Katniss to their value as food and medicine. Katniss and her family have a vast array of Appalachian plants to provide sustenance and healing. The plants that fill the pages of the Everdeen book include many that would have been readily familiar to earlier mountain people, from the blackberries, strawberries, and wild plums Katniss and Gale use for both food and trade, to the spring greens, including all parts of the evocative dandelion, once the staple of spring tonics meant to restore the health and digestive balance of people who had gone months without fresh produce.

One such green, pokeweed, traditionally harvested and enjoyed in its early leaf stage, produces toxic fruit that is reflected in the dangerous nightlock berries that Katniss repurposes as a weapon to thwart not other tributes, but President Snow's entire unjust dictatorship. As a futuristic aberration, perhaps even a muttation, nightlock combines the toxicity of both hemlock and pokeweed berries. While the name suggests the hemlocks, as well as deadly nightshade, the appearance is much like that of the poke berry, which is poisonous, but hardly so fatal as to kill an unwary eater before the berry hit her stomach. When Katniss describes plants as "tricky," she is well aware of both their danger and their value. With her own name, like that of so many other characters, originating with a plant, Katniss well knows that people, like plants, can heal like primrose, can be as powerful as clove, or can be food, medicine, or poison, like rue.

Also presenting certain dangers and benefits are the many Appalachian animals that inhabit District 12's vast wilderness. Though the packs of wild dogs Katniss occasionally flees from or shoots for Greasy Sae's soup pot are feral, the descendants of pets left to fend for themselves in the wake of civilization's collapse, others, such as the bear she once unwisely challenged for honey, would have been familiar to her Appalachian ancestors. The abundant squirrels and rabbits also fed early hunters and settlers as well as later Appalachian farmers seeking to protect and supplement the family's resources.

While wild felines, like the lynx that follows Katniss until she has to kill it, are less populous in Appalachia, they too, are native to the region. Human settlement and habitat loss have all but removed the panthers from Appalachia, along with the once-common wolves. Efforts to reintroduce the red wolf have met with little success, and the absence of native predators in the region has led to the overpopulation of deer and other wildlife, along with the arrival of the invasive, non-native coyotes, which, like the wild dogs in the District 12 forest, have taken over the link left vacant in the food chain by native predators. Interestingly, other, once-prominent Appalachian species, such as megafauna like buffalo and elk, have apparently not returned in the distant future.

Some of the most important Appalachian animals Katniss encounters are birds. Throughout the trilogy, there is a variety of birds, both actual and symbolic: Prim's shirt making a ducktail; Rue and her wings, flying from tree to tree; Maysilee Donner, murdered in the arena by colorful birds and leaving behind her songbird for Katniss' mother and a gold pin that later inspires Katniss' transformation into a bird that sparks a revolution. In addition to the fictional mockingjay, the story is filled with encounters with very real birds common to the very real Appalachian region. Like the turkeys Katniss and Gale hunt, many of these birds provide important resources for survival. However, they also provide other services. The owl whose cry warns Katniss of the re-electrified fence not only saves her, but also echoes traditional mountain beliefs about the owl as a messenger, warning of imminent death. The birds that fall silent at the approach of the hovercraft serve a similar function, illustrating the importance of birds in Appalachia's ecosystem and culture. This cultural value can be seen in everything from the legends of the Cherokee, describing the great buzzard whose wing flaps formed Appalachia's mountains and valleys, to the many songs that feature birds.

Though time and human choices have clearly altered the District 12 ecosystem, its plants and animals largely continue to reflect the character of the Appalachian forest of the past, a world that was already being altered by natural and human forces long before the creation of Panem. Before the first chestnut succumbed to the blight or the first wolf was shot by a cautious farmer, Appalachia was changing, even as it retained so many of the elements that connect to Katniss' world.

"Overcoming the barbarism of your District"
The forest was further transformed by the large-scale logging operations that swept through the region on early twentieth-century railroads whose spurs took workers into the mountains and carried out timber and coal. Though the Appalachian region is one rich in abundant biological and geological resources, the people of the region, both in the actual past and the fictional future, have often been denied access to those resources. While the denizens of District 12 are fenced in and forbidden to collect the bounty

Critical Insights

of the vast woodland around the inhabited sector of the District to feed themselves, they must slave away long hours mining coal that is not used to feed them, warm them, or power their homes. Katniss notes that they must still use a portion of their extremely low wages to buy the coal unless they track in the dust on their feet, and the District only gets a few hours of electricity each day unless mandatory programming, like the Games, is on television. This strange paradox of a rich region inhabited by a poor people is a painfully accurate interpretation of the plight of many real Appalachian communities: "the profits taken from the rich natural resources of the region flowed out of the mountains with little benefit to the mountain people themselves" (Eller xxiv). While absentee landowners and large companies benefited from the exploitation of mountain resources, the mountain people themselves, historically, were often dependent upon and impoverished by their employers, companies that had turned farmland into mines and transformed farmers into miners reliant upon the company store. Undoubtedly, many Appalachian people have benefitted greatly from the resources in the region, gaining employment and success by harvesting timber or mining coal, but, all too often, these resources were owned by outside interests who merely exploited the area and its workforce.

Though, thankfully, District 12 is a hyperbolic fictional treatment of the region, both District 12 and the real Appalachia are home to incredible resources that, instead of being used to benefit residents, are taken and used by those who then scorn the region's inhabitants as violent, dangerous creatures, justifying their position in society and their neglect and denigration by the larger culture.

The iconic image of the violent, brutish hillbilly is a pervasive stereotype that has lingered long after other such culturally offensive images have vanished from mainstream media and marketing. The idea that mountain people are intrinsically, perhaps even genetically, less intelligent and more prone to viciousness than everyone else is one that is advanced by movies, television shows, and advertising, all drawing on a long tradition of regarding the region and its people as dangerous, alien, and remote. The best illustration of this media trend is the treatment of the infamous feuds of the late nineteenth and early twentieth centuries. While the newspapers of the period described them as the results of the Appalachian people's flawed characters or warped codes of justice, a large number of those "mountain feuds" in fact took place outside the mountains, in the bluegrass regions of Kentucky and further west, and were conducted by wealthy, upper-class families and their entourages, who resorted to violence when their lawyers did not get results in economic and legal disputes—an outgrowth of the behavior and attitudes that once condoned dueling as a civilized way to settle insults to one's honor.

The disputes that did take place in the mountains, like the legendary Hatfield and McCoy feud, were often the result not of mountain people's genetic brutishness, but of reactions to outside events, such as the American Civil War and the advent of industrialization. They were often political in nature: "most were directly related to political party conflict and featured participants who were frequently wealthy merchants and prominent community leaders [but] the press described them as irrational and barbaric" (Waller 361–62). Thus, the violence that is generally ascribed to Appalachian people was often a reaction to events that happened outside the region, in a larger culture that subsequently blamed the mountain people themselves rather than the external events that fueled violent reactions in the mountains. When coal miners rose up in arms against mistreatment by their employers or when crimes committed by runaway convict railroad laborers drove uneasy locals to mob violence, the mainstream media inevitably blamed the people of Appalachia rather than investigating the more complex social forces at work.

Likewise, the Capitol creates the violence, but then sneers at the brutality it fosters. It is the bloodthirsty Capitol audience and its appetite for bloodsport that drive the Games to ever-greater levels of barbarism; the Capitol Gamemakers are the ones who arm frightened, angry, confused, and imprisoned children with the most vicious weapons possible and concoct ever-more horrifying strategies to kill them or force them to kill one another. Yet, the Capitol citizens regard themselves as far more civilized and cultured than the savage cretins in District 12. In similar fashion, much of the frenzy about the legendary feuds was fueled by the sensationalized newspaper accounts that depicted Appalachia as a land filled with shoeless, toothless barbarians lurking in the bracken, brandishing Winchesters "and, for no apparent reason, attempting to exterminate one another" (Waller 347). The readers of these highly colorful accounts, often the inhabitants of cities with their own disturbing crime problems, consumed these stories with a voracious appetite, leading to more and more exaggerations—even outright manufacturing of accounts—of the region's people as a separate, violent race. Such stories assured the residents of other areas that they were superior to the murderous mountaineers, while justifying and condoning the exploitation of those mountain people for economic advantage.

Even the iconic moonshiner is a product of outside forces far more than an indigenous element indicative of genetic or moral failings. Like Ripper and her Hob colleagues, Appalachian distillers of untaxed liquor, or moonshiners, have historically relied upon manufacturing and selling a product that would produce a reliable income even in the grimmest of economic times. The practice itself is not illegal; the illegality lies in the distillers' not paying federal taxes on sales of their product. Thus, the defining criminal activity of the region is one that has been criminalized by outside forces, just as the one-armed Ripper, "a victim of a mine accident who was smart enough to find a way to stay alive" (Collins, *Catching Fire* 10), has turned to the practice because her workplace injuries precluded other options.

Haymitch Abernathy, the familiar, pathetic drunk, is a reminder that the stereotypes of District 12 and Appalachia, when they actually do represent reality, are often more a complex product of the larger culture than a result of mountain people's poor character. Haymitch has become an alcoholic as a direct result of the Capitol's abuses, both in the arena and afterward. Just as the morphlings of District 6 use drugs, he has relied upon alcohol to cope with his emotional and psychological trauma, and the Capitol has relegated him to the role of drunken hillbilly, like the larger culture has often done with Appalachian people, ignoring their complexities in favor of a cute, convenient, and cruel image. "Few other regions in the United States confound and fascinate Americans like Appalachia.... No other region has been so misrepresented by the media" (Biggers xii). Like the gun-toting, moonshine-swilling hillbilly of early twentieth-century America, the knuckle-dragging savages of District 12 are images promoted by a larger culture that has derived entertainment and economic benefit from the exploitation of the region's inhabitants.

"The end of the line"

These stereotypes both stem from a tendency for the larger culture to view the mountains as somehow "Other," a region cut off, separated from the rest of the world. Both the real Appalachia and the fictional District 12 of Panem are subjected to the perception of being completely isolated. In some contexts, this misperception has at least slightly positive connotations, presenting a view of Appalachia as a pristine, unsullied wilderness, a replica of a lost past, and its people as charming relics of a bygone age, uncontaminated by modern influences. The paradoxical, oversimplified Appalachian stereotype thus includes both the feuding brute and the quaint, rustic pioneer. "By the turn of the century, two basic images of the people of Appalachia had been created. One image was positive, the other negative, and both were frequently intertwined. At the heart of both conceptions was the 'fact' of the region's isolation from the mainstream, modern America" (Lentz 73). Though the citizens of the Capitol do not wax poetic about the beauties of unspoiled District 12, they generally ignore and underestimate the coal miners, dismissing the region as the most isolated and unsophisticated in Panem. Ironically, this tendency to treat District 12 as the "least prestigious, poorest, most ridiculed district in the country has its advantages. Such as, being largely ignored by the Capitol as long as we produce our coal quotas" (Collins, *Hunger Games* 283). The rebellion that recreates Panem thus finds its spark in Katniss and one of its masterminds in Haymitch, underestimated, overlooked inhabitants of the country's least-regarded district.

Strangely enough, however, the idea that either Appalachia or District 12 is completely isolated is a misconception. Travel has sometimes been difficult and time-consuming, but not impossible. Railroads have, historically, reached into some of the most remote communities, and even those without reliable rail service or high-quality roads were often well aware of events in the larger world, as newspapers, mail-order catalogs, and radio provided connection. Like rural people throughout the United States, Appalachian people have enjoyed a degree of privacy and distance from large urban centers, though few other regions are labeled as cut off from the modern world.

As with the image of the violent, drunken hillbilly, the image of the isolated mountaineer, whether positive or negative, was one reinforced, if not created, by the larger culture, often through visual media. The people of Panem know about District 12 primarily through the misleading images of its tributes and footage shot during the annual visit of the Capitol escort for the reaping. These images are edited and controlled as part of the Capitol's efforts to dehumanize the districts and to limit the amount of information the citizens have about one another. Many of the iconic images of Appalachian people are photographs that have been portrayed as "accurate" depictions of mountaineers, though they used staged props and settings to create the illusion that all Appalachian people were impoverished relics of a bygone era. While some of these images were accurate, and, like those taken of struggling people elsewhere in the United States, even helped to raise awareness of real issues, many others were the product of imaginative photographers whose work, like the riveting Capitol portraits series produced for the promotion of the film adaptations, both separates and romanticizes those the larger culture wants to imagine as Other.

Though the communities of Appalachia have never actually been completely cut off, mountain people have, historically, felt they were on their own. The location of state capitals, generally far from the mountainous regions of the states that contain the Appalachian range, has reinforced the impression that mountain people have developed of themselves as overlooked and neglected by government. For example, the Lost State of Franklin episode clearly illustrates the Appalachian sense of abandonment by distant governments: shortly after the American Revolution, there was an effort to establish a fourteenth state, named Franklin to elicit support from Benjamin Franklin, from lands ceded to the new American government by the former colonies in their process of transforming into states. Covering territory eventually absorbed into other southern states, primarily North Carolina and Tennessee, Franklin was never recognized by Congress, leading to confusion and civil unrest and further contributing to the Appalachian resentment and distrust of distant governments.

"I understand, about owing"

This distrust, compounded by a myriad of other historical events, has been one of the most important elements in shaping Appalachian culture and its remarkably keen sense of self-sufficiency. Like Katniss, many Appalachian people do exhibit reticence in trusting others and abhor taking charity. Even if she had not been forced to become her family's sole provider, Katniss, like other Seam residents, would still understand the importance of exchange and would have resisted owing anyone or being the recipient of charity. Katniss does not accept gifts easily, so her friend Madge Undersee must physically attach the mockingjay pin to her bosom, rather than handing it to her. For Katniss, gifts require repayment, so those she cannot repay, like Mr. Mellark's cookies, she rejects.

Though he struggles with this concept, as a member of District 12's slightly better-off social echelon, Peeta is also a product of the mountain mindset, so he burns the bread he gives to Katniss, not just because his mother will order it thrown out, but also because he knows that Katniss will only take the bread if it is being discarded anyway. She has, after all, been skulking in trash cans, not begging at back doors, to find food to keep herself and her mother and sister alive. His confusion about why Katniss thinks she still owes him for his life-saving gesture is not because he does not understand her desire for independence; it is because he is puzzled by Katniss' inability to see his obvious love for her as genuine.

Perhaps no character better understands Katniss' need for self-sufficiency than Haymitch, who withholds water from Katniss in the arena not because he hates or neglects her, but because he knows she can find it herself and that such an accomplishment will both impress her potential sponsors and encourage her resourcefulness. By allowing her to find her own water, Haymitch also confirms the method of communication that he and Katniss will use throughout both her Games and beyond. Even when she is broken and exiled and feels Haymitch has forgotten her in a drunken stupor, it is far more likely that he is allowing her to heal and recover in her own way, without feeling she owes him, as she feels she owes Thresh when he spares her life as payment of his own debt for the kindness shown Rue and as she feels she will always owe Peeta for the bread.

The independence of Appalachian people is very closely tied to relationships, as self-sufficiency is not limited to the individual. In Katniss' world, as in the historic Appalachia, the landscape and the lifestyle of mountain farms have helped shape mountain families and communities that were at once fiercely independent and yet reliant on one another. Like Appalachian people before them, Katniss and her family choose to rely on themselves, whether it is through hunting or gathering or working with a hard-earned animal, like Prim's goat, Lady. As a true Appalachian person, Katniss has trouble admitting that Lady, or even the awful cat Buttercup, is loved for reasons other than the provision of milk and mousing services. This pragmatism is a result of her experience of being abandoned by the double loss of her father to death and her mother to crippling depression, a loss that is particularly devastating for someone culturally conditioned to regard family as a crucial element, an extension of oneself.

Devotion to family, even at the risk of one's own ambition and goals, is one of Katniss' most distinctly Appalachian traits. This is not to imply that sacrificing oneself for a family member is a trait that only Appalachian people exhibit. Rather, it explains many of the choices made by Katniss, from her pivotal volunteering to save Prim to the hesitation she expresses at the prospect of abandoning her family and the Hawthornes to flee the district. Their families are the reason she and Gale cannot leave, even when it would be in their own best interest.

By making Gale Katniss' cousin, by general community agreement, the people of District 12 acknowledge the power of family to direct the choices made by an individual, while also allowing Collins to address the prevalence of the cruel incest jokes the larger culture often makes about presumably backwoods mountain people so ignorant or isolated that they become inbred. Seeing Gale as Katniss' cousin would not cause the Capitol viewers to completely dismiss him as a romantic partner, but would confirm their suspicions about the district's "Otherness" and depravity. Ironically, it is to prevent the possibility of inbreeding that the District 12 survivors are welcomed into the population-depleted District 13, but even here, they are often regarded as "Other," with Greasy Sae having a hard time convincing the District 13 cooks to be more broad-minded: "a woman who came up with a palatable wild dog and rhubarb stew is bound to feel as if her hands are tied here" (Collins, *Mockingjay* 55). Their self-sufficiency, which has shaped Greasy Sae's rather remarkable menu, is not celebrated; they are regarded as savages who will eat anything, rather than as resourceful survivors capable of making a meal of materials others would discard.

"Stay alive"
The ability of Appalachian people to survive, and sometimes even to thrive, in harsh conditions has strongly contributed to their outlook on life. The profound combination of fatalism and humor that colors Katniss' voice is a clear connection to her Appalachian roots. Like Katniss, mountain people have not historically been known for their optimism. Her consolation in being tossed into an arena with Peeta, to whom she feels obligated, is that with twenty-two other tributes, it is highly likely that someone else will kill him first.

Though Appalachian culture often reflects a bleak outlook, its emphasis on meaningful activity and self-sufficiency does not allow room to condone the sort of depression that renders Katniss' mother completely useless. Rather, mountain people often address their certainty that they are doomed not with despair but with a wry sense of humor that dulls the pain of difficulties while also serving as a social tool. "Here in Appalachia, we have seen our loved ones die in hazardous occupations and from unchecked diseases. We have been bilked of land, minerals, and ballads. We have been gerrymandered, lied to, and done unto. But we have endured, partially, at least, because we could laugh" (Jones 613). Thus, even though their lives are often incredibly difficult, the people of District 12 can and do use humor to cope. In *Catching Fire*, one of the most amusing scenes is the one in which Katniss, having dropped over the newly re-electrified fence and injured herself, plays along with Prim, Haymitch, and Peeta in an elaborate cover story about getting the goat pregnant; their quick wits and humor not only conceal real stress and concern, but they allow Katniss to escape detection. In a region where the inhabitants have, historically, often been exploited, abused, or scorned by outside forces, humor can serve a variety of powerful functions. One reason the culture privileges humor is its use as a leveling agent, making those in power less terrifying by pointing out their foibles. For example, on the morning of the reaping for the seventy-fourth Games, Katniss and Gale defuse the very real threat Effie Trinket represents when she reaches into those glass bowls by making fun of her goofy Capitol accent, just as Appalachian people have devised jokes at the expense of politicians, the wealthy, and city folks.

Appalachian culture also frequently employs humor as a form of affection. Teasing, rather than indicting a mean-spirited attitude, is evidence of fondness. This teasing can encompass nicknames, ranging from Gale's labeling Katniss with the moniker "Catnip" to Katniss' habit of creating names for others. Sometimes she does this because actual names are not critical to her; she calls District 5's tribute Foxface, the only name she ever uses for the wily redhead, while she does not know the name of her Avox servant until Peeta later describes her death under torture. She doesn't even reveal the names of her own parents and children, but the names she gives others reveal her affection for them. Peeta, as the "boy with the bread" is thus labeled by his kindness, the trait that most fascinates and puzzles Katniss, while Prim's "little duck" nickname, referring to her untucked shirttail, connects directly to Katniss' maternal instincts both at the seventy-fourth reaping and at the attack of the double-exploding parachute bombs in *Mockingjay*. It is the sight of Prim's untucked shirt as she rushes to aid the victims of the first bombs that identifies her to Katniss, who is unable to save her sister this time.

Humor, whether manifested in nicknames or otherwise, also reflects acceptance and trust in Appalachian culture. When Peeta, buried almost entirely in mud and plants, drily tells Katniss "just don't step on me," he is not only attempting to downplay his considerable jeopardy, but also demonstrating his trust in her as an ally. This same use of humor as an indicator of trust can be seen when Katniss and Finnick, smeared with the cream that turns them a ghastly color, wake Peeta by putting their faces directly in front of him. By teaming up with Finnick to play a joke, Katniss begins to indicate that she trusts him, just as she later decides to like Boggs only when he scoffs at Fulvia's effusive comments about Gale's good looks: "Well, don't expect us to be too impressed. We just saw Finnick Odair in his underwear" (Collins, *Mockingjay* 82). Since the citizens of District 13 are largely humorless, his jibe gives Katniss the encouragement to connect with Boggs, later feeling "sure that he, and maybe he alone, is completely on my side" (*Mockingjay* 281). Appalachia, including District 12, is a place where difficulties can be overcome with laughter, though it may be rather dry.

As Appalachian people, Katniss, and particularly Haymitch, rely upon fairly dark humor. Sometimes it is merely deadpan humor, such as in Katniss' description of her rocky relationship with Buttercup: "Entrails, no hissing. This is the closest we will ever come to love" (*The Hunger Games* 3-4). At other times, mountain wit can manifest as gallows humor meant to neutralize difficult circumstances, such as Haymitch's gruff admonition to Katniss to stay alive. In a culture that recognizes the ever-present possibility of certain death, but which resolves to put a brave face on matters, Appalachian humor can temper Appalachian fatalism, but it can also result in humor that is bleak, or even cruel, such as the brutally honest and painful observations made by a hijacked Peeta or a drunken Haymitch.

Critical Insights

"Making the birds fall silent"

Both the humor of Appalachian culture and its frequent fatalism manifest themselves in a rich and complex oral culture of music and storytelling. Despite her frequent protests to the contrary, Katniss is both a gifted musician and an effective storyteller. Like many actual Appalachian songs, the ones Katniss performs revolve around love and death. Traditional ballads include the folk, or popular, ballads, many of which were preserved and transformed in southern Appalachia after their arrival from the Old World. These ancient narrative songs usually involved stock characters like knights and ladies, and though some were comical, like "The Farmer's Curst Wife," most, like "The Brown Girl," "Tam Lin," "Fair Ellender," "The House Carpenter," and "Barbary Ellen," center around forbidden love, curses, death, and the supernatural. Many, like "The Cruel Sister," have countless variations because of their age and the changes, intentional and accidental, imposed with each transmission. It is not unlikely that a song like "The Hanging Tree" could eventually evolve from these actual songs, many of which even feature hanging. For example, one well-known ballad, popularized by Peter, Paul, and Mary in the 1960s, "Hangman," shares many elements with the song forbidden by Mrs. Everdeen after finding her daughters making their own nooses. However, its ending, in which a woman sentenced to death is finally ransomed by her true love after being abandoned by a string of callous family members, is far more positive than that of "The Hanging Tree," or of other hanging-themed ballads, including the many broadside ballads that feature the protagonist at the end of a rope. Unlike the folk ballads, the broadsides were based on actual events, often shocking and scandalous ones that included illicit affairs, unwanted pregnancies, and violent death. While some, like "Pretty Polly," actually originated in Europe, others were distinctly Appalachian, such as the much-fictionalized ballads chronicling the North Carolina executions of Tom Dula (Dooley) and Frankie Silver.

In addition to the ballads, other musical elements of District 12 culture also appear to be connected to the real culture of Appalachian folk music, with its use of fiddles and its inclusion of geographical references. Though the "Deep in the Meadow" song Katniss sings for

Rue is completely fictional, its use of the willow tree is reminiscent of a number of songs popular in the Appalachian South, including, interestingly enough, "Listen to the Mockingbird," a nineteenth-century favorite still popular with traditional musicians. "The Valley Song," which Katniss sang on her first day of school, prompting Peeta Mellark to lose his heart to her then and there, may be connected to "Down in the Valley," the "popular Appalachian courting song … descended from a British air" ("Down in the Valley"); some of its verses cast the speaker as a prisoner declaring his love for the sweetheart his imprisonment has caused him to leave behind. Like so many songs connected to the region, this one combines a lively tune, one any mockingjay would love to mimic, with a mournful subject, neatly encapsulating the Appalachian paradox of fatalism expressed with flippancy, of gloom interspersed with gaiety.

Appalachian storytelling also covers a strangely paradoxical span, including fairly structured, amusing stories of tricksters like Jack, who is at once remarkably lazy and incredibly successful in nearly every venture, as well as personal stories both poignant and humorous. A skilled Appalachian storyteller can take a story that the audience has heard a dozen times and make it riveting and delightful, or turn a commonplace event into an entertaining or meaningful tale. These stories, like the ballads that intrinsically warn about the repercussions of immoral behavior, frequently transmit cultural values, history, and knowledge. Similarly, Mr. Everdeen's stories, and the skills that go with them, later provide Katniss with crucial survival tools. Though Appalachian stories are frequently based on actual events, they are just as often fictionalized and streamlined to provide both narrative cohesion and entertainment value. Legendary mountain storyteller Ray Hicks frequently said of his beloved Jack Tales, "they ain't true, but there's a lot of truth in them," a sentiment equally true of Appalachian stories the tellers craft from their own and their families' experiences.

Thus, when Katniss deliberately alters the story of giving Prim her goat, Lady, in order to conceal the illegal means by which she acquired the money for the purchase, she is engaging in a typical Appalachian practice of changing details that do not add to the narrative in order to achieve her own purposes. In this case, she wants to fulfill Peeta's request for a story with an innocuous selection that will be appropriate for the circumstances and the eavesdropping Capitol viewers, the type of people who will only see the story as a story, just as they might be fooled into thinking the mountain song was cheerful due to its sprightly tune, rather than detecting its underlying tale of misery. Peeta, a much more discerning listener than those in the Capitol, does not acknowledge that Katniss has changed elements of the story, though he has to realize that a girl who was starving in the rain behind his house because she could not sell baby clothes was unlikely to later have a locket to sell for disposable income for a birthday gift. But he clearly recognizes that Katniss is making narrative choices when she claims economics were her primary motivation for purchasing Lady. He sees both the truth behind Katniss' decision to purchase the goat and the tough exterior that motivates her narrative. After all, Peeta, whose fabrications help mold himself and Katniss into Panem's most beloved and, arguably, most powerful victors ever, is an adept storyteller himself, using humor and pathos in perfect balance. However, unlike Peeta, Katniss does not see herself as a crafter of tales, which is ironic, considering she is, in fact, the storyteller of the entire trilogy.

"This is our home"

Katniss' natural abilities as a storyteller, along with her lack of recognition of the effect she has on others, make her the ideal narrator, despite, or perhaps because of, her ignorance about the forces controlling her life. As an Appalachian woman, she focuses less on trying to puzzle out other people, a practice at which she generally fails miserably, and instead finds structure and meaning for her story in the cyclical perspective of her culture. Since she is a hunter, particularly one who identifies with and connects to the moon, Katniss is acutely aware of the cycles of life and nature, but this cyclical approach is also deeply rooted in traditional southern Appalachian culture. While the modernistic worldview is primarily egocentric, future-oriented, and linear in its approach to time, a more traditional view, like that connected to Appalachian culture, tends to be more family-oriented and community-centered, acutely aware of the past, and focused on time as a circle instead of a line.

There is no doubt that The Hunger Games is a story that is shot through with circles. From the ring of Katniss' token pin to the City Circle that figures prominently in each book, the circle is the trilogy's defining structure. Any doubts about Collins' use of circular imagery should be completely eradicated by the moment in the first novel when Katniss rises into the arena, one of twenty-four tributes arranged on circles, in a circle, around the circular cornucopia, within an arena that is likely circular. Even before the Quarter Quell and its clever clock arena, the circles that fill the text convey the traditional Appalachian concept of time as circular, coming back on itself in the cycle of days and seasons.

By making the story itself a circle, Collins continues to reinforce the power of the cyclical, traditional worldview. Each novel works cyclically, but the entire trilogy is best seen as circular, meeting itself at the end, when Katniss is back in District 12, where she started. Of course, she has to return, emphasizing the circles and cycles of the story. Her exile to District 12, and the decision of so many of her neighbors to leave sterile, safe 13 for their own miserable, burned-out, corpse- and ash-covered district is a reminder of the Appalachian need for place. That same craving for the mountains has, for generations, beckoned mountain people back to Appalachia despite hardship there and opportunity elsewhere. Katniss must return to 12, because she cannot leave. She is tied to place in a way Appalachian people can truly understand. Like the circle, the dedication to place is both completing and restricting, both comforting and confining. She must return there to heal, to be part of the cycle of seasons and to take part in the restoration of the district to which she belongs. In the lines of Appalachian poet James Still, Katniss "cannot leave"; this character, though fictional, is like so many Appalachian people who would also say, "Being of these hills, I cannot pass beyond" (Still 15). They, too, would return to the desolate, sorrow-ridden, war-torn mountains, as Katniss does, for it is there that they find not only the cultural milestones that connect the literary District 12 to the literal Appalachia, but they also find the place where their stories come full circle.

Works Cited

Appalachia: A History of Mountains and People. Dir. Ross Spears. Perf. Sissy Spacek and Sharyn McCrumb. PBS, 9 Apr. 2009. Television.

Biggers, Jeff. *The United Sates of Appalachia: How Southern Mountaineers Brought Independence, Culture, and Enlightenment to America.* Emeryville, CA: Shoemaker Hoard, 2006. Print.

Bolgiano, Chris. *The Appalachian Forest: A Search for Roots and Renewal.* Mechanicsburg, PA: Stackpole Books, 1998. Print.

Collins, Suzanne. *Catching Fire.* New York: Scholastic, 2009. Print.

_____. *The Hunger Games.* New York: Scholastic, 2008. Print.

_____. *Mockingjay.* New York: Scholastic, 2010. Print.

"District Heroes." *The Capitol.* Lionsgate Entertainment, 30 Nov. 2014. Web. 19 May 205.

"Down in the Valley." *Ballad of America: American Heritage Music.* Ballad of America, 2016. Web. 19 May 2015.

Eller, Ronald D. *Miners, Millhands, and Mountaineers: Industrialization in the Appalachian South 1880–1930.* Knoxville: U of Tennessee P, 1982. Print.

Jones, Loyal. "Appalachian Humor." *Appalachia Inside Out.* Vol. 2. Ed. Robert J. Higgs, Ambrose N. Manning, and Jim Wayne Miller. Knoxville, TN: U of Tennessee P, 1995. 613–20. Print.

Lentz Ralph, II. *W. R. Trivett, Appalachian Pictureman: Photographs of a Bygone Time.* West Jefferson, NC: McFarland, 2001. Print.

Palen, Tim. *Tim Palen: Photographs from the Hunger Games.* New York: Assouline, 2015. Print.

Still, James. "Heritage." *The Wolfpen Poems.* Berea, KY: Berea College Press, 1986. 15. Print.

"Suzanne Collins Reads Aloud an Excerpt from *The Hunger Games.*" *Scholastic Teacher.* Scholastic Inc., 20 Aug. 2010. Web. 19 May 2015.

Waller, Altina L. "Feuding in Appalachia: Evolution of a Cultural Stereotype." *Appalachia in the Making: The Mountain South in the*

   Nineteenth Century. Chapel Hill, NC: U of North Carolina P, 1995. 347–76. Print.

Walls, David S. "On the Naming of Appalachia." *An Appalachian Symposium: Essays Written in Honor of Cratis D. Williams.* Ed. J. W. Williamson. Boone, NC: Appalachian State UP, 1977. 56–76. Print.

"What I did was a radical thing": Panem's Corrupted Gift Economy

Amy Bennett-Zendzian

Katniss Everdeen is obsessed with gifts and the concept of owing. To her, they are the same thing: to receive a gift is to owe a debt. The only person from whom Katniss can accept gifts without reservation is her sister Prim, while gifts from others are received only with reluctance or even thrown away. Why? Katniss instinctually understands that accepting a gift results in not only forming an emotional bond with the giver but also incurring a spiritual debt beyond the gift's monetary value. Katniss—who has what we might call a gift for survival—is right to be wary of these obligations because as often as not in Suzanne Collins' Hunger Games series, gifts are literally a matter of life and death.

Recognizing how gifts and debts work in Panem is key to understanding some of the most important themes of Collins' novels. In the series' first book, *The Hunger Games*, the word "debt" appears four times; variations on "owe," eight times; and the word "gift," sixteen times—all together, twenty-eight occurrences. (For the sake of comparison: the thematically important word "mockingjay" appears about twenty-five times in the first book.) Early on in the series, important gifts save lives: Peeta's gift of bread rescues Katniss and her family from starvation, and rival tribute Thresh chooses to spare Katniss' life in the arena to repay the debt he owes her—and then there are all the gifts from sponsors, in the form of parachutes bringing food and medicine in the arena. But by *Mockingjay*, gifts cause death: the suicide pill that Cinna sews into the Mockingjay outfit—Katniss calls it "Cinna's last gift"—and the parachutes that the hostage children in the City Circle think are food or medicine, but which are actually bombs (373, 346). The very last use of the word "gift" in the series is when Plutarch Heavensbee admits that he doesn't believe that anything has really changed, or that humanity has finished destroying itself through war; he says that humans are "fickle, stupid beings with poor memories and a great gift for self-destruction" (Collins, *Mockingjay* 379).

Plutarch's comment reveals that what's going on with gifts in The Hunger Games series is about more than Katniss' personal trust issues, her desire for self-sufficiency, or even her survival instincts; it's about the world of Panem. The gift economy in Panem is broken, corrupted by the governing strategies of the Capitol. Even in commodity-based economies, the rules of gift economies control the exchange of whatever is considered too sacred to be purchased. However, in this dystopia, what should be sacred has been commodified—turned into something that can be bought and sold—including, most significantly, children's bodies. Despite her distrust of gifts, or perhaps because she understands their nature so well, Katniss is in a position to be a catalyst for revolutionary change, beginning with her gift of her own body to take the place of her sister's in the arena. She does not expect others to follow her example, explaining, "What I did was a radical thing" (Collins, *Hunger Games* 26). But they do follow her example, and as she discovers, it is only through radical gifts that Panem might be transformed.

Giving, Receiving, and Repaying: Understanding Gift Theory

Many gift theorists base their work on the premises formulated by Marcel Mauss in his foundational text *The Gift*. Mauss analyzes the economies of archaic societies in order to show that there have always been systems of exchange that are governed and restricted by societal rules and that predate the invention of money. Mauss proposes that gift economies are closed systems governed by three interconnected obligations: an obligation to give, an obligation to receive, and an obligation to reciprocate (*Gift* 39). And they are obligations: if recipients don't fulfill them, they will experience both social and spiritual consequences. Unlike a commodity economy, in which strangers directly exchange goods or services for the amount of money the things are agreed to be worth, a gift economy is essentially a circular one: after giving a gift, the giver will eventually be repaid, though not necessarily by the same person to whom the gift is originally given. Instead, the gift has a "spirit" that moves through the community and eventually comes back to the giver, perhaps in the form of another gift from someone else (10). The two kinds of economies, gift and commodity, are not mutually exclusive; in fact, they frequently coexist, if sometimes uncomfortably. But gift transactions, unlike exchange of capital, create a bond of feeling between giver and receiver. Ideally, the receiver is grateful to the giver, and the giver feels good about the receiver—although as we will see, the feeling-bonds created by gift exchange are not universally positive.

In some ways, this simple model of a gift economy is replicated straightforwardly in the world of The Hunger Games. Gift exchange is shown to create a relationship between giver and receiver in a way that commodity exchange does not. For example, early on, Collins introduces Madge Undersee, the Mayor's daughter, who, according to Katniss, may or may not be her friend. They eat lunch together at school, but Katniss suggests that maybe it's just because they're both oddballs with no real friends (Collins, *Hunger Games* 12). On the day of the reaping, Gale and Katniss go to see Madge with strawberries to sell, and Gale harshly reminds Madge that their chances of being reaped are much higher than hers. The next line is, "Madge's face has become closed off. She puts the money for the berries in my hand" (12). The exchange of money is directly linked to the "closing off" of emotional connection. But after Katniss has volunteered for the reaping, Madge comes to see her and gives her the gift of the gold mockingjay pin. Not until *Catching Fire* do readers learn that this gift once belonged to Madge's aunt, Maysilee Donner, who was Katniss' mother's friend and, as it turns out, Haymitch's ally in the arena; therefore, it is a gift with much history and emotional significance for both of them, although Katniss doesn't know that until later. After Madge gives her the pin, Katniss says, "I'm getting all kinds of gifts today. Madge gives me one more. A kiss on the cheek. Then she's gone and I'm left thinking that maybe Madge really has been my friend all along" (Collins, *Hunger Games* 38).

The gift is what makes Katniss admit that they have an emotional relationship, whether she likes it or not.

In the impoverished economy of District 12, gift exchange and commodity exchange coexist with a third option: barter. Barter comes across in the novels as less cold than commodity exchange, but less dangerous (in terms of its likelihood to create emotional attachments) than outright gifts, at least to Katniss. When Gale and Katniss are feasting on the morning of the reaping, Gale says that the baker gave him bread in exchange for "just a squirrel," maybe because he was feeling sentimental, and Katniss comments that they "all feel a little closer" on reaping day (Collins, *Hunger Games* 7). This communal feeling of closeness before the reaping might also help explain why in the film version of *The Hunger Games*, Katniss actually accepts the gift of the mockingjay pin from the Hob dealer, which might otherwise be out of character for her. In the first film, the pin appears cheap, not valuable like Madge's real gold pin, but it gains sentimental value very quickly by being given as a gift from the Hob dealer to Katniss, from Katniss to Prim, from Prim back to Katniss, and then from Cinna to Katniss as a secret present just before she enters the Games. Even though the character of Madge is eliminated, the team behind the films (which includes Collins) understands the connection between the theme of gifts and the symbol of the mockingjay.

"The effect she can have": Katniss, Gifts, and Relational Bonds

Since gifts create a relationship between giver and receiver, it is no surprise that the antisocial Katniss has a deeply anxious relationship with gifts (and the people who give them). She can accept gifts from Prim, who is the only person she is sure she loves, but gifts from her mother or even Gale, her best friend, are received with hesitation. She admits that it took a long time for her and Gale "to even become friends, to stop haggling over every trade and begin helping each other out" (Collins, *Hunger Games* 10). Often as not, she rejects gifts, whether consciously or unconsciously. For example, on reaping day, Peeta's father, the baker, gives her a gift of cookies, which she tosses out the window (49). Her mother gives Katniss a blue dress, but even though she knows that it is "precious" to her mother because it is "from her past," Katniss leaves it crumpled up on the floor of the train (15, 63). She even accidentally leaves Madge's mockingjay pinned to an abandoned outfit; later, after Cinna restores it to her, she tries to give it away to Rue (145, 212). Katniss has a real problem with gifts, and when Peeta implies that the people of District 12 who barter with Katniss give her especially good deals because of the "effect she can have"—implying that they care about her—she is simultaneously confused and infuriated, "sure he meant to insult me," she says (91). Nor is it any wonder that she can't accept that they might have been giving her anything: as Lewis Hyde explains, "When we refuse relationship, we must refuse gift exchange as well" (95). For most of the first book, Katniss remains grimly determined *not* to form relationships with anyone, and much of the emotional arc of *Catching Fire* involves Katniss' reluctance to accept the truth about just how many people she has formed relational bonds with after all.

Fortunately for Katniss, she is not at risk of forming relational bonds with those who give her "false gifts," donated out of an intent to harm her (Hyde 91). Wealthy Capitol sponsors might help Haymitch send Katniss gifts that save her life, but as long as they see her not as a person but just as a tribute to bet on, their gifts don't create real bonds between themselves and Katniss. Those arena gifts do, however, create bonds between Katniss and Haymitch. At the start of the Games in the first book, Katniss tries to persuade herself that Haymitch's gifts somehow don't count by telling herself "he hates me," but by *Catching Fire*, she admits freely that she owes him for her own life and Peeta's, "And that's for always" (Collins, *Hunger Games* 168; *Catching Fire* 10). Arena gifts also create bonds between Katniss and the people of District 11, who send her bread after the death of her ally Rue, and between Katniss and the people of the Hob who set up a collection to send her a gift. That's why in *Catching Fire* Katniss eventually has to admit that Peeta was right about "the effect she can have" and the fact that the connection is reciprocal. The circle of people she is willing to let herself care about continues to grow, until the point when she wants to run away into the woods to escape Snow's persecution but wants to take half of District 12 with her.

"The first gift is hardest to pay back": Dangerous Gifts

However, there is more to Katniss' aversion to gifts than her fear of the feeling-bond she might inadvertently form with the giver. She understands that if gifts are a matter of life and death, that means they are dangerous; owing someone can interfere with her own chances for survival. When Katniss tries to explain to Peeta that Thresh spared her life at the Cornucopia because he was "paying off a debt of sorts," Peeta cannot believe it: he says, "He let you go because he didn't want to owe you anything?" (Collins, *Hunger Games* 292). Katniss responds, "I don't expect *you* to understand it. You've always had enough" (292). The conversation leads inevitably to Peeta's gift of bread that had saved Katniss and her family from starvation five years earlier. Katniss says, "I never seem to get over owing you for that" (293). Peeta suggests that they can call it even now that she has saved his life in return, but Katniss says it's not that simple because "it's the first gift that's always the hardest to pay back" (293).

Here, Katniss articulates one of the key premises of gift economies. As Mauss explains, a gift, especially the first gift, carries with it something *more* than its official value as a commodity, and recipients can't discharge the debt just by giving the original giver something of equal value. They have to "reciprocate with interest," to give back something more; and the longer it takes to repay the debt, the more is owed (Mauss, *Gift* 42). In Katniss' case, Peeta's bread saved her life, as well as her mother's and sister's lives, so she is in the position of feeling that she owes him something *more* than her life. How can she ever pay that back?

Katniss also understands that Peeta doesn't know any of this, and why. When Thresh spares Katniss, he yells: "Just this one time, I let you go. For the little girl. You and me, we're even. No more owed. You understand?" and Katniss says, "I nod because I do understand. About owing. About hating it. I understand that if

Thresh wins, he'll have to go back and face a district that has already broken all the rules to thank me, and he is breaking the rules to thank me, too" (Collins, *Hunger Games* 288). Katniss tells Peeta that if *he* had come from a background of starvation and need like her and Thresh, then he would understand "About owing. About hating it." This hatred doesn't come out of nowhere. Hyde explains, "Between the time a gift comes to us and the time we pass it along, we suffer gratitude" (47). In Panem, where oppressed characters lack the resources to reciprocate, no one is more aware of this danger of "*suffering* gratitude" than Katniss.

The down side of a gift economy is the intensity of negative feeling (not to mention the threat of a loss of social status) that is generated when the cycle breaks down because the recipients of gifts cannot fulfill their obligation to reciprocate. The philosopher Nietzsche warns against accepting gifts if one has "nothing to give" because "[g]reat indebtedness does not make men grateful, but vengeful; and if a little charity is not forgotten, it turns into a gnawing worm" (201). It is no wonder that Katniss and Thresh are both desperate to find a way to discharge their debts. For the impoverished and downtrodden of Panem, reciprocating gifts becomes an unbearable obligation that threatens to crush them.

Reaping Children: Panem's Corrupted Gift Economy

The gift economy in Panem is corrupted in two ways. The first is due to extreme income inequality. The economic chasm between the super-affluent Capitol and the struggling districts is also replicated within the districts, such as District 12, where a small merchant class does relatively well compared to the impoverished Seam dwellers. As Gale observes, turning people inside the districts against one another is a strategy on the part of the Capitol, just as the Hunger Games are meant to turn all the districts against each another: "It's to the Capitol's advantage to have us divided among ourselves," he says (Collins, *Hunger Games* 14). So when Katniss is suspicious of or outright refuses gifts, it is a sign that the Capitol has been able to turn the potential positive energy of gift exchange into negative energy. The Capitol is winning in its strategy to keep the people divided, unable to form true relationships with one another. Peeta is able to save Katniss' life only because he is from the merchant class and has resources to spare, but she can't pay him back because she is from the Seam and consequently has nothing. If Peeta's act of saving Katniss' life becomes a source of pain, confusion, resentment, and suffering for her because she can't discharge her gratitude, and if she feels that owing him hurts her chances of survival, then it is not Peeta but the Capitol that is winning.

The second way that the gift economy is corrupted in Panem is in how things that should only be given as gifts, or should not be given at all, are *treated* as commodities: specifically, children's bodies. Even in economies that are primarily commodity-based, some things are not supposed to be bought or sold. The ethics of the gift economy govern the exchange of whatever the society considers sacred: for example, love and marriage (as in the tradition of the father "giving away" his daughter); the adoption of children; the donation of blood or body (often referred to as "the gift of life"). Societies are not supposed to be able to commodify these things, only to give them away. When Katniss and Peeta become victors and realize that they will be forced to continue their public love story forever, Peeta grieves the loss of the freedom to give himself away in marriage; Katniss, by contrast, had ruled out the possibility of marriage so long ago that she "recoil[s] at even the suggestion of marriage or a family," a sure sign of her sensitivity to Panem's corruption of these institutions (Collins, *Hunger Games* 257). Even worse: according to Bill Clemente, in an article about crisis economics and disaster capitalism in Panem, "the word *reaping* reinforces the extent to which the Capitol has turned people into capital, a commodity harvested for the Capitol's appetite" (25). This use of children's bodies to feed the Capitol's hunger for blood sport is, of course, what has Katniss swearing that she will never have children.

The connection between the reaping and the system of tesserae is an excellent example of the Capitol's strategy in leveraging the logic of a corrupted gift economy to keep itself in power. Katniss explains, "Say you are poor and starving as we were. You can opt to add your name [to the reaping pool] more times in exchange for tesserae. Each tessera is worth a meager year's supply of grain and oil for one person. You may do this for each of your family members as well" (Collins, *Hunger Games* 13). On the surface, tesserae appear to be a gift from the government, a public aid program intended to save the poor from starvation. However, in Clemente's words, when the children sign up for tesserae, they are "cashing in" their odds of survival, exchanging their bodies for commodities in the form of grain and oil (25). As V. Arrow points out, "The Games-tessera system is smartly designed" because it has a sinister second purpose; it is deliberately "predicated on making its beneficiaries state-dependent," in no way helping them transition from poverty to self-sustainability (50). From the perspective of the Capitol, there is nothing broken about this system; it is working exactly as intended. Any movement that intends to fight the Capitol will have to fight its corrupt economic system, too.

"Not just a piece in their Games": Radical Gifts

How can the people of Panem transform the corrupted gift economy? I propose that they do it by giving "radical gifts." Katniss begins what becomes a nationwide movement for revolutionary change with her *donation* of her own body to take the place of her sister's in the arena, even though she believes the outcome will be her death. Her action is shocking because it is so rare; she says, "What I did was a radical thing" (Collins, *Hunger Games* 26). But it is a radical example that others, to her astonishment, start to follow. Even before Thresh spares Katniss' life in the arena, the first person to follow in her footsteps is Peeta. At some point between the reaping and the beginning of the Games, Peeta decides that he is going to show the Capitol that he is "more than just a piece in their Games"—that he's not going to play the game their way (142).

The Capitol makes its ideology clear through the rules of the Hunger Games, a zero-sum game where alliances can never be more than wary and temporary; it wants the citizens of Panem to believe that not only in the Games, but in real life, the best strategy for survival in the world is dog-eat-dog, every-woman-for-herself, extreme individualism. Not only is that how a tribute becomes a victor in the Games, but it also conveniently justifies the Capitol's winner-take-all attitude towards the districts. Not only the tributes themselves but the people watching at home have little choice but to buy into this ideology, if they care about the survival of their District's children in the arena. But Peeta goes against it; he decides that instead of trying to win himself, he's going to throw everything he has into trying to *help Katniss win*.

People often assume that Peeta acts out of love for Katniss, but there is little direct evidence for his true feelings about her until they are acting as lovers together late in their first Games. It is certainly true that his gift of bread when they were eleven gave them an important connection, and there is no reason to doubt his truthfulness when he tells Caesar Flickerman, "I've had a crush on her ever since I can remember" (Collins, *Hunger Games* 130). But while he may have liked and admired her from afar, before they were thrown together in the Games, he didn't really know her. Peeta and Haymitch explain that the "confession of love" was deliberate strategizing on their parts, intended to give Katniss an advantage in the Games (132). And the theory of gift exchange—the fact that the exchange of gifts can create powerful relational bonds—raises the possibility that the intensity of the love Peeta afterwards feels for Katniss is a natural *consequence* of his attempting to give her the radical gift of his life. It is, in fact, a mirror image of the way that Katniss' willingness to sacrifice herself for Prim is a natural consequence of the intensity of her love for her sister.

Other tributes, victors, and citizens of Panem begin to follow in Peeta's footsteps, starting with both tributes from District 11. Hiding in a tree near where the Career tributes have Katniss trapped, Rue points out the tracker jacker nest that gives Katniss the advantage she needs to survive the situation. It's possible that Rue is thinking strategically—bringing the deadly tracker jackers into the situation could only help her if it meant that any of the more powerful tributes, including Katniss herself, ended up dead—but Rue is also probably motivated by altruism, as evidenced by the fact that she doesn't take advantage of Katniss' being disabled by the stings to kill her. (In the film, she even says matter-of-factly, "I changed your leaves twice.") Katniss attempts to give Rue the mockingjay pin, but Rue won't take it (Collins, *Hunger Games* 212). Flitting around the treetops and singing as she does, Rue is already so closely associated with mockingjays that she hardly needs a material symbol; besides, she and Katniss have already exchanged food, medicine, and trust, all far more precious gifts in the arena than a gold pin.

When Rue dies, Katniss grieves, revealing the depth of the feeling-bond created by their exchange of gifts—and knows that doing so will be seen by the Capitol as rebellious. But even more radical is the gift of bread sent by District 11 afterwards. Katniss is stunned:

> What must it have cost the people of District 11 who can't even feed themselves? How many would've had to do without to scrape up a coin to put in the collection for this one loaf? It had been meant for Rue, surely. But instead of pulling the gift when she died, they'd authorized Haymitch to give it to me. As a thank-you? Or because, like me, they don't like to let debts go unpaid? For whatever reason, this is a first. A district gift to a tribute who's not your own. (Collins, *Hunger Games* 239)

And the radical gifts keep coming. In *Catching Fire*, Peeta spontaneously offers Thresh's and Rue's families "one month of our winnings every year for the duration of our lives," a shocking move that he only later understands will be taken as a sign of rebellion (59). During the Quarter Quell, Finnick saves Peeta's life by performing CPR, and Katniss is "furious because it means that I will never stop owing Finnick Odair. Ever" (Collins, *Catching Fire* 282). Since Peeta saved Katniss' life—the debt she can never repay, not even by saving his life in return—that means by extension, she also owes a debt to anyone who saves Peeta's life. Then in *Mockingjay*, Boggs and nearly every other member of Katniss' military squad lose their lives in futile pursuit of her self-appointed mission. When she tries to figure out why they followed her, Peeta tells her, "I think … you still have no idea. The effect you can have" (Collins, *Mockingjay* 325). Katniss thinks, "if he's right, and I think he is, I owe the others a debt that can only be repaid in one way"—fulfilling her promise to kill Snow.

Poison Presents: Gifts of Death and Destruction

I suggested earlier that there's a progression in the series from "gifts of life" in the beginning to "gifts of death" at the end. But maybe that distinction was an artificial one: Katniss' volunteering for her sister is a gift both of life and of death at the same time, since, as Katniss says, "the word *tribute* is pretty much synonymous with the word *corpse*" (Collins, *Hunger Games* 22). Thresh's sparing of Katniss' life creates a feeling-bond between them that Katniss never forgets, but his gift is simultaneously one of mercy and one of murder, specifically of Clove. Even Peeta's gift of bread saves Katniss only long enough for her to turn twelve and sign her odds away to the games by taking tesserae. During the Quarter Quell, the other tributes save Peeta multiple times, but then they abandon him to the Capitol when the force field goes down and rescue only Katniss, ironically robbing her of the chance to finally repay Peeta by giving him a merciful death before he can be taken and tortured. It turns out that gifts and death are closely associated all along.

Mauss points out that the word "poison" and the word "present" have the same origin in Germanic languages ("Gift, Gift" 28). Of course poison is a major theme in the books: poison berries, poison pills, the poisoning snake that is President Snow. Mauss suggests that the common origin is a word that meant "the gift of drink," and recipients would never know until they drank it whether the gift was good to drink or poison (30). Snow sends Katniss a poison present in the form of a hijacked, murderous Peeta: Katniss mourns, "Snow has stolen him from me, twisted him beyond recognition, and made me a present of him" (Collins, *Mockingjay* 194). Similarly, the bomb-parachutes that kill the children and their rescuers, including Prim, in the City Circle are another kind of poison present. Meanwhile, the French intellectual Georges Bataille theorizes that a society's excess of acquired wealth *must* be given away or wasted, most destructively through war (23–25). Thus gifts have something in common with death and destruction because they're all a way of squandering excess, a word that certainly characterizes the economy of the Capitol. This connection takes us back to Plutarch's prediction that humanity will forget the lessons it has learned and end up playing out its "great gift for self-destruction" to the grim end.

Children as Gifts: A Final Note of Hope

Nevertheless, the series doesn't end with Plutarch's prediction. Nor does it end with Katniss' long-anticipated murder of Snow, which never comes about, despite her promise to repay her debt to her dead comrades-in-arms. It ends with the birth of Katniss and Peeta's children. Despite the fact that she has had a decade and a half to recover from the trauma of her teenage years before agreeing to have a family, this ending is still surprising, coming as it does after three full books depicting Katniss' unwillingness or inability to have so much as a simple romance, not to mention her repeated flat refusal to consider *ever* having children in a world so broken. And the language surrounding Katniss' motherhood is deeply ambivalent: "When I first felt her stirring inside of me, I was consumed with a terror that felt as old as life itself. Only the joy of holding her in my arms could tame it. Carrying him was a little easier, but not much" (Collins, *Mockingjay* 389).

But I would suggest that Katniss' decision to give Peeta the children that he "wanted so badly" may be, for *her*, the most radical gift of all (Collins, *Mockingjay* 389). On one level, it's the way that Katniss can truly, finally, pay Peeta back for that gift of bread that meant she owed him something greater than her own life. But on another level, it may suggest that their relationship has fundamentally changed. Instead of being based on reciprocity and owing, they may now have the option to form a relationship based on an ethic of care—from each according to her abilities, to each according to his needs. Most importantly of all, if Katniss' children can be *gifts*, it means she finally believes that the gift economy of Panem is no longer corrupted: there is no longer a threat that her children's bodies may be sacrificed as commodities, the way hers was. Try as it might, the Capitol could not destroy Katniss' ability to give the radical gift of love.

Works Cited

Arrow, V. *The Panem Companion: An Unofficial Guide to Suzanne Collins' Hunger Games, from Mellark Bakery to Mockingjays.* Dallas: BenBella, 2012. Print.

Bataille, Georges. *The Accursed Share: An Essay on General Economy, Vol. 1: Consumption.* 1967. Trans. Robert Hurley. New York: Zone, 1988. Print.

Clemente, Bill. "Panem in America: Crisis Economics and a Call for Political Engagement." *Of Bread, Blood, and The Hunger Games: Critical Essays on the Suzanne Collins Trilogy.* Ed. Mary F. Pharr and Leisa A. Clark. Jefferson, NC: McFarland, 2012. 20–29. Critical Exploration in Science Fiction and Fantasy Ser. Print.

Collins, Suzanne. *Catching Fire.* New York: Scholastic, 2009. Print.

_____. *The Hunger Games.* New York: Scholastic, 2008. Print.

_____. *Mockingjay.* New York: Scholastic, 2010. Print.

The Hunger Games. Dir. Gary Ross. Prod. Nina Jacobson. Perf. Jennifer Lawrence, Josh Hutcherson, Woody Harrelson, Elizabeth Banks, and Lenny Kravitz. Lionsgate, 2012. Blu-Ray.

Hyde, Lewis. *The Gift: Creativity and the Artist in the Modern World.* 25th Anniversary Ed. New York: Vintage, 2007. Print.

Mauss, Marcel. *The Gift: The Form and Reason for Exchange in Archaic Societies.* Trans. W. D. Halls. London: Routledge, 1990. Print.

_____. "Gift, Gift." *The Logic of the Gift: Toward an Ethic of Generosity.* Ed. Alan D. Schrift. New York: Routledge, 1997. 28–32. Print.

Nietzsche, Friedrich. *The Portable Nietzsche.* Ed. and Trans. Walter Kaufmann. New York: Viking Penguin, 1954. Print.

"As long as you can find yourself, you'll never starve": Consuming Katniss in The Hunger Games Trilogy

Stephanie Dror

George Orwell and Aldous Huxley imagined two very distinct dystopias. In *1984* (1949), Orwell depicts the forces that held people captive as fundamentally external: coercion, espionage, laws, institutions, threats, and lies told by the ubiquitous Big Brother. The vision of freedom that Orwell presents is primarily socio-political, with the greatest threat to humans being other humans, whether the Nazi, the slave-owner, the autocrat, or another oppressor. Oppression comes through pain, not pleasure; the essence of liberty is to be without external constraint. By contrast, Huxley's *Brave New World* (1932), published just after the Wall Street crash had turned the excess of the twenties into the Great Depression of the thirties, portrays a future in which people are enslaved to forces within themselves: desire, inanity, hedonism, egotism, ignorance. Humans are free if they are able to choose, to will their own future, to decide for themselves what they will do with their lives. The cores of these dystopias are striking and fascinating and launched the dystopia into a genre of its own.

The Hunger Games trilogy (2008–2010) by Suzanne Collins is one of the latest additions to dystopian literature. Unlike its blockbuster young adult or children's literature predecessors, such as J. K. Rowling's Harry Potter series (1997–2007) and Stephanie Meyer's Twilight series (2005–2008), Collins' series is not rooted in the paranormal. There is no magic; there are no vampires. The protagonists are ordinary people, living in a dystopian society. As in Huxley and Orwell's texts, nature within the dystopian society is often restricted or lacking, and yet nature is central in the dystopian protagonists' gradual realization that they are living in a dystopia. In reflection of its literary dystopian predecessors, The Hunger Games series presents an interesting blend of *1984* and *Brave New World*.

The districts live in an Orwellian dystopia, while the Capitol exists in a world that strongly resembles *Brave New World*—many Capitol citizens don't seem to notice that they are living in a controlled society or that their government commits heinous acts in order to maintain itself. Most district citizens, on the other hand, are too preoccupied with every day survival and too frightened of the Capitol to act against it. However, one of the things that ties these two worlds together is Panem's institution of the Hunger Games. The Capitol prepares for the Games all year and, ironically, by supplying the Capitol with resources and tributes, so do the districts. While it is touted as the reconciliation for the revolution of seventy-four years before, it has really become an institution that keeps the Capitol in power. In addition, it is Panem's primary consumer product. It is televised and distributed throughout the country: a sport to the Capitol and mandatory viewing for the districts.

The Hunger Games offers a critique of contemporary Western culture's devotion to media, technology, and consumerism and its loss of connection with the natural world. The ecocritic Lawrence Buell in his introduction to *Writing for an Endangered World* says that "with accelerated techno social change has come greatly intensified anxiety about 'the environment,' and with it a redirection of traditional discourses and a plethora of new ones" (3). By "the environment," Buell is referring to "both 'natural' and 'human-built'" dimensions of the palpable world, which must be distinguished between, but are also increasingly blurred, as humans move into the twenty-first century (3). The Hunger Games series expounds on Buell's "post-modernist claim that we inhabit a prosthetic environment" and speculates about whether contemporary humanity might also inhabit a simulated human existence (Buell 5). The reality of a blended non-human environment, made up of technology and nature, is realized throughout the series but predominantly in the first installment, *The Hunger Games*. Young adult (YA) dystopian fictions, like most literature, are cultural artifacts capable of providing a contemporary cultural critique. YA dystopias like The Hunger Games series pose a kind of "what if" statement regarding the anxieties and concerns of the contemporary audience: *what* would happen to contemporary society *if* the environment collapsed? Greg Garrard's *Ecocriticism* defines ecocriticism as a "widely accepted name for cultural criticism from an environmentalist perspective" (1). Therefore, granting that literature is a cultural artifact enables us to perform a cultural critique, and an ecocritical reading of The Hunger Games series is made possible. Ecocriticism and ecomimetic texts—that is, texts that discuss the real environment—have often placed humanity and culture in an oppositional binary with the natural world: whether humans have to save the environment, live alongside the environment, or simply live bereft of it, nature is separate from human culture as opposed to an intrinsic part of human life (Gerrard 105). In The Hunger Games trilogy, this belief in the binary between nature, and culture is the hubris of the dystopian regime of the Capitol. Nature plays an interesting role as Collins' series engages in creating a model of reality that shapes the natural environment in the Districts as a dangerous space, off-limits to humans. The natural world in *The Hunger Games* is either completely extraneous and autonomous from the machinations of Panem's humanity or presented as a technology-laden, constructed environment as in the Games or the Capitol. Essential to Katniss' survival throughout the series is her forbidden relationship with the natural world, her native ecosystem. This relationship not only allows Katniss access to prohibited knowledge and skills (such as flora and fauna lore and hunting with a bow), but it also gives her a space in which she can question the system of Panem freely. Nature, then, allows Katniss to both understand and undermine the dystopian regime that presides over Panem.

Along with climate change, genetic modification, an oversaturation of media and Hollywood aesthetics, an increasing global reliance on consumerism, and technological development, dystopias are growing in relevance. Contemporary concern for not only the natural, but how the natural interacts and blends with the technological, the political, and the human is becoming more prevalent. While the books of The Hunger Games series have received criticism for what some consider unnecessary violence— children killing children is as unsavory to us as cannibalism is to the

Capitol—I would argue that the graphic content is not needlessly gratuitous but instead a reflection of our own world. Collins is quoted as saying that she was motivated to write the novels after watching footage of the invasion of Iraq and reality TV (Margolis). We need look no further than our televisions and newspapers for acts of violence similar to those portrayed in the books. Therefore, rather than criticizing the novels for gratuitous violence, a more critical gaze should be cast on the blockbuster movie box office profits. The film, directed by Gary Ross, is true to the horrors of the text, depicting child tributes in bloody battle for survival, and that is what the audience—the fictional Capitol audience and the real one sitting in the cinema—have paid to see. Indeed, it is ironic that the first film alone earned over $152.5 million in its opening weekend ("Biggest Opening Weekend"). Ross's film adaptation of *The Hunger Games* even points out the irony in an added dialogue between Gale and Katniss (2010):

> *GALE*: What if they did? Just one year. What if everyone just stopped watching?
> *KATNISS*: They won't, Gale.
> *GALE*: What if they did? What if we did.
> *KATNISS*: Won't happen.
> *GALE*: Root for your favorite, cry when they get killed. It's sick.
> *KATNISS:* Gale.
> *GALE:* If no one watches then they don't have a game. It's as simple as that. (*The Hunger Games* [Dir. Ross] 6:19)

This conversation, absent in the book, is a remarkable addition to the film, as it immediately breaks the cinematic fourth wall when Gale speculates about what might happen if the audience, Panem, but also, arguably, the movie's actual audience, stopped watching the Hunger Games. Gale and Katniss reflect on the use of media technology and the social institution of the Hunger Games, noting that the point of the Games is for them to be watched: if no one watches, then the Capitol will lose its power, no one will die, and the cycle of consumption will cease. The film begins to stimulate the revolutionary consciousness, the focus of The Hunger Games novels and the tradition of dystopian texts. Of course, the film medium requires watching in order to relay its story, and so this inkling of revolution seems mere irony as opposed to the poignant beginnings of change. The first novel, on the other hand, is at once dystopian in its critical and political discussions surrounding media, consumerism, and environmental neglect, and yet it is also poignant; it advocates against and reflects on the commodification and consumption of our most precious natural resource: children.

In order to uncover the ways in which Katniss uses her relationship with nature to undermine the dystopian regime of the Capitol, each of the three settings or environments in The Hunger Games series—Panem, the Capitol, and the arena—will be examined. In each of these locations, Katniss undermines the latent consumerist cycle of Panem and uses the natural environment in ways that destabilize the intentions of the Capitol. Nature is an entropic system that constantly adapts and evolves, even as humans continue to impinge on it, and Katniss lives within the laws of this natural system. Through Katniss, Collins invites the reader to engage critically with the ecosystem, an ecosystem that incorporates nature, technology, and culture.

Panem

Panem is "the country that rose up out of the ashes of the place that was once called North America" (Collins, *Hunger Games* 18; hereafter *HG*). The reaping, the ceremony in which the tributes for the Games are chosen, begins the novel and opens with a propaganda film justifying the Hunger Games. The film portrays the rebellion of the Districts against the Capitol as an insidious assault and the institution of the Hunger Games as a system intended to maintain peace. This is the only story of Panem's past told in the novel, and both the reader and Katniss must interpret history through the Capitol's vision. In a brief reflection on the dissemination of knowledge and history, Katniss says, "I know there must be more than they're telling us.... But I don't spend much time thinking about it.... I don't see how it will help me get food on the table" (*HG* 42). This "history" sets up the structure of the world. Tom Moylan notes,

---

"Throughout the history of dystopian fiction, the conflict of the text has often turned on the control of language and information" (148). Discussing Newspeak from Orwell's *1984* and the control over information and history in Huxley's *Brave New World*, he contends that "control over the means of language, over representation and interpellation, is a crucial weapon and strategy in dystopia" (Moylan 148–9). Knowledge is spread through media and is consumed by a public too preoccupied with their own survival (putting food on the table each night) to question it. The dystopian lifestyle of the Districts becomes a normalized narrative that is justified because it goes unquestioned.

What the people of Panem know and how they live dictates what actions are possible for them within their space. Each district has a perimeter fence that keeps residents away from the natural world, and travel between Districts is restricted. In this way, Panem's hierarchical structure is geographically organized as the difference between the Capitol and the surrounding districts and can be construed as analogous to that between center and periphery in the world. The districts are responsible for fishing and the manufacture of commodities as well as the extraction and production of raw materials, such as coal, cotton, and lumber. For example, District 1 produces diamonds. As such, there is further stratification between the districts as the lower numbered districts have preferred status over the higher numbers and are allowed more privileges, including training their tributes for the Hunger Games. The Capitol citizens, then, are left to engage in various kinds of consumption, and if they do work, it involves using the resources delivered to them from the Districts in the service industry—food preparation, aesthetics, and design or entertainment. The contrast between the Capitol's urban wastefulness and the rural, natural, industrious Districts highlights an interesting twist in Collins' text. While District 12 is an exceptionally small community, where everyone knows everybody else, the Capitol is immensely populous and unwelcoming, giving the impression that, in Panem, the rich vastly outnumber the working poor, making it all the more difficult to imagine and conduct a revolution. The Capitol's decadent technological splendor—and its apparently unlimited populace who endlessly consume—represent modern Western civilization and are vilified in direct contrast with older forms of labor, such as hunting and gathering, bartering, and a generally honest work ethic.

District 12 is located on the edge of Panem's civilization and is encircled by a disabled electrical fence, which is meant to keep wild things out but really serves to keep the citizens penned in and under surveillance. With technology and a pervasive control over knowledge, the Capitol holds the power of segregation and judgment, while its citizens have limited or no access to that power. Indeed, the social hierarchy between the Capitol and the Districts and between more and less prosperous Districts is further compounded and paralleled by the class divisions within the districts themselves. In District 12, the lower class are the working miners, who happen to have dark hair and tanned skin, and the upper class are merchants with light hair and a fair complexion. The citizens lack the courage or the insight to question their social status even within their own Districts and therefore have little agency or ability to confront the societal powers that govern the whole of Panem.

Katniss accesses the ability to question the boundaries impinging on her life by leaving the district's perimeter. Out of, at first, a necessity to hunt for food and bring outside resources into District 12, Katniss takes pleasure in leaving the eye of the Capitol and the controlled space of Panem. When she leaves the perimeter with her hunting partner, Gale Hawthorn, she gains the freedom to culture her own thoughts and reflect on the structure of Panem and the institution of the Hunger Games. As reflected in the title of this essay, Katniss searches for herself—katniss the plant—both in order to consume it and to figuratively discover her own agency, an agency that, by the end of the series, is arguably consumed by the culture of Panem. Katniss gains a sense of autonomy and freedom, revealing that she is only her genuine self with Gale in the woods, hunting (*HG* 6). Furthermore, the forest gives Katniss and Gale a space in which they can freely reflect on their society: "Deep in the woods, I've listened to him rant about how the tesserae[1] are just another tool to cause misery in our District. A way to plant hatred between the starving workers … and those who can generally count on supper and thereby ensure we will never trust one another" (*HG* 14). Nature becomes a space free from surveillance, where Gale and Katniss progress from reflecting on their culture to learning it's structure and unraveling it.

Together, Katniss and Gale build their knowledge of nature as a reciprocal, cyclical system. Whereas in Panem and the districts passivity and obedience are enforced, nature offers another method of survival, a more sustainable method. Escaping the limits of District 12 allows Katniss and Gale to question those limits. Why will the Capitol not allow them to hunt freely? Why is it illegal to bring in outside resources and sell them throughout the district? The answers are simple—because then they would move from a dependence on the Capitol's consumerism to a dependence on themselves, creating a sustainable economy that would shift the power away from the Capitol. In a natural environment, Katniss is afforded an understanding of her position within the larger cultural structure of Panem, and this environment enables her to question, agree with, or disapprove of that position. Unfortunately, although Katniss and Gale recognize the powerful and cruel system in which they are prisoners, they feel helpless and unable to enact change, as the daily struggle for survival keeps them under surveillance and, therefore, compliant.

However, unwittingly, Katniss *has* begun to undermine the segregation of the people and the carefully constructed microcosmic dystopia of District 12. The wilderness holds unpredictable dangers, yet Gale and Katniss hunt in order to survive, becoming so adept at it that Katniss says:

> The woods became our savior.… I was determined to feed us. I stole eggs from nests, caught fish in nets, sometimes managed to shoot a squirrel or rabbit for stew.… Plants are tricky. Many are edible, but one false mouthful and you're dead. I checked and double-checked the plants I harvested with my father's pictures. I kept us alive. (*HG* 51)

Nature has become a space extraneous to Panem as a construct where Katniss can practice trial and error, an essential quality for a "good" game that requires the player to reflect on and *learn* the mechanics of the game space (Boghost 132). According to *Scraps of the Untainted Sky* by Tom Moylan, a utopia and dystopia scholar, this reflecting and leaning are also a feature of dystopian literature. The narrative of the YA dystopia will focus on one subject in the dystopian world, and the storyline develops around the alienated protagonist as he or she begins to recognize the situation as dystopian and to trace the development from individual experience (the egocentricity of childhood) to the operation of the entire system (adult society) (Moylan xiii). Hunting in the forest provides Katniss with the ability to transcend social boundaries and form relationships with all castes in District 12. She deals with the black market's Greasy Sae, the town butcher, the baker, the Peacekeepers, and even the Mayor's family, as she sells strawberries at his back door (*HG* 11). This subversive commercial activity is positioned as favorable compared to Peeta's family's bakery, which works on a more classic consumer system, earning money by selling decorated cakes to rich citizens. Crossing into the natural environment around District 12 undermines the Capitol's hold on it. Nature has become a place for cultural reflection, a resource to be negotiated with, and an agent for transcending powerful social boundaries. Katniss has begun not only to learn the rules of the game within the Hunger Games but to push against these rules by leaving its limits and acquiring new knowledge, perspective, and resources. She has begun to test the limits of the system in powerful ways.

Katniss distinctly becomes an active player in the game when she volunteers to become tribute at the seventy-fourth annual Hunger Games. She refuses to let the Capitol reap the most valuable thing in her life, her little sister Prim, and, in so doing, she refuses the Capitol a victim. At age twelve, with no survival skills or fighting experience, Prim would not last long in the arena. Katniss adopts a gamer attitude, one that is tied directly to the creative, improvisational, and subversive qualities of play (Boghost 119). Katniss begins to think strategy almost immediately, demanding

Prim let go of her: "I don't want to cry … everyone will make note of my tears, and I'll be marked as an easy target. A weakling. I will give no one that satisfaction. 'Let go!'" (*HG* 23). Already, Katniss demonstrates her understanding of the power that media and perception have over the citizens of Panem and, most importantly, the citizens of the Capitol and the other tributes. She knows that she will constantly be televised and has to learn how to manage her appearance. Immediately following this exchange between sisters, the citizens of District 12 refuse to clap for Katniss as a *tribute* to the Games and instead salute Katniss as an individual *player*. This is both a foreshadowing of the use that Katniss will make of the cameras within the Games themselves and a televised blatant act of insurgence, which will be watched throughout Panem. "Silence. Which says we do not agree. We do not condone. All of this is wrong," (*HG* 23).

In District 12, the natural environment is a space where the structure of Panem can be reflected upon, where new skills can be learned and where resources extraneous to the construction of the districts can be harvested and brought in for trade. By employing these skills and sharing natural resources, Katniss breaks down social barriers within and between the districts. Katniss' sacrifice and her district's dissension are broadcast to the whole nation. Katniss knows what is wrong with Panem, and though she is preoccupied with her own survival, it is her tenacious will to survive and knowledge gleaned in nature that have begun to fan the flames of rebellion throughout Panem. Katniss, the girl on fire, has begun undermining the very intent of the Hunger Games.

The Capitol

Katniss and Peeta Mellark, the male tribute from District 12 and supporting character throughout the series, finally reach the Capitol with their mentor Haymitch, a former victor. The metropolis of the Capitol is presented as an entirely artificial world compared to the coal mines and woodlands of District 12. The distinction between the natural, humble district and the constructed environment of the Capitol is a constant point of comparison for Katniss, who cannot fathom the garish fashion of her host, Effie Trinket, and who mocks the Capitol accent and tries to calculate how much lamb stew would cost in District 12. The Capitol, metaphorically representing our Western civilization, is the epitome of decadence. Its people constantly consume media and are indoctrinated with a concern for aesthetics. As they see it, they live in a relative utopia. Through totalitarian strategies, the Capitol fashions the citizen subjects as childlike and naïve in much the same way as Huxley's elite A's of *Brave New World*. The infantilized state of the Capitol populace is produced by strict codes and regulations with the intention of maintaining an uncomplicated utopian state. The Capitol and the districts are ruled in much the same fashion: they are kept in the dark about what life is like beyond their perimeters; they experience minimal communications and travel; and their lives are preoccupied with the day-to-day, as opposed to long-term thinking. This delicate balance is largely maintained through the institution of the Hunger Games and the status of "celebrity" within the Capitol and the Hunger Games themselves. Haymitch, Katniss' coach and the only previous District 12 winner; Effie; and Cinna all emphasize how important it is that Katniss be "likeable" to Panem, the Games' audience. As Katniss' goal is to win the Hunger Games and avoid "being changed" by them, she begins to harness the power of perception in order to undermine the Capitol's power. With the help of Haymitch and with Cinna as her personal stylist, Katniss begins to win the affections of the Capitol citizens and the admiration of the districts through performance and image and walks the tenuous line between the role of obedient citizen and rebel symbol.

With the use of fashion and spectacle, Cinna creates "Katniss, the girl who was on fire," and Haymitch uses Peeta to make the pair of them "the star-crossed lovers" (*HG* 67, 135). The Capitol's citizens are not sufficiently aware of their own oppression to understand their aesthetic bombardment as process. They become "the masses," a background image that is hardly mentioned until it is useful. The reader, like Katniss, will be able to see and question how being at once preoccupied with aesthetics and simultaneously unable to read them critically makes the Capitol's citizens easy to manipulate.

Katniss begins to use the impressionable masses to her advantage, unwittingly walking the precarious line between spectacle and revolutionary. By the time Katniss has entered the Hunger Games, she has built a persona that the Capitol masses adore. She has become a symbol for resistance against the corrupt government, and she has begun to understand that through the rhetoric of media, she can control the Games of the Capitol. Perhaps this is a foreshadowing of the Gamemakers' use and simultaneous underestimation of "pretty berries." This also foreshadows how, later in the trilogy, District 13 and General Coin come to use Katniss as an icon, but underestimate her natural will to survive.

For this ecocritical reading, a particularly interesting location in the text is the garden on the rooftop of the training center in the Capitol. It is a fabricated natural space, protected by a force field— in some ways, a miniature version of the playing grounds of the Hunger Games. It is also a reflection of the natural space from District 12 in that it is a space of beauty and rest, a space where Peeta and Katniss can reflect on strategy and the construction of the Games' space and criticize the Capitol without worrying about being overheard (or so they, and the reader, are led to believe). Collins writes, "Here in the garden, on this windy night, it's enough to drown out two people who are trying not to be heard" (*HG* 81–2). In the garden, Katniss divulges the story of the red-haired Avox[2] to Peeta. The story not only demonstrates the reach of the Capitol's power and how the boundaries of Panem are carefully surveilled and guarded, but in the telling of the story, Katniss reveals how safe she feels in nature and again initiates reflection upon the structure of Panem's culture between herself and Peeta. When the two meet on the roof again, after Peeta has publicly confessed his "love" for Katniss to Caesar Flickerman, the celebrity talk-show host of Panem, Peeta says that he knows he does not stand a chance of winning and hopes his personality will not change in the arena: "I want to die as myself ... I don't want them to change me in there ... I wish I could think of a way to ... to show the Capitol they don't own me. That I'm more than just a piece in their Games" (*HG* 141). Peeta, like Gale before him, reflects on the institution of the Games and how the Capitol controls dissemination of information via television, propaganda, the use of celebrity, and other forms of media. It is only in the natural space of the rooftop that he and Katniss can share information, experience, and tactics. They engage in collaborative reflection in order to maximize their potential to win the Games.

The 'natural' space in the Capitol is interesting because it reveals two things. First, the natural world is not as safe from the Capitol and its technologies as Katniss thinks it is. For example, the mockingjay birdcall warning of the hovercraft's arrival to capture the Avox is the same as the birdcall in the Games before the hovercraft removes dead tributes (*HG* 83, 237). The ease with which the Capitol found the Avox girl and her accomplice hints at hidden surveillance in the natural surroundings of the districts and how swiftly people can be consumed by the Capitol, never to be heard from again—much like the hidden surveillance within the "natural" world of the Games themselves.

Second, Peeta, like Gale before him, has recognized that, even within the framework of the Games, he has the potential to break free long enough to express individuality. The Capitol has constructed nature as a perceived haven, where dissension and sedition are discussed and planned. However, throughout the series, it is revealed that the Capitol knows everything—even District 13's existence is sanctioned by the Capitol under an old agreement. While the possibility of insurgence maintains an unsteady peace, a rebellion is not foreseeable because inter-district resources and communications are limited. However, the Capitol mindset is ignorant of nature as an autonomous system, and Capitol media only reinforce the pervasive sense of artificiality. Interestingly, Katniss' tactic in the Capitol is to hide her ability to hunt with a bow and arrow until she is alone with the Gamemakers. Instead, throughout the training period, she demonstrates her knowledge of plants, trap-making, and basic survival skills—abilities that are discounted by the other tributes and the Capitol citizens as unimportant and signaling weakness in a tribute. Perhaps the deference to survival skills is in an attempt to perpetuate other tributes' drive to kill as opposed to outlast, but it is also another way in which *The Hunger Games*' nature/culture binary is enforced. Human culture in *The Hunger Games* is removed from nature and inundated with technology. The humans of Panem are simply ignorant of the importance of nature in their everyday lives. Katniss, who reflects within nature on how the game is won and lost, reverses the intended use of nature in the Games and outplays the Gamemakers not only in the Games, but in Panem, by breaking through the nature/culture binary. Technology lies at the heart of the Capitol's power over its people, from regulating travel and communication between districts to encouraging genetic manipulation (from blue skin to mockingjays) for power and aesthetic pleasure. Technology is both the power and the weakness of the Capitol and, arguably, of current civilization. Katniss, as wielder of natural resourcefulness, begins to undo the processes behind the broader game being played in Panem.

The Hunger Games

Katniss enters the Hunger Games armed with a character the audience loves, a sense of ease in nature, the capacity to hunt and survive, and (most importantly) the ability to assess the Game's rules, limitations, and players. The Games, held in a remote location where real nature is combined with the Gamemakers' artificial elements, are broadcast live and are mandatory viewing for all of Panem. Katniss has prepared for the Games by watching recordings of previous victors. She notes,

> There are no rules in the arena, but cannibalism doesn't play well with the Capitol audience, so they tried to head it off. There was some speculation that the avalanche that finally took Titus out was specifically engineered to ensure the victor was not a lunatic. (*HG* 143)

Here Katniss clearly demonstrates that she understands the only rule of the Hunger Games: that the Gamemakers must create the most pleasing show possible for the consumption of the Capitol audience and that they achieve this by manipulating the natural elements of the Games, which, in turn, affects the tributes.

Katniss also notes the importance of acquiring food. The beginning of the Hunger Games has Katniss determined to ensure that the audience can maintain confidence in her by showing that she is capable of survival. Demonstrating both her ability to understand a natural ecology and her media literacy, she overcomes her first obstacle: finding water. As she hunts for water, she realizes that in order to make the Games bloodier, the Gamemakers have placed the largest water source in the middle of the arena, in the hopes of drawing tributes into battle over this necessity. She realizes that the forest is a game board, technologically manipulated by the Gamemakers to look pretty, to instigate confrontation between tributes, and to make survival difficult. While the reality is that the competitors are left with their most basic needs for food, water, and shelter constantly in question, this is at odds with the point of the show—to kill the other competitors. What the competitors really need to do to survive is at odds with what they are *supposed* to do for the televised competition, which is to fulfill the Capitol's need for entertainment—or their bloodlust. The people of Panem, literally and metaphorically, consume the combatants' performance in the Games. Therefore, it is also important that Katniss show that she is able to prevail on her own, crucial that she make a good impression on the Capitol crowd. Katniss quickly adapts to her reality and learns its rules and constructs, just as game theorist Ian Boghost says that any good gamer should (Boghost 134). In a demonstration of her knowledge of nature and media literacy, she hears Haymitch's silence and understands that she must follow moss until she finally finds water.

Fulfilling her basic survival needs and effectively communicating with those outside of the Hunger Games, she begins to look for a partner. Hearkening back to the reasoning behind not running away from District 12, she enlists the help of Rue, a clever, quick, and industrious tribute from District 11 who also has knowledge of natural remedies. Befriending a girl from a different district (and a different race), who does not stand much of a chance against the larger, stronger tributes alone, endears Katniss to the district crowds and pairs her with a loyal companion. Though she notes that she "can hear Haymitch groaning as I team up with this wispy child," she disregards that awareness, citing the need for teamwork in order to survive (*HG* 281). She ignores what she is "supposed" to do (there are no "rules" after all) and, instead, takes Rue under her wing. Working in tandem, they destroy the food source of the favored tributes, making it a true game of hunger and, as they know how to live off the land and the spoiled tributes[3] do not, they gain an advantage. When Rue dies, Katniss realizes that the cameras broadcasting the Games can be used directly against the Capitol. She recognizes that the Capitol, in a display of power meant to enforce the necessity of the Hunger Games, always broadcasts the corpses of the slain tributes. Twisting the intention of this broadcast, Katniss visibly honors the slain child to dramatize the injustice of the Games, decorating her corpse with flowers (*HG* 236). She transforms Rue from a consumed commodity into an anti-consumer symbol. The white flowers, placed in the arena by the Gamemakers simply to look beautiful, now represent humanity, innocence, youth, loss; Katniss begins to unravel the constructed space of the Hunger Games. It is no longer merely aesthetic; it now also harbors real natural elements that can be a resource for her own game. She begins to use the aesthetic preoccupation of the Capitol and the Games against her most dangerous enemy—President Snow. In a direct act of defiance, Rue's native District 11 acknowledges Katniss' empathy by sending her bread, showing that she has effectively broken down the barriers between districts. She gains further traction with the Capitol and district audiences when she rescues an injured and ill Peeta and hides with him. Tethered to a wounded and sick tribute, Katniss recognizes that they are easy prey. Instead of being daunted, Katniss, prompted by Haymitch, "remembers the importance of sustaining the star-crossed lover routine," "imagine[s] the teary sighs emanating from the Capitol," and, in a deliberate attempt to manipulate the Capitol masses, she begins the "star-crossed" lover performance (*HG* 281). In response to her manipulations, the Capitol citizens begin sponsoring[4] her, and in a move meant to solicit more drama for the Capitol, the Gamemakers change the rules: two tributes can now win the seventy-fourth annual Hunger Games.

Katniss is unsure of what the rule change means but continues to play the game and the role of hopeful lover. The Gamemakers draw her and the other tributes out into battle, promising them a necessary commodity—Katniss enters the fray in order to retrieve medicine for Peeta. Interestingly, she survives only because Thresh, the male tribute from District 11, spares her life; when he realizes that she had partnered with Rue and buried her with dignity, he lets Katniss go, "for the little girl" (*HG* 288). This is a powerful moment as Katniss' subversion of the perceived nature of the Hunger Games has now not only provoked empathy from the Capitol audience and made sponsors of the outlying districts, but it has also resulted in other players sparing her life—something that is not supposed to happen in the arena. Finally, Katniss has moved from manipulating to reinventing the way in which the Hunger Games are played and consumed.

Katniss and Peeta are the last contestants standing when it is announced that the two-victor rule "has been revoked. Closer examination of the rule book has disclosed that only one winner may be allowed" (*HG* 342). The two performative lovers are tortured by the thoughts of becoming a surviving murderer, which is exactly what the Capitol wants: to revoke the power and agency that Katniss has gained by forcing the two remaining tributes to play the Games the Gamemakers' way. Katniss, thinking that "death right here, right now would be the easier of the two [options]," realizes that the only recourse for them, the only way to maintain control, would be to die on their own terms (*HG* 344). Unwilling to allow the Capitol to have a victor who has really been beaten, Katniss again changes the game. Poignantly, her alternative was presented by Gale at the beginning of the novel when he suggested escaping into the wilderness, as well as by Peeta in the rooftop garden when he says he does not want to lose himself. With these reflections in the back of her mind, Katniss' modifications come into play once more as she holds out poisonous berries. Nature is part of the Games' environment, yet it is underestimated or overlooked by the Gamemakers and is used by Katniss against the institution of the Games. She uses the threat of double suicide to checkmate the Capitol. Death in the arena ceases to be a confirmation of the Capitol's power and consumption and becomes instead an act of refusal, of agency, of rebellion against oppression. Katniss has reversed roles with the Gamemakers, who are now at her mercy. With the threat of having no winner, of being revealed as murderers to the Capitol citizens, the Gamemakers relent and allow Katniss and Peeta both to win.

Conclusion

It is critical that the millions of youth around the world who are constantly consuming media by watching advertisements, playing video games, engaging with new media, and discovering the joys of technology, are also provided with an opportunity not only to become critical media readers but to be introduced to a natural literacy as well. Technology and nature are blended in *The Hunger Games*, and, through Katniss' metacognitive narrative, the distinction between game and dystopian system collapses, and she begins to see the structure of the Hunger Games within the larger framework of Panem. Katniss' task toughens when, in *Mockingjay*, she must contend with the Capitol city as an arena space completely void of nature—indeed the only nature present, the scent of roses, is probably the most horrific aspect of the book. But despite her being out of her element, Katniss has learned to play the game and fight for survival. The Hunger Games series points to the way in which our own world's ecology incorporates culture, technology, and nature as in an ever-changing and reactive system. Recall the quotation at the beginning of this paper, wherein Gale suggests that they (meaning the districts) simply refuse to watch the Hunger Games and that this refusal might stop the entire spectacle. Just as the Games are mandatory viewing, broadcast throughout Panem, this film was broadcast worldwide in 2012, grossing hundreds of millions of dollars in revenue. It is one thing to read about children slaughtering children, especially when it is done through the meta-fictive eyes of our female protagonist, Katniss, but quite another to sit where the Capitol citizens sit and watch. Contemporary viewers have paid and continue to pay to watch and endorse the seventy-fourth annual Hunger Games in all its aesthetic beauty and harsh brutality. More recently, with the release of the second film, *Catching Fire* (2013), came the onslaught of products and advertisements for Cover Girl's Capitol Collection and Subway's "Catching Fire" Chicken Sandwiches. The marketing continues with *Mockingjay Part 1* (2014) pairing itself with Doritos and both *Mockingjay* films participating in a viral marketing scheme filled with tweets and video clips "leaked" from the Capitol and District 13—a scheme that wholly depends upon the franchise's audience continuing to consume the films for its own marketing success. It is ironic that a book, which protests against the masses' love of spectacle and global hunger and which calls for a recognition of the organic way that nature and humanity are part of the same system, has been made into a Hollywood product for universal consumption. But perhaps this commodification can be useful. A discussion of the ways in which The Hunger Games series might be used as learning tool or as a way to engage in discussion about this kind of irony helps frame a future approach to this narrative. The fascinating realm of genetic mutations as hybrid nature-technology creatures uncovers the jabberjay's evolution into the mockingjay, an unexpected outcome, which the Capitol did not expect and which it ignores. Yet, the bird's transformation is a metaphor for Katniss' own metamorphosis into the Mockingjay and the Capitol's blatant disregard for the way nature and ecology work. A discussion of the ways in which The Hunger Games series might be brought into the classroom as a media franchise would bring real world application to this study. In many ways, The Hunger Games book series challenges readers to engage critically with the text, with its speculative representations of nature, consumerism, media, the government, and learning.

The recent popularity of dystopian literature for young adults presents an opportunity. Perhaps books like The Hunger Games trilogy will encourage readers of all ages to view consumption as metaphor, to question what they consume, to consider the binary between the Capitol (i.e., the Western world) and the unseen people living in the Districts. Perhaps the film can be used to point out this irony, to question the dissemination of knowledge and history, to question government and statism, and to engage critically with our blended environment. And perhaps by reading books like The Hunger Games trilogy, young people will engage with the messages and ideas of liberty—before fiction becomes reality.

Notes

1.   Children between the ages of twelve and eighteen can apply for a tessera in order to receive a year's supply of grain and oil for one person. Each tessera taken requires the child to put an extra ballot with his or her name on it into the draw for the Hunger Games. Tesserae may be taken for family members and the tesserae are cumulative. Gale's name is in the draw for the 74th annual Hunger Games forty-two times (Collins, *Hunger Games* 13).

2.   A servant whose tongue has been removed as punishment for a crime.

3.   Those tributes from the more prosperous and privileged Districts (1–3, generally) are known as "Career" tributes. They train as children from a young age for competition in the arena, and these children will volunteer for the Games. These districts have accepted the Games to such an extent that it is a heroic fate, reminiscent of the gladiators who volunteered to fight in the ring and trained in a *ludus* (plural, *ludi*) in classical times.

4.   Capitol citizens will sponsor a tribute with money, which can be spent for supplies or weapons for that tribute in the Game.

Works Cited

Bogost, Ian. "The Rhetoric of Video Games." *The Ecology of Games: Connecting Youth, Games, and Learning.* Ed. Katie Salen. Cambridge, MA: MIT, 2008. 117–40. Print.

"Biggest Opening Weekends at the Box Office." *Internet Movie Database.* IMDb.com, Inc., 10 Dec. 2013. Web. 10 Dec. 2013.

Brandtzaeg, Petter Bae, and Jan Heim. "Children's Usage of Media Technologies and Psychosocial Factors." *New Media & Society* 9.3 (2007): 49–78. 22 Feb. 2007. *SAGE Publications.* Web. 19 Nov. 2012.

Buell, Lawrence. *Writing for an Endangered World: Literature, Culture, and Environment in the U.S. and Beyond.* Cambridge, MA: Belknap of Harvard UP, 2001. Print.

Collins, Suzanne. *Catching Fire.* New York: Scholastic, 2009. Print.

_____. *The Hunger Games*. New York: Scholastic, 2008. Print.

_____. "A Killer Story: An Interview with Suzanne Collins, Author of 'The Hunger Games.'" Interview by Rick Margolis. *School Library Journal*. Media Source. 1 Sept. 2008. Web. 14 March 2013.

_____. *Mockingjay*. New York: Scholastic, 2010. Print.

Garrard, Greg. *Ecocriticism*. London: Routledge, 2008. Print.

Hamer, Naomi. "The Lion, the Witch, and the Cereal Box: Reading Children's Literature across Multimedia Franchises." *Books, Media & the Internet: Children's Literature for Today's Classroom*. Winnipeg: Portage & Main, 2009. 121–135. Print.

The Hunger Games. Dir. Gary Ross. Prod. Nina Jacobson. Perf. Jennifer Lawrence, Josh Hutcherson, Woody Harrelson, and Donald Sutherland. Lionsgate, 2012. DVD.

Margolis, Rick. "Suzanne Collins' 'The Hunger Games' Has Plenty of Blood, Guts, and Heart." *School Library Journal*. Media Source, 1 Sept. 2008. Web. 14 Mar. 2013.

Moylan, Tom. *Scraps of the Untainted Sky: Science Fiction, Utopia, Dystopia*. Boulder, CO: Westview, 2000. Print.

Pavlov, Peeta, and PTSD: Historical and Contemporary Research on Scientific Principles Underlying Hijacking

Louise M. Freeman

The violence and death in Suzanne Collins' Hunger Games trilogy are all the more horrifying because children are both victims and perpetrators. Katniss Everdeen is described as "a sacrificial child, [who] burns with passion, desire, and eventually with literal flames, as children are forced to become killers and technology and social pressures enable the warping of the human form and mind" (Tan 55). One well-known way that the mind can be "warped" by violence is post-traumatic stress disorder (PTSD), a well-documented psychiatric condition that affects some 15 to 30 percent of trauma survivors (Johnson et al. 642). About 7 to 8 percent of people develop PTSD at some point in their lives; combat veterans have about twice the risk (Gates 361).

PTSD in Panem

District 13 mental health professionals are clearly aware that trauma can have damaging effects. Johanna is treated in the aftermath of her torture by "this head doctor who comes around every day" (Collins, *Mockingjay* 220) and annoys her by repeatedly trying to assure her she is safe. Katniss is issued a bracelet reading "mentally disoriented" in District 13 after the Quarter Quell and in the Capitol after witnessing Prim's death. Another "head doctor," Dr. Aurelius, diagnoses Katniss as a "psychological Avox" when she stops speaking after Prim's death; later, he helps get her the Panem equivalent of a "not guilty by reason of insanity" verdict for killing President Coin by presenting her as "a hopeless, shell-shocked lunatic" (Collins, *Mockingjay* 378). "Shell-shocked" is a term originally used to describe a syndrome seen in World War I veterans and now known to be a combined result of brain injury and psychological trauma that produces symptoms overlapping with those of PTSD (Jones, Fear, and Wessely 1644). However, the Panem "head doctors" never use the term "post-traumatic stress disorder," suggesting they do not have a formal name or diagnostic procedure for the condition.

Given the level of violence in The Hunger Games series, it is not surprising that many characters meet the diagnostic criteria for PTSD published by the American Psychiatric Association in the *Diagnostic and Statistical Manual of Mental Disorders*. The revised fourth edition (*DSM-IV-TR*, 2000), which was current when Collins wrote the trilogy, lists twenty-one potential symptoms; a specific combination of at least ten must be present for a diagnosis (see Table 1).

Table 1: Diagnostic criteria for post-traumatic stress disorder

A. The person experiences a traumatic event in which both of the following were present:
A1: The person experienced or witnessed or was confronted with an event or events that involved actual or threatened death or serious injury, or a threat to the physical integrity of self or others;
A2: The person's response involved intense fear, helplessness, or horror.
B. The traumatic event is persistently re-experienced in any of the following ways:
B1: Recurrent and intrusive distressing recollections of the event, including images, thoughts, or perceptions;
B2: Recurrent distressing dreams of the event;
B3: Acting or feeling as if the traumatic event were recurring (e.g., reliving the experience, illusions, hallucinations, and dissociative flashback episodes, including those on wakening or when intoxicated);
B4: Intense psychological distress at exposure to internal or external cues that symbolize or resemble an aspect of the traumatic event;
B5: Physiological reactivity on exposure to internal or external cues that symbolize or resemble an aspect of the traumatic event.

C. Persistent avoidance of stimuli associated with the trauma and numbing of general responsiveness (not present before the trauma) as indicated by at least three of the following:
C1: Efforts to avoid thoughts, feelings, or conversations associated with the trauma;
C2: Efforts to avoid activities, places, or people that arouse recollections of this trauma;
C3: Inability to recall an important aspect of the trauma;
C4 Markedly diminished interest or participation in significant activities;
C5: Feeling of detachment or estrangement from others;
C6: Restricted range of affect (e.g., unable to have loving feelings);
C7: Sense of a foreshortened future (e.g., does not expect to have a career, marriage, children, or a normal life span).
D: Persistent symptoms of increased arousal (not present before the trauma), as indicated by at least two of the following:
D1: Difficulty falling or staying asleep;
D2: Irritability or outbursts of anger;
D3 Difficulty concentrating;
D4: Hypervigilance;
D5: Exaggerated startle response.
E. The symptoms on Criteria B, C, and D last for more than one month.
F. The disturbance causes clinically significant distress or impairment in social, occupational, or other important areas of functioning.

(Source: DSM-IV-TR, 2000)

Katniss, even before she volunteered for her first Hunger Games, has enough A, B, C, D, and E symptoms to be diagnosed with PTSD, as a result of her father's death and her family's subsequent near-starvation (see Table 2). The only thing that would spare her a formal PTSD diagnosis at age sixteen is her failure to meet criterion F: her symptoms do not impair her daily functioning. Prior to the reaping, she is a successful hunter and trader, providing for her family so that they eat better than most in the Seam. She has strong bonds with both Gale and Prim and, while she may consider herself largely friendless, she has the respect of the Hob community, and both Peeta and Delly confirm that she is admired by her peers. After the 74th Hunger Games, Katniss' symptoms expand in both severity and number; she eventually displays all twenty-one symptoms listed in the *DSM-IV-TR* (see Table 2). For example, her previously occasional nightmares become nightly, and their contents become more variable:

> The old standby, the one of my father being blown to bits in the mines, is rare. Instead I relive versions of what happened in the arena. My worthless attempt to save Rue. Peeta bleeding to death. Glimmer's bloated body disintegrating in my hands. Cato's horrific end with the muttations. Those are the most frequent visitors (Collins, *Catching Fire* 54).

By *Mockingjay*, it is clear that both Haymitch and Johanna also meet the diagnostic criteria for PTSD (see Table 2). We do not see as many examples of Finnick's and Annie's behaviors, but given that Finnick is, like Katniss, classified as "mentally disoriented" and that Annie is frequently described as "mad," it is likely they have PTSD as well.

Table 2: Some examples of PTSD symptoms displayed by Hunger Games characters

PTSD SYMPTOMS	Katniss, before 74th Games	Katniss, after 74th Games	Haymitch	Johanna
A. History (must have both)				
A1: Actual or threatened death, serious injury to self or others	Katniss' father dies in mine; she and Prim nearly starve after her mother quit caring for them.	In Games: nearly dehydrates; suffers injuries, witnesses deaths. Sees combat in *Mockingjay.*	In Quell with forty-eight tributes; severely injured; Snow kills family.	Fought in two Games; tortured by Capitol.

A2: Fear, helplessness or horror	"I was terrified … all I know was that I had lost not only a father but a mother as well" (*HG* 27).	Horrified at gruesome deaths of fellow tributes in 74th Games.	Could not save Maysilee, family, or girlfriend.	"Peeta and I had adjoining cells in the Capitol. We're very familiar with each other's screams" (*MJ* 241).
B. Re-experienced trauma (1 needed)				
B1: Recurrent, intrusive memories of the event	"The pain would hit me out of nowhere, doubling me over, racking my body with sobs" (*HG* 26).	"It brings on the flood of images that torment me" (*MJ* 9).		
B2: Recurrent nightmares about event	"Five years later, I still wake up screaming for him to run" (*HG* 5).	"Nightmares—which I was no stranger to before the Games—now plague me whenever I sleep" (*CF* 53).	Haymitch has nightmares, refuses to sleep in the dark. (*CF* 54).	"Her wide-set eyes fighting to stay awake…. Terrified of what sleep may bring" (*MJ* 255).
B3: Acting or feeling as if event is recurring (flashbacks)		Attack on Nut causes Katniss to flashback to the mine explosion that killed her father. (*MJ* 207–209).	Haymitch brandishes his knife when awakened suddenly (*CF* 14).	"She had some sort of flashback. Panicked, didn't know where she was" (*MJ* 253).

B4: Psychological distress to cues		Katniss sobs uncontrollably at Buttercup, who reminds her of Prim. (*MJ* 386).		
B5: Physiological reactivity to cues		Katniss gags at scent of Snow's rose. (*CF* 14).		
C. Avoidance behaviors, numbing (3 needed)				
C1: Avoids thoughts associated with the event		"If it were up to me, I would try to forget the Hunger Games entirely" (*CF* 3).	"Haymitch has never mentioned his personal experience in the arena to me" (*CF* 37).	"Maybe they were onto something in Six. Drug yourself out" (*MJ* 228).
C2: Avoids people, situations associated with event	Avoids the lake after her father's death; swimming makes her sad (*CF* 34).	Glad to avoid Justice Building because it is "too full of sadness" (*CF* 87).		Refuses to shower after water torture in Capitol (*MJ* 253).
C3: Cannot remember parts of trauma		Does not remember breaking glass in cellar window and cutting her hand (*CF* 176).		

C4: Diminished interest, participation		"I've been in the woods for three hours, but I've made no real attempt at hunting" (*CF* 4).	Described as "blotting out the world with drink" (*CF* 46).	
C5: Detachment, estrangement from others	"I had taken a step back from my mother, put up a wall to protect myself" (*HG* 53).	"But, of course, I hate almost everyone now. Myself more than anyone" (*MJ* 8).		"True. But no one likes me" (*MJ* 221).
C6: Restricted range of affect	"Neither of us really has a group of friends" (*HG* 12).	"I'm forced to accept what I am. A badly burned girl with no wings. With no fire. And no sister" (*MJ* 358).	"He could have had his choice of any woman in the district. And he chose solitude" (*CF* 46).	"There's no one left I love." (*CF* 347).
C7: Sense of foreshortened future	"I never want to have kids" (*HG* 9).	"I'll stay in 2 until it falls, go to the Capitol and kill Snow, and then die for my trouble" (*MJ* 198).	Agrees when Katniss says he should go to arena because he "hates life" (*CF* 177).	
D: Increased Arousal (2 needed)				
D1: Difficulty sleeping		"Effie starts giving me pills to sleep, but they don't work" (*CF* 72).		Stays up all night cursing at Katniss (*MJ* 237).

D2: Irritability, outbursts of anger	"My voice has risen to a shout. It is all the anger, all the fear I felt at her abandonment" (*HG* 35).	"I lunge across the table and rake my fingernails down Haymitch's face" (*CF* 387).	Described as "surly and violent" (*CF* 18).	"I don't care if you are knocked up, I'll rip your throat out" (*CF* 328).
D3: Difficulty concentrating		"I've been sitting here for 20 minutes. Finnick isn't the only one with attention problems" (*MJ* 38).		
D4: Hypervigilance	"Any sign of danger, a distant howl, the inexplicable break of a branch, sent me flying back to the fence" (*HG* 51).	"As we travel over District 12, I watch anxiously for signs of an attack" (*MJ* 16).	Sleeps with a knife in his hand (*CF* 14).	During combat training, only Johanna and Katniss react fast enough to get gas masks on in time (*MJ* 246).
D5: Exaggerated startle reflex		"It's not an aggressive move, really, but after the arena, I react defensively to any unfamiliar touch" (*MJ* 27).	"He jumps up, kicking his chair ten feet behind him" (*CF* 14).	

E. Symptoms last longer than one month	Katniss has presumably had symptoms for at least five years, since her father's death.	Katniss shows symptoms from end of 74th Games into adulthood.	Haymitch's symptoms develop over a twenty-five-year period.	Johanna's symptoms last from rescue until the end of war.
F. Symptoms cause significant distress, interfere with functioning	No. Katniss is competent hunter, provides for family, admired by community.	Yes. Six months after Games, Katniss is distressed, relationships suffer, cannot develop her talent.	Yes. Haymitch is isolated, lives in filthy house, often too drunk to function.	Yes. Although eager to attack Capitol, Johanna relapses and cannot join fight.

HG = The Hunger Games; CF = Catching Fire; MJ = Mockingjay.

Peeta, by contrast, survives the arena without developing full-blown PTSD. He is not completely unscathed; at the beginning of *Catching Fire* (Collins 53), he, too, acknowledges frequent nightmares (B2). After the shootings at District 11 and the realization that he had endangered Rue and Thresh's families, he has an angry outburst (D2), during which he throws lamps and statues, making Katniss think, "I've never seen him like this" (Collins, *Catching Fire* 66). But, compared to Katniss, he is coping well post-Games: visiting his family, frosting baked goods, and developing his painting talent. When the terms of the Quarter Quell are announced, Katniss falls apart, runs away, gets drunk with Haymitch, then has an emotional breakdown that confines her to bed for a day. It is Peeta who dumps out the liquor and insists that he, Haymitch, and Katniss begin intensive training to give themselves the best chance of surviving.

Hijacking Induces Extreme PTSD

It takes the sadism of the Capitol's torturers to break Peeta; after the hijacking, he returns not only with enough symptoms to diagnose PTSD, but with exaggerated versions of them. For instance, his psychological (B4) and physical responses (B5) to Katniss, the stimulus most associated with his trauma, are not just "severe distress" and "reactivity" but an automatic and uncontrollable urge to attack and kill her. He has more than memory lapses (C3); he has a set of completely false memories that he cannot distinguish from real ones (Collins, *Mockingjay* 270). His detachment and estrangement (C5) from Katniss are complete; he had previously loved her enough to sacrifice his life; now he dismisses her with a cold, "Well, you're a real piece of work, aren't you?" (Collins, *Mockingjay* 232) and doesn't even consider her human (*Mockingjay* 191). He goes beyond a mere sense of foreshortened future (C7) to actively trying to bring about his demise, asking Squad 451 to kill him (*Mockingjay* 289). His outbursts exceed simple irritability or anger (D2); they are uncontrollable rages that require him to be continuously restrained. Finally, his over-responsive startle reflex requires little or nothing to trigger it; as Haymitch says, "Sometimes he's almost rational, and then, for no reason, he goes off again" (Collins, *Mockingjay* 228). Clearly, the hijacking aftereffects are long-lasting (E) and incapacitating (F). Johanna accuses the Capitol of replacing Peeta with "the evil mutt-version" of himself (Collins, *Mockingjay* 243). It might be more accurate to say that in hijacking Peeta, the Capitol has created a muttation form of PTSD.

Interestingly, the fifth and most recent version of the DSM, published in 2013, includes a dissociative subtype of PTSD (*DSM-V*) for patients who experience either depersonalization (a feeling of detachment from oneself) or derealization (the feeling of things being unreal or dream-like). Tracker jacker venom seems specifically designed to induce the latter symptom. Katniss, after being stung in the arena, cannot be certain whether Peeta's saving her is genuine or a hallucination; Peeta's hijacking leaves him wondering whether most of his life's memories are "real or not real" (Collins, *Mockingjay* 272). Although the dissociative PTSD subtype did not appear in the *DSM* until after *Mockingjay* was published, it was proposed in the psychology literature much earlier (e.g., Bremner 349; Ginzberg 7).

PTSD and Pavlovian Conditioning

Understanding PTSD's relationship to fear requires going back to psychology's earliest human fear conditioning studies. This, in turn, requires an understanding of one of the most basic types of learning, Pavlovian or classical conditioning.

Fear Conditioning—Basic Pavlovian Principles

Pavlovian conditioning builds an association between two stimuli, so that a response originally triggered by the first stimulus is subsequently triggered by the associated stimulus. Ivan Pavlov's original demonstration in dogs started with the knowledge that one unconditioned stimulus (US), food, reflexively triggered an unconditioned response (UR), salivation. When Pavlov repeatedly presented a neutral stimulus, a sound,[1] just before he showed the dog the food, the dog eventually learned to salivate in response to the sound alone. The sound became a conditioned stimulus (CS) for the conditioned response (CR) of salivation.

Pavlov also noted that animals could show generalization: conditioned responses to stimuli that resembled or were related to the original conditioned stimulus. Dogs would salivate to sounds that were similar to the sound originally used in their training. Learned Pavlovian associations can also be unlearned through a process called extinction; if the sound was presented multiple times with no further food pairings, conditioned salivation would decrease and eventually cease entirely.

Conditioned Fear

Heavily influenced by Pavlov, American psychologist John B. Watson and his student Rosalie Rayner used Pavlovian methods to condition an eleven-month old boy known as "Albert B." (or commonly, "Little Albert") to fear a stimulus he originally liked (Watson, and Rayner 1). Prior to conditioning, they exposed Albert to a variety of animals (including a dog, monkey, rabbit, and white laboratory rat) and found he responded with curiosity, not fear, to them all. He was, like most infants, afraid of loud noises; Watson and Rayner showed that the sudden sound of an unseen hammer striking a metal bar reliably caused him to startle and cry (Figure 1A). To condition Albert, Watson and Rayner put the white rat in front of him, then struck the bar as soon as he reached for it. After seven such pairings, two one week and five the next, Albert reliably cried or tried to move away from the rat whenever it was presented. Watson and Rayner wrote, "It was as convincing a case of a completely conditioned fear response as could have been theoretically pictured." The rat had become a conditioned stimulus for fear. Albert also showed stimulus generalization, reacting with fear to other animals, a fur coat, a roll of white cotton, and a bearded Santa Claus mask. It is not known how long Albert's fears endured after conditioning; his mother removed him from the hospital where Watson conducted the study after the final session.[2] However, under normal circumstances, he would have eventually undergone extinction:

> It is likely that, after the experiment was over, Little Albert encountered other rats or other furry objects in the absence of a loud noise. Eventually, he should have learned that such objects no longer predicted a frightening clang, and his fear response should have declined. (Van Elzakker 4)

Hijacking as Fear Conditioning

According to Katniss, tracker jacker venom is "carefully created to target the place where fear lives in your brain" (Collins, *The Hunger Games* 195). Beetee describes what he knows of the hijacking process:

> It's a type of fear conditioning…. Imagine I asked you to remember something—either with a verbal suggestion or by making you watch a tape of the event—and while that experienced is refreshed, I give you a dose of tracker jacker venom…. Just enough to infuse the memory with fear and doubt. And that's what your brain puts in long-term storage. (Collins, *Mockingjay* 180–181)

In simplest terms, the venom is the unconditioned stimulus and fear, the unconditioned response (Figure 1B). Memories of Katniss were used as the conditioned response. Peeta was conditioned to fear and hate his beloved Katniss, much as Little Albert learned to fear the rat he had previously enjoyed. Because tracker jacker venom so efficiently targets the neural centers of fear, it produces a long-lasting change and, eventually, completely new and terrifying memories. As Plutarch Heavensbee speculates, "Fearful memories are the hardest to root out. They're the ones we naturally remember the best, after all" (Collins, *Mockingjay* 182).

Figure 1. Comparison of Watson & Rayner's 1920 fear conditioning of Little Albert to Peeta's hijacking.

A.

At first, Albert likes the rat.

Rat is paired with loud noise.

Fear

Albert learns to fear rat.

B.

At first, Peeta loves Katniss.

Katniss is paired with venom.

Fear

Peeta learns to fear Katniss.

Artwork courtesy of Jade Walters and Katriel Cho

Fear Conditioning as a Model for PTSD

Understanding Pavlovian fear-conditioning helps to explain the development and persistence of PTSD. During combat, torture, or other cases of severe trauma, people experience unconditioned stimuli for fear that are much more threatening than the noises faced by Little Albert (Van Elzakker 7). Multiple studies suggest that PTSD patients become fear-conditioned more readily than non-patients, have more trouble distinguishing stimuli that predict the appearance of an unconditioned stimulus for fear from those that do not, and, most importantly, are slower at undergoing extinction (Blechert et al. 2019; Johnson et al. 638; Jovanovic and Ressler 648; Wessa and Flor 1684).

During combat situations, seemingly innocuous stimuli can become conditioned stimuli for fear.

> For example, after the invasion of Iraq, US troops frequently faced improvised explosive devices (IEDs) hidden in trash piles along the side of the road. If a soldier survives an IED attack, this event forms a powerful memory and powerful associations. Ideally, such a veteran who has returned to the United States should learn, upon several exposures to trash piles along his street, that they no longer predict violence. If this extinction fails to happen, then even years after the danger has passed, a previously neutral cue (trash, the conditioned stimulus) that was associated with a grave danger (IED explosions, the unconditioned stimulus) may trigger a fear response (conditioned response) and painful memories. Indeed, even internal cues such as autonomic arousal or thirst can become conditioned stimuli. For a veteran of war in Iraq, the conditioned stimulus that causes a fear response could be the sight of a trash pile, the presence of a crowd of people, the feel of hot temperatures under bright sunlight, the sound of Arabic being spoken, the smell of diesel fuel from military vehicles, internal states such as feelings of frustration, or any other cue that was present during the explosion. (Van Elzakker 8)

There is some experimental evidence that PTSD patients do, in fact, resist extinction more than non-patients. A 2007 study compared PTSD patients with people who had experienced comparable trauma but had not developed PTSD and people who had never experienced major trauma. They used a Pavlovian fear conditioning protocol with visual patterns as the conditioned stimulus, moderately painful but non-dangerous electric shock as the unconditioned stimulus, and skin conductance (a measure of perspiration, a physiological response to fear) as the unconditioned response. PTSD patients showed delayed extinction compared to the other two groups (Blechert et al. 2031). Another 2007 study compared twenty-nine survivors of a German air show disaster (fourteen with diagnosed PTSD, fifteen without) with fifteen healthy control participants who had not witnessed the original crash. The researchers conditioned the participants to respond emotionally to a neutral shape by pairing it with an explicit picture of the crash. PTSD patients rated the shape that was shown just before the crash site picture as more arousing and more unpleasant than either the non-PTSD crash witnesses or the controls and failed to undergo extinction when the shape no longer predicted the presentation of the air disaster picture (Wessa and Flor 1689).

Hunger Games characters also show failure of extinction. Even after years of familiarity with coal mines and weeks living underground at District 13, the collapse of the Nut or going into an underground tunnel triggers Katniss' painful memories of her father's death. The hijacked Peeta, too, finds that multiple cues continue to prompt his lethal attacks, even after being exposed repeatedly to Katniss in the absence of tracker jacker venom. When he is speaking to Katniss in the District 13 cafeteria, she notices, "Spasms cause Peeta's hands to tighten into fists, then splay out in a bizarre fashion. Is it all he can do to keep them from my neck?" (Collins, *Mockingjay* 243). An explosion startles Peeta in the Capitol and, at the sight of Katniss, he becomes "mad, flashing back into the land of the hijacked, his gun raised over [her], descending to crush [her] skull" (Collins, *Mockingjay* 279). Even two decades later, after he and Katniss have married and had children, she reports, "There are still moments then he clutches the back of a chair and hangs in until the flashbacks are over" (Collins, *Mockingjay* 388). It appears that Haymitch is right when he says that Peeta will never be the same (Collins, *Mockingjay* 182).

Treatments for PTSD

Remarkably, some of the treatments suggested for trauma-induced "mental disorientation" in Panem resemble modern-day treatments for PTSD and other problem fears. Prim suggests a method originally pioneered by a student of Watson's; Jackson suggests a common technique used by cognitive behavioral therapists, and both Katniss and Peeta recognize the benefits of art therapy.

Counterconditioning

Watson and Rayner had planned to "uncondition" Little Albert of his fears as the next phase of their study, but Little Albert's mother removed him before that was possible. However, in 1924, another of Watson's students, Mary Cover Jones, would experimentally demonstrate the technique today known as counterconditioning in a case "which almost seemed to be Albert grown a bit older" (Jones 318). Peter was a three-year-old boy who had a fear of animals and other furry objects, like coats; unlike Albert, it was not known how the fear developed. Jones was able to reduce Peter's fear of a rabbit by first having other children model peaceful encounters, then by trying to recondition a pleasant response: "Peter was seated in a high chair and given food that he liked. The experimenter brought the rabbit in a wire cage as close as she could without arousing a response, that would interfere with the eating" (Jones 313).

Here, the food is the unconditioned stimulus, positive emotions the unconditioned response, and the rabbit the conditioned stimulus (Figure 2A). Gradually, Peter was able to tolerate closer and closer encounters with the rabbit, eventually progressing to "fondling the rabbit affectionately" and "letting the rabbit nibble his fingers" (Jones 312), suggesting the rabbit had ceased to trigger fear and became a conditioned stimulus for positive emotions. Like Albert, Peter's newly conditioned emotional responses generalized, and he lost his fears of furry objects and other animals as well. This landmark experiment earned Jones the title of "Mother of Behavioral Therapy" (Rutherford); Beck (613) claims, "All behavior therapies trace their lineage to Mary Cover Jones's 1924 counterconditioning of Peter."

Amazingly, despite her lack of formal training in psychology, young Prim manages to independently develop this very treatment (Fig. 2B). Haymitch tells Katniss, "Prim came up with the idea of trying to hijack him back. Bring up the distorted memory of you, and then give him a big dose of a calming drug, like morphling" (Collins, *Mockingjay* 195). Unfortunately, Prim's solution did not work because the morphling is such a powerful narcotic that it put Peeta in a stupor for several hours, presumably inducing a semi-conscious state that precluded learning new associations. But, given that Prim, at the tender age of thirteen, independently reinvents a classic therapeutic technique that eluded District 13's finest "head doctors," she must be given full credit for her efforts. Perhaps, if Jones' paper had been available as a resource, Prim would have thought to try the Capitol's famous lamb stew, or some other tasty food, as an unconditioned stimulus instead.

Figure 2. Comparison of Jones' 1924 counterconditioning study to Prim's suggested treatment.

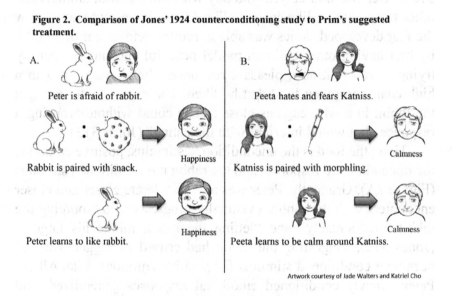

Artwork courtesy of Jade Walters and Katriel Cho

Cognitive and Behavioral Techniques

Two therapeutic approaches have proved particularly helpful in treating PTSD (Hamblen et al.). The first is prolonged exposure, which is based on the principle of extinction. It typically works by first teaching relaxation techniques, then by exposing the patient to stimuli that trigger anxiety, either virtually, through imagination, or *in vivo*, by in-person exposure. With repeated exposure, relaxation, and no reappearance of trauma or danger, the associations between the stimuli and the anxiety should diminish.

Another technique is cognitive restructuring, which teaches patients to identify and correct negative beliefs and memories associated with the event (Hamblen et al.). Many PTSD patients experience, like Peeta, difficulties with autobiographical memories (Ehlers and Clark 327), leaving them with vague or overly negative memories for the trauma. Correcting these errors can be a valuable part of recovery.

Multiple studies have confirmed the effectiveness of exposure therapy and cognitive restructuring. In a group of Cambodian refugees, cognitive behavioral therapy (CBT), combined with an antidepressant drug, provided an added benefit to PTSD patients, when compared to those who received the drug alone (Otto et al. 1274). A large study of PTSD patients who had survived assault or car crashes found that a combination of virtual and *in vivo* exposure therapy with cognitive restructuring worked better than exposure alone (Bryant et al. 702). A more recent, randomly controlled study found that exposure therapy, cognitive restructuring, and a combination of both were all effective in treating PTSD, and effectiveness was improved when patients had a strong social support network (Thrasher et al. 188). PTSD patients are reported to have increased neural activity in the amygdala, a part of the brain particularly associated with fear processing, but a 2007 study using brain scans found amygdala activity decreased following eight weeks of treatment with both exposure therapy and cognitive restructuring (Felminghan et al. 128).

Both prolonged exposure therapy and cognitive restructuring are key to aiding Peeta's recovery. His occasional encounters with Katniss prior to being assigned to Squad 451 do not seem to help him much; he clearly poses a danger to her early in the mission. However, the prolonged contact with her, particularly when he can see in person that she is his ally, not an enemy, helps. Coin have placed Peeta on Squad 451 intending that he kill Katniss, but ironically, the prolonged contact may likely helped him recover.

Learning to distinguish true from false memories is also essential. The "Real or Not Real" game that Jackson devised is a type of cognitive restructuring that helps Peeta identify and correct inaccurate memories. After some practice with this "game," Peeta discovers a cue that helps him distinguish the implanted memories from genuine ones: the false memories seem "shiny." He explains to Katniss: "I think there's a pattern emerging. The memories they altered with the tracker jacker venom have this strange quality about them. Like they're too intense or too unstable" (Collins, *Mockingjay* 302). This observation fits with that of Ehlers and Clark: intentionally recalled trauma memories are "fragmented and poorly organized," while involuntary recollections be "very vivid and emotional" (Ehlers and Clark 324).

The combination of exposure and cognitive restructuring was effective in making Peeta functional again. The first time he sees Katniss, after the mission to the Capitol is at the vote for the 76th Hunger Games. As angry as he was about her "yes" vote, he does not attack or even berate Katniss but directs his anger at Haymitch (Collins, *Mockingjay* 370). In the chaos that erupts after Katniss kills Coin, he not only refrains from harming her, but prevents her from harming herself after she draws blood biting his hand. (Collins, *Mockingjay* 373). While he may never recover fully from the hijacking, the "therapy," within the context of the social support he got from Squad 451, brought the murderous rages under control.

Art Therapy: Paintings and Books

The final recovery process that helps both Peeta and Katniss is the creation of art. Peeta takes up painting after the 74th Games, reproducing his nightmares and saying, "for me, it's better to wake up with a paint brush than a knife in my hand" (Collins, *Catching Fire* 162). After the crackdown in District 12 prevents Katniss from hunting, she and Peeta update her family's reference book on medicinal and edible plants, with Katniss providing the text and Peeta the illustrations. Katniss describes it as "quiet, absorbing work that helps take my mind off my troubles" (*Catching Fire* 161), while Peeta remarks that "this is the first time we've ever done anything normal together" (*Catching Fire* 162). The plant book inspires Katniss and Peeta to later design a scrapbook memorializing all those they have lost; Dr. Aurelius recognizes its therapeutic value and provides the parchment for it (*Mockingjay* 387).

Art therapy is frequently used in the treatment of trauma patients, particularly children and young adults. It has also been found to facilitate the goals of cognitive behavior therapy in treating trauma in sexually abused children (Pifalo 171). In a recent review, twenty of thirty-five published studies using art therapy involved children, teens, or college students (Slayton et al. 110–15). Given how readily

Katniss adopts the role of both parents in the physical absence of her father and the emotional absence of her mother (Oliver 682), it is easy to forget that she is herself still an adolescent.

An art therapy intervention with survivors of the 2004 tsunami in Sri Lanka invited 113 young girls to paint a picture of "The Day They Would Never Forget." Like Peeta in *Catching Fire*, most chose to depict their traumatic experience. When asked to make a picture of "Safe Places and Memories," many, like Katniss with her memory book, drew family and friends who had died. The artwork allowed the children to "regain emotional control that was shattered with the tsunami and to commemorate their loss" (Chilcote 161); Katniss and Peeta share a similar healing process in their painting and scrapbooking. Art therapy is specifically recommended for adults with combat-related PTSD because containing frightening images in art helps exert control over them (Collie et al. 161). Art also promotes relaxation, reduces arousal, helps express traumatic emotions and memories, and is enjoyable. Therefore, it helps curb emotional numbness and repair social connections (Collie et al. 161), something Katniss and Peeta clearly need after their ordeal.

The homemade, hand-painted books of The Hunger Games trilogy provide a clear contrast between the technical and artificial video propaganda produced by both the Capitol and District 13. The genuineness of art provides a source of healing that stretches beyond the creators. Cinna's book of costumes, for instance, allows him to coach and encourage Katniss even after his horrific death. The healing power of Katniss and Peeta's memory book is extended to Haymitch, as he is able to honor the memories of the District 12 tributes that he could not save. Even before the reaping, the edible plants in the Everdeen family book provided the family's path out of starvation, after Katniss' hope was renewed by Peeta's gift of bread. Later, its medicinal information, recorded by a long-forgotten relative, becomes a source of recovery for all of Panem, as District 12 shifts from a supplier of fiery coal to a provider of healing medicines. Art becomes therapeutic, not only as a psychological tool, but also as a source of sincere and beautiful inspiration.

Is Hijacking Possible?

Counterconditioning changes learned associations between stimuli, thereby altering the ability of one stimulus to trigger recall of a specific emotion. This is a type of rewriting of human memory; an everyday example would be the pleasant memories of a first date changing to unpleasant ones after a bad break-up (Takeuchi and Morris 323). Processes such as cognitive restructuring can be useful in correcting the distorted perception or exaggerated horror of intrusive memories in a PTSD patient. In both of those processes, details about the event, such as the restaurant in which you dined, would be unlikely to change, but the emotions triggered by the memory would shift (Takeuchi and Morris 323). To date, using a neurotoxin or other brain manipulations to intentionally rewrite the explicit content of human memory—as happened when Peeta falsely remembered Katniss killing his family (Collins, *Catching Fire* 190)—remains in the realm of science fiction. However, neuroscientists are understanding more about how memories are formed, and how, under some circumstances, they can be altered by physiologically manipulating the brain.

Two recent experiments in mice have succeeded in 1) implanting a false memory during sleep (de Lavilléon et al. 493) and 2) changing pleasant memories to unpleasant ones (Redondo et al. 426). Both of these studies involved stimulating specific neurons in the brain, not with tracker jacker venom, but with either electrodes or light.

Creating a False Memory

In the first study (de Lavilléon et al. 493), scientists identified specific nerve cells in an area of the brain called the hippocampus. These cells are called "place cells" because they fire whenever an animal is in a specific location in a test box. Interestingly, place cells also fire spontaneously when a mouse is asleep, probably during dreams (Guitchounts). In this experiment, scientists first let the mice wander around a test box while they recorded from hippocampal nerve cells and identified place cells that reliably fired when a mouse was in a certain position; let's call it Point X.

Next, they moved the mice to a different cage to sleep. Whenever a particular place cell associated with Point X fired in the sleeping mouse, the scientists stimulated a different part of the brain called the medial forebrain bundle, a part of a recognized reinforcement center that fires with exposure to desirable things like addictive drugs. After the mice had slept for an hour, the scientists woke them up and put them back in the test box. This time, instead of randomly wandering around, the mice lingered around Point X. In other words, they behaved like animals that had a memory of a reinforcing experience at that location, even though they had never experienced any such thing. The concurrent activation of the place cells and the medial forebrain bundle during sleep was apparently enough to create a false memory.

Turning Good Memories Bad

The other study (Redondo et al. 426) is even more similar to what happened to Peeta, when hijacking changed his love for Katniss to fear and hate. This study used a specially engineered group of mice that, thanks to the recently developed technology of optogenetics, allows scientists to label a neural engram (a group of neurons that fire when a memory is formed) and reactivate that same engram later by shining a tiny blue light within the animal's brain. (Liu et al. 381). Redondo and colleagues used this method to label hippocampal engrams in two groups of male mice: one that formed an unpleasant memory and another that formed a pleasant one. For the unpleasant memory, they placed the mice in a distinctive chamber for slightly over eight minutes and delivered four shocks to the mice's feet during that period. For the pleasant memory, the mice each got to spend two hours in their home cage with a female mouse. Two days later, the mice were placed in a larger preference chamber and were allowed to roam freely, but whenever they entered a specified area, the scientists turned on the light that activated the engram neurons labeled in their earlier memory (Takeuchi and Morris 323). The mice in the group that had been shocked quickly learned to avoid the area where the light went on, while the group that had been allowed access to a female learned to prefer it. Activating the engram with light seemed to trigger the same emotions (either fear or pleasure) associated with the original memory.

Next, in a method similar to counterconditioning, the scientists tried to reverse the memory. Two days later, they took the group that had the pleasant memories of the female mouse, put them in the shock chamber, and activated the female-associated engram with light at the same time the mice received the shocks. Two days later, in the preference chamber, the mice now avoided the area where the neuron-activating light was turned on. The same memory engram that was previously rewarding was now aversive.[3]

Were Redondo's Mice Hijacked?
Since we cannot ask the mice, there is no way of assessing the actual content of their memory when the light turns on. It is highly unlikely that these mice are consciously connecting the memory of the female mouse with the distress and fear of electric shock. Moreover, the researchers did not test to see if the experimental mice, when reintroduced to the female, would react with fear or aggression, as a truly "hijacked" mouse would be expected to do. It is more likely that, since the engram is a set of hippocampal cells associated with place, the reactivation triggers a memory of the location the mouse met the female. Reactivation of those neurons concurrently with shock creates connections with parts of the brain associated with fear, overriding the previous connections to neurons associated with the pleasure of sexual arousal (Redondo et al. 428). More simply, "light is used to selectively reactivate the representation of the 'where' component of a memory and then change its 'what' association" (Takeuchi and Morris, 323).

Potential Applications
Although the Capitol used its hijacking technique to turn Peeta into a weapon, there are potentially beneficial uses to reducing or changing the negative emotional content of memories: for example, in the treatment of PTSD, depression, or anxiety disorders. Tonegawa, the lead researcher in the memory reversal study, states, "In the future,

---

one may be able to develop methods that help people to remember positive memories more strongly than negative ones" (Trafton). However, he also emphasizes that his work has no immediate clinical applications, as optogenetic techniques cannot yet be used in humans (Howard Hughes Medical Institute).

Clearly, better understanding of the basic science underlying memory formation, storage, and retrieval could be useful in understanding mental disorders. But the example of hijacking in The Hunger Games series reminds us that scientific advances in memory manipulation must be applied ethically. As Guitchounts states, "The simple yet powerful experiments by de Lavilléon and colleagues not only represent a neat addition to our understanding of memory and navigation, but may also pave a path for fascinating (though potentially sinister) techniques of neurobiological manipulation in the future" (Guitchounts).

Conclusion

The Hunger Games trilogy, though in the genre of dystopian fantasy, draws heavily from the modern sciences of psychology and neuroscience, particularly research in the area of fear. Understanding the history of behaviorism, particularly the contributions of the Pavlov and Watson laboratories, is crucial to understanding the Capitol's use of hijacking as a form of memory-altering torture. Collins presents multiple literary depictions of PTSD in both major and minor characters and uses them to illustrate the permanent damage inflicted by war and oppression. Finally, she seems to anticipate developments in the behavioral sciences, both by depicting the dissociative symptoms of PTSD several years before they would be added to the official diagnostic criteria and by imagining mechanisms for rewriting memories, aspects of which have since been partially achieved in laboratory mice. Psychological and neurobiological constructs enrich the fictional world of Panem and make it a more believable and, therefore, a more frightening dystopia. In a similar fashion, study of the behavioral sciences, from historical breakthroughs in psychology to cutting-edge technical advances in neuroscience, can enhance the readers' appreciation of the trilogy.

Notes

1. Pavlov's experiments are commonly described as using a bell for the controlled stimulus. However, he probably used other sounds, like metronomes and buzzers, much more frequently than bells (Black 426; Todes 492).

2. The true identity of "Little Albert" and what became of him after the experiment has long been a mystery. However, recent research (Beck et al. 605; Griggs 14) has identified two boys as possible candidates. Which one is the true Little Albert is still debated, but one of them, Albert Barger, is reported to have disliked furry animals even as an adult (Powell 609). Watson and Rayner originally speculated that Albert's fears "are likely to persist indefinitely, unless an accidental method for removing them is hit upon" (Watson and Rayner 1). Modern ethics rules would prevent similar stressful experiments on children today.

3. This experiment worked in reverse as well. The mice that had originally been shocked learned to prefer the area of the preference box where the light stimulated their brains after the shock-associated neural engram was activated while the mice were paired with females.

Works Cited

American Psychiatric Association. *Diagnostic and Statistical Manual of Mental Disorders, (DSM-5®)*. Washington, DC: American Psychiatric Association, 2013. Print.

_____. *Diagnostic and Statistical Manual of Mental Disorders, Text Revision (DSM-IV-TR)*. Washington, DC: American Psychiatric Association, 2000. Print.

Beck, Hall P., Sharman Levinson, and Gary Irons. "Finding Little Albert: A Journey to John B. Watson's Infant Laboratory." *American Psychologist* 64.7 (2009): 605–14. Print.

Black, Stephen L. "Pavlov's Dogs: For Whom the Bell Rarely Tolled." *Current Biology* 13.11 (2003): R426. Print.

Blechert, J., T. Michael, N. Vriends, J. Margraf, and F. H. Wilhelm. "Fear Conditioning in Posttraumatic Stress Disorder: Evidence for Delayed

Extinction of Autonomic, Experiential, and Behavioural Responses."
Behaviour Research and Therapy 45.9 (2007): 2019–33. Print.

Bremner, J. Douglas. "Acute and Chronic Responses to Psychological Trauma: Where Do We Go from Here?" *American Journal of Psychiatry* 156.3 (1999): 349–51. Print.

Bryant, Richard A., et al. "A Randomized Controlled Trial of Exposure Therapy and Cognitive Restructuring for Posttraumatic Stress Disorder." *Journal of Consulting and Clinical Psychology* 76.4 (2008): 695–703. Print.

Chilcote, R. L. "Art Therapy with Child Tsunami Survivors in Sri Lanka." *Art Therapy* 24.4 (2007): 156–62. Print.

Collie, Kate, et al. "Art Therapy for Combat-Related PTSD: Recommendations for Research and Practice." *Art Therapy: Journal of the American Art Therapy Association* 23.4 (2004): 157–64. Print.

Collins, Suzanne. *Catching Fire.* New York: Scholastic, 2009. Print.

_____. *The Hunger Games.* New York: Scholastic, 2008. Print.

_____. *Mockingjay.* New York: Scholastic, 2010. Print.

de Lavilléon, Gaetan, et al. "Explicit Memory Creation During Sleep Demonstrates a Causal Role of Place Cells in Navigation." *Nature Neuroscience* 18.4 (2015): 493–95. Print.

Ehlers, Anke, and David M. Clark. "A Cognitive Model of Posttraumatic Stress Disorder." *Behaviour Research and Therapy* 38.4 (2000): 319–45. Print.

Felmingham, Kim, et al. "Changes in Anterior Cingulate and Amygdala after Cognitive Behavior Therapy of Posttraumatic Stress Disorder." *Psychological Science* 18.2 (2007): 127–29. Print.

Gates, Margaret A., et al. "Posttraumatic Stress Disorder in Veterans and Military Personnel: Epidemiology, Screening, and Case Recognition." *Psychological Services* 9.4 (2012): 361–82. Print.

Ginzburg, Karni, et al. "Evidence for a Dissociative Subtype of Posttraumatic Stress Disorder Among Help-seeking Childhood Sexual Abuse Survivors." *Journal of Trauma & Dissociation* 7.2 (2006): 7–27. Print.

Griggs, Richard A. "Psychology's Lost Boy: Will the Real Little Albert Please Stand Up?" *Teaching of Psychology* 42.1 (2015): 14–18. Print.

Guitchounts, Grigori. "Inception Helps Mice Navigate." *SITN: Science in the News*. Harvard Medical School, 16 Apr. 2015. Web. 23 Jan. 2016.

Hamblen, Schnurr, Rosenberg, and Eftekhari. "Overview of Psychotherapy for PTSD." *PTSD: National Center for PTSD*. U.S. Department of Veterans Affairs. 27 Feb. 2014. Web. 23 Jan. 2016.

Howard Hughes Medical Institute. "Emotional Association of Memories Changed by Researchers." *ScienceDaily*. ScienceDaily, 27 August 2014. Web. 23 Jan. 2016.

Johnson, Luke R., et al. "Pavlovian Fear Memory Circuits and Phenotype Models of PTSD." *Neuropharmacology* 62.2 (2012): 638–46. Print.

Jones, Edgar, Nicola T. Fear, and Simon Wessely. "Shell Shock and Mild Traumatic Brain Injury: A Historical Review." *American Journal of Psychiatry* 164.11 (2007): 1641–45. Print.

Jones, Mary C. "A Laboratory Study of Fear." *Pedagogical Seminary* 31 (1924): 308–15. Print.

Jovanovic, Tanja, and Kerry J. Ressler. "How the Neurocircuitry and Genetics of Fear Inhibition May Inform Our Understanding of PTSD." *The American Journal of Psychiatry* 67.6 (2010): 648–62. Print.

Liu, Xu, et al. "Optogenetic Stimulation of a Hippocampal Engram Activates Fear Memory Recall." *Nature* 484.7394 (2012): 381–85. Print.

Oliver, Kelly. "Ambiguity, Ambivalence and Extravagance in *The Hunger Games*." *Humanities* 3.4 (2014): 675–86. Print.

Otto, Michael W., et al. "Treatment of Pharmacotherapy-refractory Posttraumatic Stress Disorder among Cambodian Refugees: A Pilot Study of Combination Treatment with Cognitive-behavior Therapy vs Sertraline Alone." *Behaviour Research and Therapy* 41.11 (2003): 1271–76. Print.

Pifalo, Terry. "Jogging the Cogs: Trauma-focused Art Therapy and Cognitive Behavioral Therapy with Sexually Abused Children." *Art Therapy* 24.4 (2007): 170–75. Print.

Powell, Russell A., et al. "Correcting the Record on Watson, Rayner, and Little Albert: Albert Barger as 'Psychology's Lost Boy.'" *American Psychologist* 69.6 (2014): 600–11. Print.

Redondo, Roger L., et al. "Bidirectional Switch of the Valence Associated with a Hippocampal Contextual Memory Engram." *Nature* 513 (2014): 426–30. Print.

Rutherford, Alexandra. "Mary Cover Jones (1896–1987)." *The Feminist Psychologist* 27.3 (Summer 2000). Dept. of Psychology, University of York, Ontario, n.d. Web. 23 Jan. 2016.

Slayton, Sarah C., Jeanne D'Archer, and Frances Kaplan. "Outcome Studies on the Efficacy of Art Therapy: A Review of Findings." *Art Therapy* 27.3 (2010): 108–18. Print.

Takeuchi, Tomonori, and Richard G. M. Morris. "Neuroscience: Shedding Light on a Change of Mind." *Nature* 513 (2014): 323–24. Print.

Tan, Susan Shau Ming. "Burn with Us: Sacrificing Childhood in *The Hunger Games*." *The Lion and the Unicorn* 37.1 (2013): 54–73. Print.

Thrasher, Sian, et al. "Social Support Moderates Outcome in a Randomized Controlled Trial of Exposure Therapy and (or) Cognitive Restructuring for Chronic Posttraumatic Stress Disorder." *Canadian Journal of Psychiatry. Revue Canadienne de Psychiatrie* 55.3 (2010): 187–90. Print.

Todes, Daniel P. *Ivan Pavlov: A Russian Life in Science.* New York: Oxford UP, 2008. Print.

Trafton, Ann. "Neuroscientists Reverse Memories' Emotional Associations." *MIT News*. Massachusetts Institute of Technology, 27 Aug. 2014. Web. 23 Jan. 2016.

Van Elzakker, Michael B., et al. "From Pavlov to PTSD: The Extinction of Conditioned Fear in Rodents, Humans, and Anxiety Disorders." *Neurobiology of Learning and Memory* 113 (2014): 3–18. Print.

Watson, John B., and Rosalie Rayner. "Conditioned Emotional Reactions." *Journal of Experimental Psychology* 3.1 (1920): 1–13. *Classics in the History of Psychology*. Web. 23 Jan. 2016.

Wessa, Michèle, and Herta Flor. "Failure of Extinction of Fear Responses in Post-traumatic Stress Disorder: Evidence from Second-order Conditioning." *American Journal of Psychiatry* 164.11 (2007): 1684–92. Print.

Labyrinthine Challenges and Degenerate Strategies in *The Hunger Games*

Lars Schmeink

According to Dutch cultural historian Johan Huizinga, the concept of play is a cultural phenomenon that permeates social activity and can be found as an element of almost everything humans do, from the way we construct language to the way we enact our beliefs: "law and order, commerce and profit, craft and art, poetry, wisdom, and science. All are rooted in the primaeval soil of play" (5). What engrains play into cultural activities is its simulation of specific *sets of rules* that define a social system in which we operate, "a rule-based formal system," that can produce differently evaluated outcomes—winning and losing (Juul 6; Sniderman). Key to all play is its dependence upon rules and their regulation of behavior within a given system. But just from looking at Huizinga's list, it becomes clear that a concept as encompassing as play runs the risk of losing its scientific value for any kind of specific inquiry. To counteract this diversity of forms, games scholar Brian Sutton-Smith proposes to differentiate the concept into seven distinct rhetorics, meaning specific ways of thinking and talking about play. At the heart of this argument is what he calls the "rhetoric of play as progress," which holds that we learn and develop by playing, that play can function as "socialization and moral, social, and cognitive growth" (Sutton-Smith 9f).

Sutton-Smith shows that it is possible to understand play as contributing to a variety of developmental steps such as the "real-life adaptive skills for survival" or "skills for cognition and education," that play may function as "an imitation of adult activities" or "a form of learning or socialization" (50). In this very general pedagogical function then, play is related to other cultural forms, such as mythology or literature. In regards to myth, Joseph Campbell argues that one of its functions is "to validate and maintain a certain sociological system: a shared set of rights and wrongs, proprieties or improprieties" (10), and another is "the pedagogical" (14). Myth thus functions as a moral guideline for right and wrong behavior, teaching younger members of society "to become self-reliant" (Campbell 14). Moreover, young adult literature fulfills a similar function, encouraging development and learning, foregrounding stories that deal with adolescents' quests for "self-identity and self-discovery ... [and] define their journey toward self-understanding" (Kaplan qtd. in Canavan, and Petrovic 46).

To sum up: many aspects of culture (myth, literature, play) provide young adults with a guideline (with the *rules*) as to what is considered an acceptable or a desirable action within a given social system. Suzanne Collins' The Hunger Games series might be read as such a cultural rulebook—one that appropriates Greek mythology to reveal a behavioral strategy that allows survival in a dystopian social reality. Key to this reading is the understanding of the world presented in the novels as deeply and unjustly prejudiced against the inhabitants of the districts. The only chance to escape the systemic exploitation, while adhering to the rules of the system, is participation in the Hunger Games, which itself is a game system that is unjust towards its players. A strategy to deal with such unjust systems (both the social reality of the novels and the Games) thus has to be making use of any means available to ensure not only survival but a change in the system. The Hunger Games present us with examples of systems that warrant the use of what game theory refers to as *degenerate strategies* as a legitimate and necessary path to victory.

The Labyrinth Metaphor

When talking about inspiration for the books, Suzanne Collins points towards the Greek myth of Theseus and the Minotaur. Especially the aspect of a "punishment for past deeds" seems to have captured her imagination because of its ruthless violence and the inherited guilt of the crime: "Crete was sending a very clear message: 'Mess with us and we'll do something worse than kill you. We'll kill your children'" (Everett 1). It is this unjust system, punishing children for crimes of generations past, which inspires a heroic rebellion—both in the myth and in *The Hunger Games*, as Collins points out: "I guess in her own way, Katniss is a futuristic Theseus" (Everett 1). In order to understand these parallels, a recapitulation of the myth seems helpful.[1]

In a conflict between the King of Crete, Minos, and Aegeus, the King of Athens, Minos had the upper hand, due to his vast fleet, and threatened the city of Athens with destruction unless Aegeus paid tribute every nine years by sending seven boys and seven girls to be sacrificed to a fearsome creature, the Minotaur. The Minotaur, a monster that was half-man and half-bull, was kept in a labyrinth and devoured the youths as they tried to escape the confusing maze. When the third sacrifice was ready, Theseus, the son of King Aegeus, volunteered to go, so that he could to slay the Minotaur. When he arrived at Crete, King Minos' daughter Ariadne fell deeply in love with Theseus and did not want him to die, so she secretly helped him defeat the Minotaur. She gave him a ball of thread, with which he could retrace his steps and safely maneuver the maze without getting lost. In some more recent versions of the myth, she even gave him a sword to fight with. Theseus attached one end of the thread to the entrance door and unwound the ball as he went into the maze, found the Minotaur, killed him, and then returned by following the thread back to the entrance.

Central to the myth's connection with The Hunger Games series is the challenge set before Theseus in the form of the labyrinth and the unjust system it represents. In contemporary (Western) culture, the labyrinth has become a trope that metaphorically represents a loss of orientation in society, an inability to find safety and meaning, a search for an individual path to self-determination, as well as a form of initiation and development. The labyrinth is thus suited to represent not only the loss of orientation in twenty-first century society in general and more specifically after the events of 9/11, but also the anxieties felt by adolescents when confronted with the task of identity-formation. The latter is especially important, as the labyrinth functions as a site for a rite of passage, an initiation into adult society. Craig Wright argues that the labyrinth of Crete "signified a gloomy, tortuous Underworld," and that as such, it served as "an arena for trial and ordeal, for confrontation and conquest, for initiatory rites in which the hero undergoes a process of self-discovery" (15). Manfred Schmeling specifies the function of such an initiation for society by claiming that the fight against the Minotaur as a ritual is focused on "rectifying a social injustice" (33, translation mine). Theseus volunteers to be sacrificed to the Minotaur, because he sees the slaughter of children as a social injustice. By crossing the threshold into the labyrinth, Theseus leaves behind the status as child/son, and the social security associated with this, to enter the mythological realm, which bears no orientation or security. All categories of stability are suspended here. Theseus has to navigate the mythical space and time of the labyrinth, entry into and reemergence from which represents death and rebirth, the maze itself becoming a sort of Underworld (cf. Wright 15). By slaying the Minotaur and returning safely from the labyrinth, Theseus thus claims his rightful place as an adult, as a hero, and as a leader, restoring order and eliminating the previous social injustice.

In a mythopoetic retelling, such as Collins' novels, the elements of the myth become more complex and adapted to the contemporary situation. The conflict between two city-states becomes a civil war in which the districts rebel against and are subdued by the Capitol and, as punishment, have to offer up one boy and one girl each as surrogate sacrifices. However, Collins escalates the ruthlessness of the sacrificial system: not fourteen but twenty-four tributes are demanded, not every nine years, but each year, and, of course, Katniss as "future Theseus" emerges not in the third but the seventy-fourth round of sacrifices. Also, it is interesting to note that though Katniss volunteers to become a tribute, she does so to stave off the unjust reaping of her younger sister, not to balance out the more dominant injustice of the system in general. In the end, she succeeds in both, but the socio-political injustice is addressed only later in the series, when her conflict with the Capitol escalates, and Katniss' actions become symbolic for a political movement.

In a metaphorical sense, Katniss has to overcome more than one opponent (e.g., the tributes, the mutts, Snow, Coin) and has to navigate more than one labyrinth (e.g., the Capitol's entertainment structure, the Games' arena—twice, the warzone) during the course of the novel series, but the first book and the Hunger Games competition ring truest to the original myth. Here Katniss volunteers as a tribute, is brought to the arena, and has to survive both disorientation and obstacles before finally defeating Cato. She enters the arena as a tribute, a teenager to be sacrificed for the sins of past generations, and reemerges from it a grown-up victor, a revered leader for the districts. A detailed comparison of any novel and classical mythology will, of course, yield differences, but it is easy to see that the overall structure of Katniss' challenge in the Hunger Games resembles that of the labyrinth.

Beating the Labyrinth

In talking about the pedagogical function of the labyrinth myth and especially Collins' appropriation of it in *The Hunger Games*, I will concentrate on an aspect that has been generally overlooked: that of Ariadne's thread and its function in the myth. Following from the original discussion of play as elementary to rituals and cultural behavior, readers can understand the labyrinth as a system governed by game-like rules. Analyzing it according to game theory should thus offer up new insights, especially in regards to the rules in such a system and how to "beat the game," so to speak, and survive.

In their book *Rules of Play*, Katie Salen and Eric Zimmerman argue that there are three kinds of rules: operational, constitutive, and implicit rules (130). Operational rules are explicitly spelled-out, and in the case of the labyrinth they are thus probably found in the (oral) contract between Crete and Athens: every nine years seven youths and seven maidens are to be sacrificed to the Minotaur. In return, Crete will not attack Athens. The constitutive rules are rather abstract, determined by "the underlying formal structures" (Salen, and Zimmerman 130), such as the logical movements in navigating the maze: when coming to a crossroads, one can either go left, go right, or go straight to progress; moving backwards will not help.

Most interesting, though, are the implicit rules, which are so variable and so numerous that it is hard to determine them for each game. These deal with the fundamental social dynamics when playing, but as Sniderman argues, we cannot possibly know all the rules of a game, as "some deeper rules are always operating … without the player's being aware of them" (par. 1). In the case of the labyrinth, the implicit rules are complex, opaque, capricious, and unjust towards the players. King Minos wants the Minotaur to devour the Athenians because he wants to appease the beast (something he will not advertise in the rules), while at the same time keeping his enemy in line. So, implicit in the rules—which Ariadne, daughter of Minos, should know—is that the Minotaur needs to eat the sacrifices in order for Minos to keep his power. In this game, the odds are never in the Athenians' favor (because Minos, as game designer, systematically favors the other side), and there can only be one victor: the Minotaur.

The game rules implicitly work so that the sacrifices are defenseless, disoriented, and scared to death to go into the maze, but Ariadne's gifts negate this. Since Theseus receives a ball of thread and a sword, he is the first person to enter the labyrinth equipped with tools not intended to be in play and thus not covered by the rules. Though they are not expressly forbidden, thread and sword were not foreseen as part of the game. Theseus can backtrack his path, should he get lost, and he can fight the monster. Thus, for him, the ultimate fear of entering a disorienting, chaotic space in which a superior opponent lurks is mitigated by the fact that he has tools to his favor. In terms of the rules of play, Theseus is thus cheating—or better, he uses degenerate strategies to outwit the design of the game.

Also called "exploits," degenerate strategies are described by Salen and Zimmerman as a "way of playing a game that takes advantage of a weakness in the game design, so that the play strategy guarantees success" (271). In game theory, this behavior is not referred to as cheating, as it does not involve breaking explicit rules, but reflects the most efficient strategy to beat the game:

> Taking advantage of the game's weakness in this way would not exactly constitute cheating, but it does exploit the game's structure as a means of winning. Although games are not designed to be exploited by players, what makes a degenerate strategy degenerate is not just that it goes against the intentions of the designers. Using an exploit

is a way of playing that violates the spirit of the game. (Salen, and
Zimmerman 272)

It is important to point out that the spirit of the labyrinth as a game
is ruthlessly evil and highly prejudiced against the Athenian players.
In fact, the intention of the game design is to kill the players.
Consequently, the labyrinth does not really qualify as a *game* (which
according to most definitions needs to be voluntary), but only exhibits
game-like qualities. Nonetheless, in terms of rule-based systems,
the skewed nature of the rules of play offers an interesting point
of analysis: In a system that is unjust and threatening, divergent or
degenerate strategies can become necessary to survive. In such an
environment, using an exploit feels justified, and that is probably
why Theseus has been seen as a hero and not an unsportsman-like
player or even a cheat.

Strategies for Survival

The mythical use of degenerate strategies becomes a model for *The
Hunger Games*, but Collins takes great care to make her variant
of the myth more complex by rearranging aspects of Ariadne and
Theseus into Katniss and the rest of her team. Ariadne and Theseus
have clear roles in their strategy: Ariadne knows the exploits and
provides the tools, whereas Theseus executes the strategy and
beats the system; Katniss, on the other hand, sometimes devises
the strategy and at other times executes it. Haymitch, Peeta, Cinna,
and even Effie provide additional aid and guidance. What the novel
emphasizes is that in order to make use of degenerate strategies
(i.e., become Theseus), one needs to decipher the implicit rules and
devise a plan (i.e., become Ariadne). The novel reimagines the myth
and foregrounds the ability to spot the exploits, to observe a system
and find its flaws, to "game the game" so to speak.

Already in the beginning of the novel, Katniss shows an acute
awareness of how the society of District 12 works and how to
manipulate the rules in order to survive. Food is scarce in the district,
and hunting in the woods is forbidden and severely punished. But
since the Peacekeepers, who would enforce these rules, are just "as

Critical Insights

hungry for fresh meat as anybody is" (Collins, *Hunger Games* 5), Katniss is able to exploit this as a flaw in the system. She is also very aware of the outright injustice of the reaping and of the Hunger Games, with its systemic prejudice against the poor, who are forced to add their names "more times in exchange for tesserae" (13) to provide their families with additional food. This system Katniss knows and handles rather well until her sister Prim is chosen as a tribute. With her name in the bowl only once, she should have been "as safe as you can get" (15)—that she is chosen against the odds proves that Katniss is "powerless against the reaping" (15) though. It also forces her to volunteer in Prim's stead and enter a world with new rules, which she has to learn to exploit for survival.

On the train towards the Capitol, Haymitch hits Peeta and reminds him that appearances matter. When Peeta protests, that the bruise suggests a breach of rules—no fighting between tributes outside the arena—Haymitch reveals his knowledge of the implicit rules and of degenerate strategies: "Only if they catch you. That bruise will say you fought, you weren't caught, even better" (Collins, *Hunger Games* 57). Later, when the train arrives at the Capitol, and Peeta is waving at the crowds, Katniss realizes that the Games have begun, that every moment counts, and that Peeta is "already fighting hard to stay alive" (60) and winning sponsors for himself. The rules of the Hunger Games are much more complex and opaque, and Katniss has to learn them fast.

At the presentation ceremony, Katniss for the first time grasps the reality of the Games: the need to play the crowd, as the Games are mostly about entertainment, and the tributes are judged for sympathy and admiration. When Cinna tells them to hold hands and stand confident, Katniss feels the force of the image: "Cinna has given me a great advantage. No one will forget me.... Surely, there must be one sponsor willing to take me on!" (Collins, *Hunger Games* 70). But it takes Haymitch to point out the gesture's power as degenerate strategy: "Just the perfect touch of rebellion" (79). In terms of the operational rules, the hand-holding is simply a way to earn sympathy, but in terms of the implicit rules—that only one tribute remain—it becomes symbolic, rebellious in that it defies the spirit of deadly competition.

During the final evaluations in training, the operational rules state that each tribute is granted a private session in front of the Gamemakers to rank his or her skills, giving "the audience a starting place for the betting" (Collins, *Hunger Games* 184). The implicit rules suggest that tributes show off their skills to their best ability to impress the Gamemakers. Further, in the spirit of the situation, tributes should display a respectful behavior towards the Gamemakers—the judges who decide their fates. When it is Katniss' turn, she realizes that the Gamemakers are bored: "Instantly, I know I'm in trouble. They've been here too long…. Sat through twenty-three other demonstrations. Had too much wine…. The majority of them are fixated on a roast pig that has just arrived" (100). Katniss is enraged: "[W]ith my life on the line, they don't even have the decency to pay attention to me…. I'm being upstaged by a dead pig" (101). She fires an arrow at the pig's mouth and then storms off. Behind this brash act is the knowledge of the implicit rules that the Gamemakers will need to remember her in order to rank her high. Shooting at them is no breach of the operational rules, but it is a degenerate strategy, as it certainly "violates the spirit" of the session and the "intentions of the designers" (272), as Salen and Zimmerman put it. It is indeed such a violation that a year later (in *Catching Fire*), the Gamemakers' booth is secured by a force field—thus preventing another similar exploit. Metaphorically, as Shannon Mortimore-Smith argues, Katniss' arrow "declares her presence, her dignity, and her threat" (165) to the Gamemakers, thus foreshadowing the disruption to the rules of play of the Hunger Games and the dissolution of the fascist district system that will follow over the course of the trilogy.

In the arena it becomes clear, that the Gamemakers control all aspects of the Games, but may change the rules to get better audience ratings. Keeping with the idea of a spectacle, Katniss realizes the underlying rules of this entertainment and the options to exploit them. The audience consequently becomes a key component in the rules of play, as Vivienne Muller argues:

Critical Insights

The supervisors ... are responsible for setting up and controlling the killing fields. The topography, the flora and fauna and the weather are artificially manipulated and dangerous and deadly obstacles are deliberately put in the way of the participants to direct the action ... [But t]he audience can become sponsors, providing food, medicine or weaponry to help their favourite tribute win. In this they are recruited as associate directors of the simulation, players of and in the game, contributing to its theatricality and its sub-plots, aiding and abetting murder and violence. (55)

Katniss manipulates the audience's desire for the star-crossed lovers theme in order to receive food from her sponsors (Collins, *Hunger Games* 261), but she is also keenly aware of the repercussions her actions could have in District 12: "Because my words go out all over Panem" (268). She and Haymitch take on the roles of Theseus and Ariadne, Haymitch communicating the implicit design via the sponsored goods (or lack thereof), guiding Katniss to natural water (169) or sending medicine to steady her after the fire attack (188). She muses on the Gamemakers' need to keep entertainment levels up, arguing that water and food can be found, as "barren landscapes are dull and the Games resolve too quickly without them" (140). The "real sport of the Hunger Games is watching the tributes kill one another" (177) not watching tributes die from exhaustion or killing them off too swiftly. The fire attack is a device to manipulate the in-game situation to make it more entertaining: "This fire is designed to flush us out, to drive us together" (173), creating a more dynamic interaction.

So the audience and its reaction play a role in determining Katniss' behavior, leading to specific options for degenerate strategies. The strongest example of this is Katniss' decision to give Rue a burial ceremony after her death. She not only refuses to leave and let the game-rules take over, but also provides a defiant reading of the situation by decorating Rue's body with flowers and paying respect: "I press the three middle fingers of my left hand against my lips and hold them out in her direction" (Collins, *Hunger Games* 237). This clearly violates the competitive spirit of the Games and negates the intentions of the designers: "I want to do something ...

to shame them, to make them accountable, to show the Capitol that whatever they do or force us to do there is a part of every tribute they can't own. That Rue was more than a piece in their Games. And so am I" (236).

Katniss realizes the violation of the rules, which state that she should remove herself from the body so that it can be collected. Her gesture is defiant of those rules—deliberately using an exploit to send a message. She knows that the cameras will have to show the body being collected, and by decorating Rue, she signals love and respect for Rue as a person, effectively undermining the dehumanization that the Games represent. Muller suggests that the tributes function as "avatars" (55) for the districts in a punishment simulation. But punishment functions best, according to Andrew Shaffer, when the avatars are dehumanized, so that the audience can feel "a sense of justice" when they witness "perpetrators of a crime actually punished" (79). By re-humanizing Rue, Katniss robs the audience of its distance, forcing them to acknowledge their complicity (cf. Mortimore-Smith 165).

That this degenerate strategy completely violates the spirit of the Hunger Games becomes obvious when District 11, Rue's home, sends Katniss a loaf of bread. The gesture in itself is a degenerate strategy, as the intention of the Games is to pit the districts against each other: "For whatever reason, this is a first. A district gift to a tribute who's not your own. I lift my face and step into the last falling rays of sunlight. 'My thanks to the people of District Eleven,' I say. I want them to know I know where it came from. That the full value of their gift has been recognized." (Collins, *Hunger Games* 238). As Tom Henthorne has argued, the viewers "ultimately determine the Games['] meanings" as:

> ideological content cannot be fixed by producers, however much they try.... In effect, viewers are able to use the Games' interactivity to subvert the producer's ideological intent: sponsoring Katniss while she is in the arena becomes a means of defying the Capitol's power since to them Katniss has come to represent resistance. (104)

At this point, the novel for the first time acknowledges that Katniss' actions are not merely part of the Hunger Games but also part of a larger social system with similarly strict and complex rules governing the relation between the Capitol and districts.

Degenerate strategies also reverberate outside of the context of the Games arena and apply to the social system at large; just how deeply they apply becomes apparent in Katniss' last act of resistance in the book. For the Capitol, the "stunt with the berries" (Collins, *Hunger Games* 372) is an outright act of cheating and is viewed as subverting not only the spirit of the Games but its power as a tool for suppression. After the back-and-forth changes of the Hunger Games' operational rules—allowing for two victors, then again denying that opportunity, Katniss realizes "they have to have a victor" (344) and that both remaining tributes dying would mean the audience would be denied their greatest entertainment— the after-show and the Victory Tour. It is at this point that Katniss reveals the deepest understanding of the implicit rules of the game. By threatening to eat the poisonous berries, Katniss and Peeta can turn the game rules completely against their intentions. In effect, as Helen Day has argued, this strategy "exposes the war between ratings (which require the editors to show this climactic gesture) and deterrent (which requires the censorship of such an incendiary act)" (174); thus, the gesture completely undermines the Gamemakers' intentions.

Furthermore, her act of exploiting the unwritten rules of the televised spectacle is read as the ultimate defiance against an unjust system. "By refusing to play by the established rules, Katniss forces all of the players into a new game, the ramifications of which reverberate through the second and third books," as Andrew Jones has stated (246). But it is important to note here that Katniss uses this as a degenerate strategy for the Hunger Games—in order to survive. The political message of rebellion is a product of the mediated process: "In the arena—I was only thinking of outsmarting the Gamemakers, not how my actions would reflect on the Capitol. But the Hunger Games are their weapon and you are not supposed to be able to defeat it" (Collins, *Hunger Games* 358). The degenerate strategy is doubly effective; not only does it secure Katniss' survival in the arena, but it also sparks the change in the unjust system, turning her into a hero and a role model.

Unjust Systems

Just as Ariadne's thread helped Theseus dismantle the social injustice of the Athenian sacrifices by killing the Minotaur, so Katniss uses degenerate strategies to topple an unjust system of sacrifice and state control. The moral message that both transport is thus clear: When the system is prejudiced and stacked against those acting within it, it is necessary to explore the rules that govern that system and use any exploit possible. We are all subject to rules and regulations, taking part in a complex web of intricate and often implicit, unwritten rules. Understanding those rules is paramount. As Salen and Zimmerman point out: "In a social context, the exploit unbalances the level playing field of conflict and shrinks the space of possibility to a very narrow range, threatening the meaningful play of the game" (273). But what about a game, in which the playing field is skewed from the beginning? What about a social context in which the odds are *never* in your favor? Here, degenerate strategies are an act of defiance, an act of rebellion against the rules and the system itself. In an unjust system, one that stacks the odds against the players and threatens their lives, knowing the rules that bind the system and exploiting them to one's advantage becomes a heroic deed. Degenerate strategies, because of their willingness to undermine the spirit of the game and the intentions of the system designers, are ideal guidelines for dystopian and unjust systems, be they game systems or social systems.

Note

1. As with all classical mythology, there are many versions of the myth. None of the variants is the *correct* version; instead myth can be seen as a "system of communication that depends on a body of pre-worked material, a system that brings with it a host of associations, connotations, and interpretive baggage" (Dougherty 13). Every telling of a myth thus adds to the baggage and emphasizes a different aspect, adapting the myth to its specific time. I am here referring to

versions given by Apollodorus (E1: 7–9), Plutarch (*Life of Theseus*, XIX: 1–3), Diodorus Siculus (IV: 61.4–7), and Ovid (*Metamorphoses*, VIII: 152–82), as well as modern scholarly interpretations by Robert Graves (Chapter 98: 336–48) and W. H. Matthews (17–22).

Works Cited

Campbell, Joseph. *Pathways to Bliss: Mythology and Personal Transformation*. Ed. David Kudler. Novato, CA: New World Library, 2004. Print.

Canavan, Anne M., and Sarah N. Petrovic. "Tipping the Odds Ever in Her Favor: An Exploration of Narrative Control and Agency in the Novel and Film." *Space and Place in The Hunger Games: New Readings of the Novels*. Ed. Deidre Garriott, Anne Evans, Whitney Elaine Jones, and Julie Elizabeth Tyler. Jefferson, NC: McFarland, 2014. 45–58. Print.

Day, Helen. "Simulacra, Sacrifice and Survival in the *Hunger Games*, *Battle Royale*, and the *Running Man*." *Of Bread, Blood and The Hunger Games: Critical Essays on the Suzanne Collins Trilogy*. Ed. Mary F. Pharr and Leisa A. Clark. Jefferson, NC: McFarland, 2012. 167–77. Print.

Dougherty, Carol. *Prometheus*. London: Routledge, 2006. Print.

Everett, Sheila Marie. "A Conversation. Questions & Answers: Suzanne Collins, Author of Hunger Games." *Scholastic*. Scolastic, Inc., n.d. Web. 13 Aug, 2014.

Graves, Robert. *The Greek Myths*. Harmondsworth, UK: Penguin, 1955. Print.

Huizinga, Johan. *Homo Ludens: A Study of the Play-Element in Culture*. London: Routledge, 1949. Print.

Jones, Andrew Zimmerman. "The Tribute's Dilemma: The Hunger Games and Game Theory." *The Hunger Games and Philosophy: A Critique of Pure Treason*. Ed. George A. Dunn and Nicolas Michaud. Hoboken, NJ: Wiley, 2012. 253–49. Print.

Juul, Jesper. *Half-Real: Video Games between Real Rules and Fictional Worlds*. Cambridge, MA: MIT Press, 2005. Print.

Matthews, W. H. *Mazes and Labyrinths: Their History and Development*. 1922. New York: Dover, 1970. Print.

Mortimore-Smith, Shannon R. "Fueling the Spectacle: Audience as 'Gamemaker.'" *Of Bread, Blood and the Hunger Games: Critical Essays on the Suzanne Collins Trilogy.* Ed. Mary F. Pharr and Leisa A. Clark. Jefferson, NC: McFarland, 2012. 158–66. Print.

Muller, Vivienne. "Virtually Real: Suzanne Collins' *The Hunger Games* Trilogy." *International Research in Children's Literature* 5.1 (2012): 51–63. Print.

Salen, Katie, and Eric Zimmerman. *Rules of Play: Game Design Fundamentals.* Cambridge, MA: MIT Press, 2004. Print.

Schmeling, Manfred. *Der labyrinthische Diskurs: Vom Mythos zum Erzählmodell.* Frankfurt am Main: Athenäum, 1987. Print.

Shaffer, Andrew. "The Joy of Watching Others Suffer: Schadenfreude and The Hunger Games." *The Hunger Games and Philosophy: A Critique of Pure Treason.* Eds. George A. Dunn and Nicolas Michaud. Hoboken, NJ: Wiley, 2012. 75–89. Print.

Sniderman, Stephen. "Unwritten Rules." *The Life of Games.* Kadon Enterprises, Inc., Oct. 1999. Web. 13 Aug. 2014.

Sutton-Smith, Brian. *The Ambiguity of Play.* Cambridge, MA: Harvard UP, 1997. Print.

Wright, Craig. *The Maze and the Warrior: Symbols in Architecture, Theology, and Music.* Cambridge, MA: Harvard UP, 2001. Print.

The Girl within the Mockingjay: Roman Allusions, Repercussions of War, and Ideological Transformation

Amalia L. Selle

In Flanders fields the poppies blow
Between the crosses, row on row,
That mark our place, and in the sky
The larks, still bravely singing, fly
Scarce heard amid the guns below.

We are the dead; short days ago
We lived, felt dawn, saw sunset glow,
Loved and were loved, and now we lie
In Flanders fields.

Take up our quarrel with the foe!
To you from failing hands we throw
The torch; be yours to hold it high!
If ye break faith with us who die
We shall not sleep, though poppies grow
In Flanders fields.

(John McCrae)

Five years after her father returned from fighting in Vietnam, thirteen-year-old Suzanne Collins stood before a field of poppies as her father recited this poem from memory. In a "transformative" moment, Collins suddenly wondered if these beautiful flowers hid a graveyard (Dominus). This memory echoes the ending of *Mockingjay*, when Katniss and Peeta's children play in the Meadow, unaware that below the flowers lie the remains of District 12 citizens killed because of Katniss' revolutionary actions. Disturbing images such as these show The Hunger Games series as about more than mere entertainment. Collins' conclusion refuses to grant readers a sunset ending. She unflinchingly portrays the lasting physical and emotional wounds caused by war because education, rather than entertainment, is Collins' end goal.

With this end in mind, Collins created Katniss, a character steeped both in heroic lore and the horror of modern warfare. The combination leads to a character trapped by fate, cruel enemies, suspicious friends, and perhaps her own mind. *Mockingjay* involves the intricate interplay among three tropes—the story of Spartacus, the theme of war, and the Mockingjay image—and how these tropes influence the character development of Katniss.

Before considering these tropes, thought must be given to Katniss' cultural education throughout *The Hunger Games* and *Catching Fire* as she, through Peeta's influence, recognizes the lies of the Capitol and moves toward becoming the Mockingjay, despite the cost. The first two books showcase the struggle against the evils of the Capitol. This struggle leads to traumatic effects and tension between the Katniss Peeta loves and the Mockingjay Katniss becomes to survive. Collins sets the stage for *Mockingjay*'s message as Katniss experiences loss and trauma as well as the healing power of friendship.

Katniss and Spartacus

As related in her interview with Rick Margolis, Collins originally came up with the idea of the Hunger Games when a reality TV show and real war footage blurred together in her mind. From there, a Roman-reminiscent arena and children fighting to the death as gladiators came quickly. The Roman allusions go beyond references to the Roman games and the name of Panem, reminding readers of the Latin saying "*panem et circenses*," meaning "bread and circuses." From Juvenal in *Satire X*, the quote refers to Rome's political usage of food and entertainment, specifically gladiator games, to prevent civil unrest.

Collins has revealed that although the story of Theseus finding his way through the labyrinth to defeat the Minotaur formed the beginning inspiration for the series, the historical figure of Spartacus became her ending inspiration. Collins notes that Spartacus "caused the Romans quite a bit of trouble. And, ultimately, he died"

(Margolis). Collins' vision for a flawed, realistic heroine becomes clear when the reader views Katniss as a Spartacus-figure. The similarities between Spartacus and Katniss reveal how individual identities become trapped within political propaganda and history.

The link between Spartacus and Katniss begins with their improbable origins. Spartacus began as either a former Roman auxiliary or war captive turned gladiator. A man taught to fight for entertainment became a charismatic leader who successfully evaded the greatest military machine of the ancient world. In a similar way, Suzanne Collins notes how the unexpected mutation of jabberjays symbolizes Katniss' transformation from "a girl who should never have existed" into "the mockingjay, which is Katniss" (Margolis). Created by the Capitol as a weapon and abandoned when no longer useful, jabberjays mated with female mockingbirds, giving birth to mockingjays (Collins, *Hunger Games* 43). While the Capitol urges unresisting faith in the system, Katniss receives a different sort of education because of the relative freedom of the woods. Deep in the woods, Katniss can voice the revolutionary thoughts unutterable within the fence. Doubtless without this education, Katniss would have followed cultural norms and remained silent when Prim's name was called.

Katniss' actions of rebellion within the Hunger Games and Spartacus' actions of breaking out of bondage begin as a struggle for survival. Spartacus began as an enslaved gladiator; Katniss grows up within a system that celebrated murder for entertainment. Both Katniss and Spartacus came from a vanquished people and were trapped into fighting for the entertainment of others, with little hope of long-term survival. Historians know little of Spartacus' true motives, yet he does not seem to have been motivated by lofty ideals of rebelling against Rome or abolishing slavery. Likewise when Plutarch's original propaganda features a carefully staged Katniss, her performance is laughable. Haymitch sarcastically comments, "And that, my friends, is how a revolution dies" (Collins, *Mockingjay* 72). Spartacus, and Katniss likewise, shine through the heroic struggles of the battlefield. Not makers of insincere speeches, they are people of action.

Katniss fails to inspire when others stage her behavior. Spartacus also received a retelling by another Plutarch, and as this retelling took place years after Spartacus' death, we can only guess between embellishment and truth. In fact, as Brent Shaw has noted in *Spartacus and the Slave Wars*, all Greek and Roman sources were "deliberately crafted, self-conscious interpretations of earlier events. It is critical to bear in mind that *not one* of these documents was written by a slave or a former slave" (25). As Katniss' true identity becomes swallowed by the Mockingjay image, so Spartacus has become inseparable from the myth. The leaders of both District 13 and the Capitol use the well-crafted propaganda version of Katniss to control, inspire, and propagate their own political endgame.

Without a doubt, Katniss and Spartacus share a common charisma. Spartacus' rebellion quickly swelled to include tens of thousands of slaves. While Rome quickly crushed two other slave rebellions, Spartacus' daring raids and clever maneuvers lasted for two years and made the Roman fighting machine look decidedly foolish. Largely untrained slaves defeating Roman armies is just as improbable as a young girl inspiring a rebellion. Scores of girls had fought bravely in the Hunger Games, yet Katniss, by her acts of mercy toward both Rue and Peeta, inspired rebellion.

Furthermore, Katniss and Spartacus became trapped within the very movements they began. According to Plutarch, Spartacus knew the Roman army would ultimately prevail. Therefore, he urged his army toward the Alps in the hope that, once over the mountains, his troops could dissolve and live out their lives in freedom. Spartacus found himself unable to control his men, who "had confidence in their great number and had grander ideas in their heads" (qtd. in Shaw 133). When their looting and destruction reached the level that Rome could no longer ignore, high-ranking military commanders were dispatched and eventually Spartacus was defeated.

Similarly, Katniss sees surrender to the Capitol as unthinkable, yet the just war tactics of District 13 trap her within a morally questionable battle. Katniss realizes this when she witnesses the bombing of the underground stronghold where hundreds of civilians are callously sacrificed for the greater good. Later, one of the few survivors asks for one reason why he shouldn't kill her. Katniss admits she doesn't have one, saying she's done killing the Capitol's slaves.

> "I'm not their slave," the man mutters.
> "I am," I say. "That's why I killed Cato ... and he killed Thresh ... It just goes around and around, and who wins? Not us ... But I'm tired of being a piece in their Games." (Collins, *Mockingjay* 215)

Collins wishes her readers to see war as complicated; all sides have hidden agendas and no government has completely pure motives. Facing evil is complicated. After all, evil itself is not always easy to define or see, especially when the evil is within ourselves.

The true Spartacus remains foggy in history; it's the legend, with the focus on heroics rather than the real identity of Spartacus, which concerns us most. Likewise the leaders of District 13 and the Capitol, Coin and Snow, focus on furthering their political agendas. Modern romantics desire to paint a flattering picture of Spartacus, yet just like Katniss, some accounts show a dark desire for revenge. Appian mentions Spartacus sacrificing three hundred Roman prisoners (qtd. in Shaw 141). Orosius relates, "They staged gladiatorial games, using four hundred prisoners they had taken. Those who had once been the spectacle were now to be the spectators" (qtd. in Shaw 151). This account brings to mind Katniss' vote for a renewal of the Hunger Games to punish the Capitol (Collins, *Mockingjay* 370). Perhaps this is just a ruse to fool Coin into complacency, but it also shows a certain ruthlessness.

Therefore, much of the power of Spartacus' story comes from his death rather than his life. Plutarch's version of Spartacus' ultimate end calls to mind the impassioned Katniss yelling, "If we burn, you burn with us!" (Collins, *Mockingjay* 100). Plutarch writes that Spartacus called for his horse; then he "drew his sword and shouted that if he won the battle, he would have many fine horses that belonged to the enemy, but if he lost, he would have no need of a horse. With that, he killed the animal" (qtd. in Shaw 136). Spartacus rushed toward the Roman general and "[s]urrounded by a great many of the enemy, he was cut down" (qtd. in Shaw 136).

Florus also favorably described Spartacus' end, saying, "Spartacus himself died fighting bravely at the front of his men, just like a true general" (qtd. in Shaw 155). Had his end been less heroic, these sources—with their Roman concern for a noble death—would no doubt have scornfully related his cowardice. If Spartacus had escaped over the Alps and died peacefully as an old man, would future politicians, such as Karl Marx, have used his story in quite the same way? Herein lies the problem with heroes. Heroic people are fallible and will eventually make mistakes; dead heroes can be shaped to the propagandist's agenda.

Katniss also realizes, as a living and unpredictable individual, her usefulness remains limited. Coin publicizes the Mockingjay brand for her own benefit, yet finds Katniss uncontainable. The Mockingjay would become controllable only with Katniss' death. As Boggs puts it, the best help Katniss can give to the rebellion might be as "a martyr to fight for" (266). With this goal in mind and to eliminate a possible rival, Coin purposely assigns a hijacked Peeta to Katniss' unit. Both Spartacus and Katniss are little more than figureheads exploited for political ends.

Ultimately, the paths Katniss and Spartacus follow have consequences for their followers. Appian recounts how 6,000 captured rebels were crucified along the highway running from Capua to Rome (qtd. in Shaw 143–144). Rome did not tolerate challenges to its absolute authority. Why else would it crucify 6,000 men—many of them valuable slaves and gladiators? Trailed by a film crew and a small group of District 13 soldiers, the Mockingjay ignores Coin's commands and heads into the heart of the Capitol. Following and protecting Katniss, six of her supporters die. She arrives just in time to see Prim perish. Perhaps Prim would still have been there, even if Katniss hadn't agreed to become the Mockingjay. Maybe District 12 would still have been destroyed. However, Collins implies that Katniss' challenge to the Capitol government and District 13 authority directly caused these events.

A War Story for Children

Literary agent Rosemary Stimola, shocked by the violent deaths of Prim, Finnick, and others as she read the first draft of *Mockingjay*, called Suzanne Collins to question these literary sacrifices. Yet Collins stood firm, insisting war and mourning could not be separated (Dominus). With this troubling climax, Collins moves beyond references to the ancient world and into the costly no man's land of modern warfare. At the end of *Mockingjay*, Collins' acknowledgements honor her father's "deep commitment to educating his children on war and peace" (392). Collins vividly remembers her father's war stories from his service in Vietnam. Instead of keeping children in ignorance, Collins believes education of children in war is paramount; children should understand and recognize the cost of war. Additionally, her father recognized how story powerfully impacts the world. No doubt some of these true stories were not pleasant for him to re-experience with the telling, yet they allowed his children to understand and engage with hard topics in a safe way. Collins remembers her father's war stories saying, "he would discuss these things at a level that he thought we could understand and [that was] acceptable for our age. But, really, he thought a lot was acceptable for our age, and I approach my books in the same way (Margolis).

Collins acknowledges that parents hesitate to expose their children to difficult issues, thinking that heavy topics are too much for children. Yet she insists that children are able to understand complex issues far better than we think. Collins believes thoughtful writing will lead to thoughtful readers, and, in turn, to adults attuned to the ambiguities of war. Her portrayal of war follows in her father's legacy, as she presents characters emotionally broken from the effects of war. Jack Zipes writes that literature should expand children's understanding of their world. Although written in 1981, his words apply to *Mockingjay*, as this book certainly "seduces and challenges children to take sides, see, grasp, tolerate, hate, dream, escape, and hope.... The frame has borders, sets limits, and curtails the view of the young reader, yet, it sometimes even seeks to contain the mind with contests that dare children to go beyond the borders"

(Zipes 19). If children's books focused on addressing the cost of war, we'd have a new generation equipped with a greater understanding and compassion for those suffering the seen and unseen scars of violence.

This education is so needed because of how our society glorifies war. Battle wounds are "cool" as long as they are only physical and not too extreme. In contrast, Katniss and Peeta's struggles with post-traumatic stress show the true cost of violence. Through Katniss' emotional and disjointed narrative, Collins addresses the unseen scars of war, also a factor of her childhood. Collins remembers waking to the sound of her father weeping; his nightmares lasted for the rest of his life (Dominus).

Katniss and Peeta: Battle Buddies

Katniss and Peeta should have absorbed their culture's acceptance of violence and concern for self over community. Instead, they learned to heal the best they could. Peeta seems to have coped through his artistically iced cakes. Through hunting with Gale, Katniss gained both an environment free of trauma and an education on freedom. Escaping to the woods was Katniss' most important coping mechanism. Jon G. Allen would describe this process as Katniss choosing and constructing her own healthier environment: "The new environment will foster new learning: The world is dangerous; people are dangerous—but not that dangerous. The world can be relatively safe...." (22).

Once Katniss reaches District 13, PTSD explains why Katniss insists on hunting. Yet, hunting alone is not enough because Katniss needs human support. The act of being in the open calms her, yet Gale can no longer be a secure attachment figure, as their values have changed. Gale fails to understand her concern over the mistreatment of her Capitol prep team, and this foreshadows her need for Peeta as a secure attachment figure. Through their experiences within two arenas, Katniss had formed a unique relationship with Peeta. In an environment inherently dangerous, he became the reason to keep going. The attachment relationship with Peeta develops slowly as she initially mistrusts his every action. Allen notes that "individuals who have been hampered in forming attachments need more than just the mere availability of a good 'attachment figure'… they must overcome distrust, avoidance, resistance, and ambivalence" (48).

Peeta becomes the one who calms her during her nightmares, both real and imagined. A notable moment comes when Katniss and Finnick become trapped within a section of the arena where mockingjays imitate the tortured screams of loved ones. Only Peeta's voice is able to return a catatonic Katniss to herself (Collins, *Catching Fire* 344–45). Allen writes "because attachments are healing, establishing or reestablishing a sense of secure attachment is a cornerstone of treatment" (36).

Because of this attachment relationship, Peeta and Katniss' relationship can be seen as an unbreakable bond forged through war rather than a typical teen romance. There are several passion-filled scenes between the two, yet in Katniss' world of uncertainty, the idea of love is threatening rather than safe. After all, she witnessed the effect of her father's absence on her mother. Despite her resistance, Katniss does feel affection for both Gale and Peeta, but this caring is complicated by her dependence on both men to provide self-knowledge. Gale lets her return to her post-Hunger Games self; Peeta loves her despite the scars of the Hunger Games. When examining her motivation within all three books, almost every major decision is made because of her key relationship with Peeta. At the core, Katniss is a survivor, and Peeta is the one person Katniss cannot survive without. How this attachment works can be understood through the military idea of a battle buddy.

Modern warfare has created endless uncertainties; the enemy can now be anyone—man, woman, child, even a fellow soldier. Yet without some level of trust, the human race would completely destroy itself. Human nature still desires community. If devoid of community, Collins' landscape would be dark and hopeless. Typical war stories contain some understanding of community and Collins creates her strongest example through the battle-buddy relationship between the two main protagonists. A battle buddy is defined as, the person to whom a Soldier can turn in time of need, stress, and emotional highs and lows, who will not turn the Soldier away, no matter what. This person knows exactly what the Soldier is experiencing because he or she is currently going through a similar experience or has been through a similar experience and/or situation before. (Orsingher, Lopez, and Rinehart 1)

Although Katniss originally mistrusts Peeta's every move, by the end of *The Hunger Games*, she cannot escape her nightmares unless he is there. In *Catching Fire*, Peeta has become another Prim, for whom she is willing to sacrifice everything. In the first two books, the battle-buddy relationship is largely dependent on Peeta, as he makes the choice to care for a girl who does not return his affection. This continual support establishes Peeta as the most important force in Katniss' life. In times of uncertainty, Katniss remembers his words and often changes her actions.

The events of *Mockingjay* almost destroy this battle-buddy relationship, for Snow, president of Panem, transforms Peeta into a weapon specifically programmed to kill Katniss. The roles are reversed, and Katniss must decide whether she will risk her life or seek to save his, no matter what. She first responds in self-defensive anger, yet Haymitch raises the question of how Peeta would act if the roles were reversed. She realizes Peeta "would be trying to get me back at any cost. Not shutting me out, abandoning me, greeting me with hostility at every turn" (Collins, *Mockingjay* 269). This battle-buddy loyalty, despite even Peeta's own death wish, prevents Katniss from acting out of self-preservation when her Mockingjay side would have eliminated the threat represented by mutt-Peeta. Her reasoning: "Because that's what you and I do. Protect each other" (302).

The Mockingjay Transformation
Finally, truth about Katniss' nature is distorted by the existing dichotomy between the Katniss Peeta loves and the Mockingjay she becomes to survive. Collins hints at this early in *Mockingjay* with Peeta's words, "To murder innocent people? It costs everything you are" (23). Transforming Katniss into the mutt version of herself is yet

another way Collins reiterates the reality of war. Katniss constantly mistrusts everything around her and, ultimately, herself. District 13, which promised new freedom, proves just as manipulative as the Capitol, and Katniss finds herself without Peeta—her attachment figure, her battle buddy, the one person who really knows her. She falls apart. Drifting in uncertainty, she spends most of her time sleeping in random places where she feels safe.

This stage of Katniss' development presents a frightening portrayal of how the lack of community leads to despair. The war-ravaged wreck would gladly die, and only the hope of a living Peeta roots Katniss in District 13. Katniss the person is aimless; Katniss the Mockingjay has a goal. In order to save Peeta, she strikes a deal with Coin and agrees to become the rebel figurehead. Yet the rescue of Peeta fails to help her mental state, as his first action is to try to kill her. He has always seen Katniss as beautiful; now love veers to loathing. Peeta's view of Katniss becomes identical to the way in which Katniss views herself: a monster stained with the blood of her innocent victims. Lacking Peeta's focus on truth, Katniss' understanding becomes distorted, her life purposeless. The girl Katniss is broken by the loss of Peeta's love.

The Mockingjay takes over. She grasps at her memories of "the boy with the bread ... to make myself put a name to the thing I've lost. But what's the use? It's gone. He's gone. Whatever existed between us is gone. All that's left is my promise to kill Snow. I tell myself this ten times a day" (195). Hope is the name of what she has lost. Collins shows that in the absence of hope, a realistic view of the corrupt world leads to self-corruption. In pursuit of her new goal of killing Snow, Katniss truly becomes the Mockingjay in its most ruthless form. After a time of playing by Coin's rules, the Mockingjay defies them and takes off through Capitol streets, aiming for Snow's mansion. The deaths of Finnick and the other District 13 soldiers disturb the girl Katniss, but not enough to stop her headlong spiral into hatred. Even the refusal to kill Peeta is mixed with doubtful motives because to kill Peeta would be to let Snow win, and the Mockingjay refuses to let that happen (Collins, *Mockingjay* 297).

The first clear example of the Mockingjay's power comes when Katniss kills a defenseless Capitol citizen. The description of the woman's smeared lipstick makes her appear foolish, inconsequential, and unworthy of pity (Collins, *Mockingjay* 314). Contrast this with Katniss' first kill during the initial Hunger Games where, despite having acted out of self-defense, Katniss feels lasting guilt over the death of Rue's murderer. In wondering about his mother and family, she humanizes this kill and recognizes the cost (Collins, *Hunger Games* 243). By the third book, the Mockingjay takes over; Katniss sees hatred rather than empathy as the only emotion keeping her going.

Prim's death continues Katniss' plummet into mental collapse. Now her mantra ends with "I am the Mockingjay. I brought down the Capitol. President Snow hates me. He killed my sister. Now I will kill him. And then the Hunger Games will be over" (Collins, *Mockingjay* 352). An accidental meeting with Snow causes confusion once again, as he refuses responsibility for Prim's death. Katniss sees Coin played her as a pawn. So when Coin proposes one last Hunger Games, only this time with Capitol children, the Mockingjay knows the danger Coin represents and takes steps to appear agreeable in order to eliminate the threat. Katniss votes for the last Hunger Games, horrifying Peeta. Yet Haymitch, with his words, "I'm with the Mockingjay," recognizes the origin of her choice (370). After assassinating Coin, the Mockingjay seeks her own death, and only Peeta stops Katniss from swallowing her nightlock pill. Her goal accomplished, the mutt Mockingjay lacks any reason to live. The compassionate girl, who felt sorrow for the loss of human life, has been destroyed by trauma and remade over and over again to serve the ends of those more powerful. Katniss is more Mockingjay than girl.

As the Mockingjay legend is kept alive by Katniss' passionate stand for justice, so the Mockingjay ensures Katniss' survival. Katniss, a creature of survival, melds almost seamlessly into the image of this bird who survives at all costs. The Mockingjay lives only to save those she loves and ruthlessly kills those in her way. Yet in the end, this image must die so that Katniss, the real Katniss loved by Peeta, can survive. After Coin's assassination, Katniss refuses food, and slowly, the Mockingjay part of her perishes. As her body dies, she unexpectedly begins to sing. This is the first time in all three books when Katniss sings without being prompted by others. Gant notes the soul healing effect of these songs. "Without the discord of other voices, she learns to trust her own voice above any other. As she passes through this dark night of the soul, she discovers the strength and beauty of her own voice" (Gant 95). While the songs are redemptive to the girl Katniss, they also signal the death of the Mockingjay.

Parts of Katniss and Peeta have died, and they will never be free of the costs of war, yet they make choices not to live in their pain. While Peeta plays a significant role in this, it's important to note that this healing is a decision Katniss makes. After a winter of being paralyzed by grief, Katniss sheds and burns her clothes in a symbolic, snake-like ridding of Snow's scent of roses. Together Peeta and Katniss begin a book of memories to commemorate those they lost. They "seal the pages with salt water and promises to live well to make their deaths count" (Collins, *Mockingjay* 387). The former mutts of the Capitol and District 13 choose to live not according to what society tells them, but according to their own understanding of right and wrong. Their love for each other is a choice, a choice mixed with confusion, pain, and the final realization that only through each other can they find hope.

Through Katniss as Spartacus, battle buddy, and Mockingjay, Collins wishes her readers to consider their own role and responsibility in the world. She says regarding her readers, "You have to at some time in your life begin to question the environment, the political situation around you and decide whether it's right or not and if it isn't, what part you're going to play in that" (Neary). Ironically, many of Collins' readers join in the Capitol's and District 13's disregard for human life by their reading of the books as mere entertainment. They contribute to the Hunger Games franchise through the consumption of clothes, soundtracks, and paraphernalia of all kinds. Since the release of the first film, many fans have become fans without having read the books at all. Many leave the theater entertained rather than thoughtful. Does Collins' message get lost in all the glitz? Surely some readers will miss Collins' message on human suffering and our responsibility not to turn away. The first two books were more palatable to fans, but the final book could be interpreted as disjointed, confusing, and traumatic.

For this reason, *Mockingjay* provides a masterful conclusion precisely because Katniss' disturbed narrative refuses to allow readers mere entertainment. It forces the question: should great literature be easy to understand? Should literature for young people be simplified? Should young adult literature challenge or reassure readers? Young readers need challenge rather than simplification. It would be wrong to make a book more acceptable simply because not all will understand. As Tony Watkins argues, we should provide stories that "make sense of cultural experience, constitute a kind of mapping, maps of meaning that enable our children to make sense of the world. They contribute to children's sense of identity, an identity that is simultaneously personal and social" (183).

Spartacus, the moral ambiguity of war, and the Katniss/Mockingjay dichotomy all weave together in Collins' arena. Within the Games, the truth is often distorted and always costly. The author presents a true picture of the ambiguity of war and the fear that in defeating evil, good risks becoming evil. Yet Collins wishes to leave her reader with hope. Pointedly, the epilogue is about Katniss and Peeta's children, who innocently play in the graveyard Meadow. Katniss wonders "how to tell them about that world without frightening them to death," yet she acknowledges that some day they will need to know, because through knowledge there is hope for change (Collins, *Mockingjay* 389). Determined not to be paralyzed by fearful memories, Katniss resolves to live in the memories of all the good actions others have done. In a manner reminiscent of John McCrae's poem, Katniss takes up a torch, but as a weapon of love rather than war. She keeps the faith of those who died by living well. Collins wishes for the bravery of Katniss to cause us—both young and old—to question, struggle, cry for the pain of this world, and then go forth to change it through how we live.

Works Cited

Allen, Jon G. *Coping with Trauma: A Guide to Self-understanding.* Arlington, VA: American Psychiatric Press, 1995. Print.

Collins, Suzanne. *Catching Fire.* New York: Scholastic, 2009. Print.

_____. *The Hunger Games.* New York: Scholastic, 2008. Print.

_____. *Mockingjay.* New York: Scholastic, 2010. Print.

Dominus, Susan. "Suzanne Collins' War Stories for Kids." *New York Times.* The New York Times Company, 8 Apr. 2011. Web. 4 Aug. 2011.

Gant, Tammy L. "Hungering for Righteousness; Music, Spirituality and Katniss Everdeen." *Of Bread, Blood and The Hunger Games: Critical Essays on the Suzanne Collins Trilogy.* Ed. Mary F. Pharr and Leisa A. Clark. Jefferson, NC: McFarland, 2012. 89–97. Print.

Margolis, Rick. "The Last Battle: With 'Mockingjay' on Its Way, Suzanne Collins Weighs in on Katniss and the Capitol." *School Library Journal.* SLJ, 1 Aug. 2010. Web. 31 Oct. 2015.

McCrae, John. "In Flanders Fields." 1915. *Poets.org.* Academy of American Poets, n.d. Web. 10 Jun. 2013.

Neary, Lynn. "Edgy, Violent Thrillers for The Teen-Age Set." *NPR Books.* NPR, 1 Sept. 2009. Web. 31 Oct. 2015. Transcript.

Orsingher, John M., Andrew T. Lopez, and Michael E. Rinehart. "Battlemind Training System: 'Armor for Your Mind.'" *U.S. Army Medical Department Journal* (2008): 66–71. Print.

Shaw, Brent D. *Spartacus and the Slave Wars: A Brief History with Documents.* Boston: Bedford/St. Martin's, 2001. Print.

Watkins, Tony. "Cultural Studies, New Historicism and Children's Literature." *Literature for Children: Contemporary Criticism.* Ed. Peter Hunt. London: Routledge, 1992. Print.

Zipes, Jack. "Second Thoughts on Socialization through Literature for Children." *The Lion and Unicorn* 5.1 (1981): 19–32. *Project MUSE.* Web. 27 May. 2013. Print.

The Presidents and Power: Machiavellian Elements in The Hunger Games Series

Todd Ide

Machiavelli wrote his famous dissertation on power, *The Prince*, in 1517. In this treatise, Machiavelli offers political leaders (royal or otherwise) rules for gaining, using, and keeping power. *The Prince* has been called "the greatest single study of power on record" (Berle 19). Since the sixteenth century, it has served as a blueprint for countless coups and acts of political maneuvering. Scholars see *The Prince* as a clear and often brutally honest explanation of the nature of power. Despite the characterization of Machiavelli's ideas as evil, *The Prince* continues to be read and studied widely.

It is important to note that this essay, like Machiavelli himself, does not in any way attempt to consider, defend, or justify the ethical or moral questions raised within *The Prince*. Machiavelli penned *The Prince* because he sought "to write something of use" and, as such, deemed

> it best to stick to [the] practical truth of things rather than to fancies. [For] many men have imagined republics and principalities that never existed at all. Yet the way men live is so far removed from the way they ought to live that anyone who abandons what is, for what should be, pursues his downfall rather than his preservation. (66)

Daniel Donno, in the introduction to his 1981 translation of *The Prince*, echoes this sentiment when he states that Machiavelli freed "political action from moral consideration" (6).

This separation between political action and morality plays out nowhere more vividly than within the pages of The Hunger Games series. Both President Snow and President Coin repeatedly employ Machiavellian ideals in their efforts to hold and/or gain power throughout the series. Through a close examination of the text, the reader will observe the ideas Machiavelli outlines within

The Prince and how these are portrayed within The Hunger Games. Further, it can be argued that Machiavelli's recommendations are the *only* logical course for President Snow and President Coin to pursue, given the situation outlined within the novels. Such an examination is valuable because it deepens our understanding of the complex political climate of the novels and provides an accessible framework to illustrate and develop the reader's understanding of Machiavellianism. Thus, we will examine the various lessons or themes Machiavelli sets out within *The Prince* with illustrative examples from The Hunger Games series.

Principalities and Maintaining Power

The first three chapters of *The Prince* focus on the type of principality or state that a ruler/prince[1] may find himself leading. Machiavelli writes that "All states and dominions that hold or have held sway over men are either republics or principalities" (7). Given the nature of *The Prince* and its intended audience, Machiavelli focuses on principalities. Further, he refines his analysis by dividing principalities into two main types. The first is hereditary principalities.[2] These are states that are currently ruled by a prince or hereditary family. Machiavelli argues that as long as the existing prince has "no extraordinary vices [that] make [him] hated" and he "is ordinarily industrious," these types of states are very difficult to conquer and hold (8).

It is the second type of principality identified by Machiavelli that presents a prince with challenges. These principalities are identified as "either entirely new ... or added to the hereditary state of the Prince who acquires them" (Machiavelli 7). A new principality is defined as a former republic or hereditary state that has been acquired through force of arms, fortune, or virtue.[3] In the case of a hereditary state, the former monarch has been replaced with a new prince. This second form also includes what Machiavelli calls mixed principalities. These former republics or hereditary principalities have been acquired in a manner similar to an entirely new principality, except that, in these instances, they have been annexed or added to an existing state's territory.

Despite the fact that the leaders of both Panem and District 13 hold the title of president, both can be considered monarchs in the context of this paper. It is clear within the novels that neither Panem nor District 13 is a democracy. This is first shown in *Catching Fire*, when Katniss and Peeta see President Snow presiding over the Second Quarter Quell twenty-five years earlier (195). Within a functioning democracy, it would be unheard of for an individual to serve twenty-five years or more in office.

Furthermore, in *Mockingjay*, Plutarch explains to Gale that if the rebellion is successful, the districts will "form a republic where the people of each district and the Capitol can elect their own representatives to be their voice in a centralized government" (83). Plutarch also adds that this sort of government has worked before. This can be read as implying that neither Panem nor District 13 is a functioning democracy. As a result, both President Coin and President Snow should be viewed as the monarchs of their respective principalities.

Due to this reality, the lessons Machiavelli offers on power, its acquisition, and its use manifest themselves throughout The Hunger Games series. Also, given the long rule of both President Snow and President Coin, both Panem and District 13 could be seen as well-established principalities. This, Machiavelli would argue, should mean that Snow and Coin are "legitimate Prince[s, and, as such, should have] fewer reasons and less need to harm [their] subjects, [and] it follows that [the people] would love [them] more" (8). However, this is not the case as both Snow and Coin are unable to control their own "extraordinary vices,"[4] resulting in their "mak[ing] them[selves] hated" (Machiavelli 8).

Despite the failure noted above, both Snow and Coin embrace the concepts within *The Prince*. President Snow is well versed in Machiavelli's ideas within these chapters. For example, Snow does attempt to strengthen his control over the districts through the establishment of colonies of a sort, with outside Peacekeepers supervising each. These are meant to serve as "the shackles of the state," without the necessity of keeping "a large force of men at arms and infantry there" (Machiavelli 12). While this is not a perfect analogy, as the Peacekeepers serve as both law enforcement and infantry, it is still an apt one.

Katniss' description of many of the District 12 Peacekeepers regularly purchasing her illegally acquired game (Collins, *Hunger Games* 5) and of Darius in *Catching Fire* (11) demonstrates that, at least in District 12, some Peacekeepers do become part of the community. The colonist analogy is shown to be accurate at least as it relates to the Peacekeepers of District 12 based on the impact their replacement by the Capitol has on the community. This results in a dramatic shift in the life of the community. These newly arrived Peacekeepers become the infantry that Machiavelli warns against. They not only disrupt the workings of the District, but also significantly worsen the situation by increasing the injuries suffered by the populace at the hands of the Capitol. This increases not only the resentment, but also the hostility the citizens feel toward the Capitol and Snow. Further, these additional Peacekeepers consume more of the "revenues of the state in order to guard it … and much greater harm is done" by their presence in these new districts than gains made by the Capitol with these actions. Each of these impacts undermines Snow's ability to maintain his grip on power.

Snow's Machiavellian streak is further demonstrated by his use of the Dark Days as a pretext to justify the torture and murder of opponents and his tyranny over the districts. The Games and many of his actions following the beginning of the second uprising are portrayed by Snow as being necessary to "secure his position [and that of the state] by punishing offenders, clarifying suspicions, and strengthen[ing]" his control over Panem (Machiavelli 10). However, Snow follows this dictate for far too long and at the expense of pursuing other aspects of the advice offered within *The Prince*. As a result, it becomes one of his "extraordinary vices [that] make him hated" (8).

The leadership of President Coin in District 13 is similarly marked by Machiavellian concepts. For example, Coin clearly understands that "a new [monarch] must always inflict harm on those over whom [she] rules, both from [her] men at arms and with countless other injuries [her] new conquest entails" (Machiavelli

10). It may be argued that Coin could also be seen as both an established ruler *and* a new monarch, due to the recent large influx of new refugees arriving from Panem. Throughout *Mockingjay*, Coin is shown to be a cold and calculating leader, who embraces the use of brutal military tactics and offers little mercy to her enemies. This is clearly demonstrated by her willingness to engage in total warfare against Panem with little concern for civilian casualties.[5]

President Coin also demonstrates her adherence to Machiavellian principles in her dealings with Katniss. Coin understands that "men change rulers willingly, hoping to better their lot, and this belief makes them take [up] arms against their ruler" (Machiavelli 10). To achieve this end, Coin sees the value of Katniss as a symbol that will unite Panem behind her and District 13 in this civil war. However, Coin realizes that she will not be able to "maintain the friendship of those who helped put [her in power], since [she] will not be able to satisfy them as they expected, nor can [she] treat them with strong medicine, since [she is] obligated to them" (Machiavelli 10). In an effort to firmly establish that she is in control and what happens if she is not obeyed, Coin orders the imprisonment and torture of Katniss' prep team (Collins, *Mockingjay* 46–50). This message is not lost on Katniss.

Finally, within these first three chapters, Machiavelli offers a warning to all those who might assist a would-be prince in gaining power. He states that there is "a general rule which never, or rarely, fails: that whoever is the cause of another's becoming powerful will come to ruin himself, because that power is created by him through either his industriousness or his force, and both of these qualities are suspect to the one who has become powerful" (Machiavelli 16–17). President Snow proves this rule when it is revealed that his rise to power was marked not only by the "mysterious [poisoning] death[s] of [his] adversaries" but also the untimely demise in a similar manner of "his allies who had the potential to become threats" (Collins, *Mockingjay* 171).

President Coin also demonstrates the reliability of this rule in a number of ways. One of the first instances is the proviso that Coin adds when she announces the granting of amnesty for past

Hunger Games victors, provided Katniss fulfills and meets all of her responsibilities. This addition, Katniss comes to realize, is an effort by Coin to be "the first to publicly brand [her] as a threat" (Collins, *Mockingjay* 59) and to "publicly remind her people that [Katniss is] not in control" (91). Further, Coin demonstrates the rule's efficacy through her efforts to kill Katniss. Coin's first attempt comes when she assigns a mentally unstable Peeta to Katniss' unit during the invasion of the Capitol in hopes that he will become unhinged again, then attack and kill her (261). When this fails, Coin orders Katniss and the Star Squad to clear "a special block [that] has been set aside for" them in an effort to get footage for additional propaganda films (273). However, the block proves to be far more lethal than they have been led to believe, costing lives and cutting off the survivors from the rest of the rebel army. Katniss survives, but only barely.

Fortune vs. Virtue

Machiavelli returns several times within *The Prince* to the concepts of fortune and virtue. As has been previously noted, Machiavelli argues in favor of virtue over fortune. For it is virtue that will enable a prince to build a stable foundation for his state, thereby allowing him to overcome future adversity and shifts in fortune. Both President Snow and President Coin take this maxim to heart. Throughout the novels, both are seen utilizing all of their skill and intelligence in an effort to maintain and/or expand their positions of power. Neither relies on the fickle nature of fortune.

In Chapter 7 of *The Prince*, Machiavelli demonstrates how to use underlings to enhance and maintain one's power. Machiavelli refers to the example of Messer Remirro de Orco to illustrate this lesson. De Orco was selected by Cesare Borgia to bring order to a state that he had newly acquired. He was a "cruel and decisive man," who quickly achieved his assigned task (Machiavelli 31). However, Borgia feared that the "rigorous measures [used by de Orco would] generate a certain amount of hatred toward him, in order to purge the minds of the people and to win them over for himself completely[;] he wanted to show that if any cruelty had taken place, it did not come from him, but from the harsh nature of his minister" (31). To this end, Borgia ordered the execution of de Orco and had his body "put in the piazza at Cesena in two pieces, with a piece of wood and a bloody knife by his side. The ferocity of such a spectacle left those people both satisfied and stunned" (31).

Political leaders, fictional and real alike, have embraced the spirit of this piece of advice. While most underlings of today's modern political leaders are not executed and put on public display, this does not mean that they are not symbolically sacrificed. Instead, they are offered up for public humiliation by being fired and/or prosecuted, all in an effort to distance their actions from the "official" policies of the president or other leader. At the same time, these actions provide the type of political cover and public accountability that is necessary to preserve the power of the president, that is, the prince.

Both President Snow and President Coin readily employ underlings to do the dirty work necessary to achieve their goals. While these individuals are held to account for their failures,[6] nowhere within the novels are they punished for excessive cruelty or brutality. Instead, both seem to encourage their subordinates to adopt the approach of de Orco. Snow criticizes Seneca Crane's weakness and the sentimentality that prevents him from killing both Katniss and Peeta at the end of the 74th Hunger Games. Coin demonstrates this principle through her ironfisted rule of District 13 and the harsh punishment that is meted out to anyone who opposes her or violates even the most minor of laws.

Armies, Fortresses, and the Study of War

In addition to virtue, Machiavelli espoused the necessity of any prince to spend considerable time and energy thinking of and preparing for war. *The Prince* begins this discussion by making it clear that princes must have "an abundance of men or of money, so that they can put together [a] sufficient army [to] fight a battle in the field against anyone who comes to attack them" (Machiavelli 46). Those monarchs who are unable to do so "are obliged to seek refuge within their walls and defend them" (46). A prince who has "a strong city and does not make himself hated, cannot be attacked, and if

---

there were someone who attacked them, he [the attacker] would depart with shame" (47).

Machiavelli's advice again plays out within the pages of The Hunger Games series. First, the Capitol establishes a new military stronghold (The Nut),

> directly after the Dark Days, when the Capitol had lost 13 and was desperate for a new underground stronghold. [The Capitol] had some of their military resources situated on the outskirts of the Capitol itself—nuclear missiles, aircraft, troops—but a significant chunk of their power was now under an enemy's control. (Collins, *Mockingjay* 192)

This fact, combined with the just-quelled uprising, necessitated that the Capitol leaders fortify the city to maintain their hold on power. These strongholds, combined with the Capitol's vast wealth and the fact that many of District 2's residents serve in the Capitol's military, enable President Snow to field an army.

These fortifications also support Machiavelli's contention that a "Prince who fears his own people more than foreigners ought to build fortresses" (Machiavelli 92). Machiavelli argues that "the best fortress that exists is not to be hated by the people, for even though you have fortresses, they will not save you if the people hate you, because when once the people have taken up arms, they will never lack outsiders to come to their assistance" (92). President Snow ignores this advice and instead places his trust "in fortresses, [and] thinks it of little [concern] to be hated by the people," much to his detriment (92).

The leaders of District 13 and President Coin take a similar course of action. Despite having ample weapons and equipment they seized from the Capitol, District 13 lacks the manpower or money to field an army. Unable to do so, District 13 fortifies its city and lays in provisions to prepare for a possible attack (Collins, *Mockingjay* 17). Coin and the other leaders of District 13 make no efforts to engage with the Capitol militarily until the districts of Panem are ready to rebel once again. This provides Coin with the soldiers necessary to field an army.

Throughout the chapters of his treatise, Machiavelli also stresses the need for a prince not only to constantly prepare for war but to become a student of the art of war. He argues that "a prince, therefore, must have no other object or thought, or take up anything as his profession, except war and its rules and discipline, for that is the only art that befits one who commands" (Machiavelli 63). Machiavelli even goes so far as to suggest that if princes think "more of luxurious living than of arms, they have lost their state" (63).

President Snow lost sight of this over the course of his reign. Life in the Capitol offered much in the way of comfort, luxury, and a host of other distractions. This lack of focus by President Snow ultimately costs him his kingdom. In contrast, District 13's existence requires constant fear of another attack by the Capitol. The result of this was "strenuous discipline, and constant vigilance against any further attacks" (Collins, *Mockingjay* 17). A lifestyle that forced President Coin to condition herself for the hardships of war also made her a student of it.

The Ruin of Extravagance

Not only does the luxurious lifestyle of President Snow take his focus off the study of war, but it causes him and the citizens of the Capitol to engage in the type of "sumptuous display" that eventually requires a prince to "consume all his wealth in such activities" (Machiavelli 68). As a result, Snow is forced "to impose a heavy tax burden on the people, and become an extortionist, and do everything that can be done to get money" (Machiavelli 68). This action causes him to become greatly despised by his subjects. An example of the extravagance enjoyed by the Capitol occurs during Katniss and Peeta's Victory Tour. During the banquet hosted by President Snow, Flavius and Octavia overhear that Katniss is too full to eat anymore. In response, they take her over "to a table that holds tiny stemmed wine glasses filled with clear liquid" and explain that if she drinks the liquid, it will cause her to vomit, thereby emptying her stomach, and allowing her to continue to eat (Collins, *Catching Fire* 79). The absurdity of this is not lost on either Katniss or Peeta, who have witnessed and known the hunger of those in the districts.

Love, Hate, Fear, and Cruelty

It is the advice offered by Machiavelli in Chapter 17 of *The Prince* that draws the most criticism and condemnation. The first lesson Machiavelli offers comes in the example of the King of Syracuse, who calls together all of the nobility in his kingdom, and "at a prearranged signal, [they are all]... killed by his soldiers" (Machiavelli 36). Thus, the King rids himself of potential opponents and is then able to rule unchallenged. Machiavelli acknowledges this action as an example of cruelty. Cruelty, Machiavelli writes, can be used "well or badly. Those can be called well used (if it is permissible to say 'well' about evil) which are done at one stroke, out of the need to make oneself secure, and which afterwards are not persisted in, but are converted into the greatest benefits possible for one's subjects" (39).

In this regard, both President Snow and President Coin fail to use cruelty well. Snow, for instance, allows these incidents to "grow over time rather than being extinguished"; this is shown through the continued staging of the Hunger Games and the suffering of and injustices against the citizens of Panem at the hands of the Peacekeepers (Machiavelli 39). President Coin does little better. Coin continually renews the cruelties she heaps upon Katniss through her mistreatment of Katniss' prep team, her initial insistence that past Hunger Games victors be tried as criminals, her attempts to kill Katniss, and finally, her murder of Prim. As a result, Coin fails to reassure Katniss or win her support. Both Snow and Coin would have been wise to remember that any ruler who inflicts "fresh and continual injuries" will never be able to make his or her "subjects the foundation of [his or her] rule," and will "always [be] obliged to hold a knife in his [or her] hand" out of fear of the subjects (Machiavelli 39).

Within *The Prince*, Machiavelli explains that a ruler should strive "to keep his word and to live with integrity," but that it is important to realize that there are "princes [who] have done great things who have had little regard for keeping their word" (75). These individuals have realized

> that there are two methods of fighting, one with laws, the other with force: the first one is proper to man, the second to beasts; but because the first one often does not suffice, one has to have recourse to the second. Therefore, it is necessary for the Prince to know well how to use the beast and the man. (Machiavelli 75)

Machiavelli extends this analogy by explaining that a prince must be able to choose between the fox and the lion.

It is essential for a prince to be able to use the cunning of the fox to recognize and avoid traps and use the strength and ferocity of the lion to frighten off wolves or other would-be attackers (Machiavelli 75). Part of this ability is to know which to use. For example, a fox must be able to recognize when he "cannot, must not, keep his word, when keeping it would work against him, and when the reasons which made him promise it have been removed" (75). This is especially true since men, being the "sadly wicked" creatures that they are, "would not keep their word to you" (75). A prince must "be able to color over this character well, and to be a great hypocrite and dissembler; and men are so simple and so obedient to present necessities that he who deceives will always find someone who'll let himself be deceived" (76).

Both President Snow and President Coin demonstrate their ability to be both human and beast. President Snow demonstrates his ability to shift from man to beast throughout the series. One such example is Snow's order to have Haymitch's family and girlfriend killed, both to warn any other victor of the Games who may cause problems and to punish him for being too clever (Collins, *Mockingjay* 172–73). Snow displays his cunning when Katniss attempts to convince him of her love for Peeta. In reality, Snow wants to know if Peeta can be used as a weapon against her (Collins, *Mockingjay* 156). These incidents, as well as many others, are each designed by Snow to either expand or secure his hold on power.

Coin is equally skilled at demonstrating her human and beastly aspects. Indeed, Katniss recognizes this trait within Coin. As a result of this realization, Katniss demands that Coin give her promise of immunity for the other victors publicly, in front of what remains of the citizens of District 12 and those of District 13 (Collins, *Mockingjay* 40). Near the end of *Mockingjay*, President Coin further demonstrates her bestial side through her use of a false flag[7] tactic to eliminate any of the final vestiges of support that Snow may have enjoyed, and, as a possible side benefit, to destroy Katniss emotionally.

Machiavelli cautions a would-be prince against both being cruel and using mercy badly (71). A prince, therefore, "must not mind acquiring a reputation for cruelty" if it means keeping his principality united, loyal, and orderly because such actions are necessary in order to protect the community as a whole. Further, "a new prince cannot avoid a reputation for cruelty, because new states are always full of dangers" (Machiavelli 71). It is within this section that Machiavelli poses one of his most infamous questions: "Whether it is better to be loved than feared, or the contrary" (71).

Machiavelli's "reply is that one should like to be both the one and the other, but as it is difficult to bring them together, it is much safer to be feared than to be loved if one of the two has to be lacking" (71–72). Machiavelli refers again to a fact that he noted earlier, that men, in general, cannot be trusted to act as they have promised and will instead take "every opportunity to serve their self-interest" (72). Machiavelli argues that "Men love at their own will and fear at the will of the prince, [so] a wise prince must build his foundation on what is his own and not what belongs to others; he must only contrive to escape hatred" (73).

In *The Prince*, Machiavelli explains that a ruler can avoid hatred if he does not "touch the goods and the women of his citizens and subjects,… for men sooner forget the death of their father than the loss of their patrimony" (72). Unfortunately, President Snow does not heed this advice. While it is very clear throughout the entire series that Snow is widely feared, his actions have made him deeply despised and hated. Snow looks the other way concerning atrocities such as Cray's exploitation of starving women for sexual purposes[8] and acts as a pimp when he forces past Hunger Games victors, such as Finnick Odair, to prostitute themselves to the highest bidder (Collins, *Catching Fire*; *Mockingjay*). However, it is not these actions alone that make Snow hated.

Machiavelli left out the necessity of a prince to leave unmolested not only the women and property of his subjects, but also their children. Snow forces the citizens of Panem not only to sacrifice twenty-four of their offspring each year as participants in blood sport for the entertainment of the Capitol but also to watch the gruesome spectacle nightly. This, combined with the "fresh and continual injuries" that life in the districts inflicts on his subjects, guarantees that Snow is deeply loathed and hated (Machiavelli 39).

As far as can be discerned from the novels in the series, Coin is neither loved nor hated, and it is unclear whether or not she is feared. The description of District 13 in *Mockingjay* mentions the "strenuous discipline" of the district (17). Additionally, there are some allusions indicating that Coin may not enjoy widespread support among the people of District 13. For example, Katniss wonders why Coin would feel the need to secure District 13's weapons with two different levels of security and a total of eight separate biometric scans (Collins, *Mockingjay* 67). While Katniss may be correct in her guess that these measures may have been put in place in response to the influx of Panem refugees, the complexity of these measures leads one to question whether life in District 13 is as harmonious as it seems, or whether the appearance of harmony is merely another façade.

Conclusion

Roughly five hundred years separate the publication of *The Prince* and Suzanne Collins' *The Hunger Games*. No longer is the world broken up into individual city-states and kingdoms ruled by nobility. Instead, we find ourselves in a time when republics, which used to be the exception, are now the norm. Some would argue that Machiavelli's work is no longer relevant to these modern times. Indeed, they would suggest that the observations found in *The Prince* are not relevant to today's world. They would dismiss them as reflections of the violent and often unstable times in which Machiavelli lived.

There is some truth to this view. However, I believe there is still much to be learned from Machiavelli's work. He was right when he wrote that men live far removed from the way they ought to. The sad reality is that ethical and moral considerations seldom guide the actions of rulers and nations. One only needs to watch the news on any given night to see these principles play out on the screen.

The desire of some in humanity to seize, hold, and expand their power and control over others is not new. Indeed, it stretches all the way back to the beginning of civilization. It should not be surprising, then, that the decisions and actions made by both President Snow and President Coin follow this same well-worn path within the pages of The Hunger Games series. While fictional, these actions are not random choices made by the author. Instead, these decisions are shaped and informed by something much more basic and ingrained within humanity's genetic code: our desire for power, our desire to control our environment and those around us, and our desire to rule over all we survey.

This is not to say that we are doomed to follow this path. I like to believe that we can be better than our basest desires, that we have the ability to rise above what Machiavelli saw so long ago. To do this, however, requires us to be familiar with our darker nature, to be able to recognize when we are on the path of *The Prince* and, when we realize this, to turn back, so that we can change course and become a better version of ourselves.

Notes

1. I recognize that this paper often uses only the masculine pronoun or reference. This was a conscious decision made to reflect the style used by Machiavelli, one which reflected the times in which he lived and the limited public role that women were allowed to play. However, there are examples of female political and business leaders in the past and present, as well as within literary works, whose actions and decisions could easily be labeled as Machiavellian. I do deviate from this when referring to President Coin.

2. Machiavelli uses this term to distinguish areas formally ruled by a prince or other hereditary leader.

3. Virtue, as Machiavelli uses it, is not the moral, ethical, or religious concept that many associate with this term. Machiavelli's concept of virtue is an individual's ability to pursue whatever course of action necessary to achieve one's goal or objective(s). Machiavelli employs a very narrowly constructed concept of virtue, one based on political necessity, rather than the Christian ethics of his time.

4. Coin's vice is her thirst for unquestioning obedience and hunger for power. It could be argued that Snow's vices include lavish living. However, I would argue that his vice also is his desire for absolute power and control.

5. For example, the use of Gale and Beetee's bomb designs was intended to inflict maximum casualties by incorporating a second explosion—one that seeks to kill individuals trying to escape or come to the aid of those that are wounded (Collins, *Mockingjay* 185–86).

6. This is demonstrated by the fate of Seneca Crane (Collins, *Catching Fire* 20).

7. A false flag operation is a term used to describe a military or other type of operation that is carried out in such a way that it appears that one group or nation is carrying out the attack, when in reality it is being done by a different group or nation. This is done to shift blame and to hide who is truly responsible for the act. In this instance, the false flag refers to Snow's contention that Coin ordered the firebombing and used a hovercraft with the Capitol's seal to make it appear as if he (Snow) ordered it.

8. Katniss recalls that Cray would lure "starving young women into his bed for money" and that during "really bad times, the hungriest would gather at his door at nightfall, vying for the chance to earn a few coins to feed their families by selling their bodies" (Collins, *Catching Fire* 114–15).

Works Cited

Berle, Adolf A. *Power*. New York: Harcourt Brace & World, 1969. Print.

Collins, Suzanne. *Catching Fire*. New York: Scholastic, 2009. Print.

_____. *The Hunger Games*. New York: Scholastic, 2008. Print.

_____. *Mockingjay*. New York: Scholastic, 2010. Print.

Donno, Daniel. "Introduction." *The Prince*. Ed. and trans. Daniel Donno. New York: Bantam Classic, 1981. Print.

Machiavelli, Niccolo. *The Prince*. 1517. *The Prince and Other Writings*. Trans. Wayne A. Rebhorn. New York: Barnes & Noble Classics, 2003. Print.

The Hunger Games Series as Text for the Democracy, Justice, and Civic Engagement Classroom_____

Sandra Via

Introduction

In fall 2011, I was asked to teach a course called "Practicing Democracy, Justice, and Civic Engagement" (DJCE). The DJCE course is separate from a traditional American politics/government course and is the second of a two-course series (the first course is titled "Theories of Democracy, Justice, and Civic Engagement"). As I considered the content of the course, I began to think about the topics that I would incorporate in my lectures and the texts that I would use to supplement the course material. I was admittedly at a loss as to how I would convey the practice of these concepts in a way that would differ from a traditional American government or theory course. I knew that a traditional textbook was not going to be a good choice. I began scouring academic journals, academic blogs, and news articles for short texts that I could assign, but I still did not have an overarching text that I could use throughout the course. As I continued to think about a textbook, I thought about my students and my own experiences as an undergraduate, and I began to realize that a traditional approach was not necessarily the most effective pedagogical technique. It was soon after that I noticed the increasing media hype surrounding the anticipated theatrical release of the first Hunger Games film during the same semester that the course would be taught. I had read The Hunger Games and, like so many, became enthralled with the series' plot and characters. It then occurred to me that The Hunger Games series included all of the concepts—more specifically, included *violations* of all the concepts—that were going to be the focus of the course.

This chapter chronicles the approach that I take to apply The Hunger Games trilogy to the DJCE classroom. In the first section of the chapter, I will discuss the role of critical pedagogy in my application of the trilogy and the importance of including popular culture into the political science classroom generally. I will then outline the structure of my course, providing a discussion of some of the issues that I address. The chapter will conclude with a brief examination of the successes and challenges of teaching the trilogy in the course.

Critical Literacy and Democracy, Justices, and Civic Engagement

Concepts such as democracy, justice, and civic engagement are common in political science courses. They are central themes in the study of American government, international relations, and political theory or philosophy. However, they are also concepts that are only touched on during a typical fifteen-week semester course. This, of course, is not due to lack of focus on the subject, but rather a need to cover so many topics that pertain to each theme. Faculty hope that most college students have been introduced to these concepts prior to attending college, but often many students either forget the concepts, were not provided an opportunity to thoroughly engage the concepts, or have become apathetic, like so many in American society. Many college students then come to think of democracy and justice in terms of buzzwords and synonymous with liberty and freedom, but yet not fully comprehending their meaning or potential impact on society; furthermore, civic engagement is typically equated with only community service. Liberty and freedom are then reduced to superficial understandings of freedom of speech, press, religion, free elections, and the right to own private property, while equating civic engagement with community service prompts students to think of the concept as picking up trash, collecting food, working in a soup kitchen, or other tasks. None of these parallels is wrong. Civic engagement can involve community service, but that is only part of what civic engagement can entail. Freedom and liberty are vital components to democracy and justice, but do students really understand the concepts if they are drilled into them in an American government course or through readings of Plato or Locke?

Cynthia Weber, a feminist international relations scholar, has authored a textbook that seeks to explain, through films, international relations (IR) theories—or myths, as she calls them. According to Weber, theories such as anarchism, realism, and liberalism are myths—products of culture and ideology that converge to create apparent truths about how we see and interpret the world (8). Even though Weber is focused on IR theories, her reasoning can be applied to the concepts of democracy, justice, and civic engagement as well. Just as realism and liberalism result from cultural and ideological understandings of the world, so do the concepts of democracy, justice, and civic engagement.

Weber argues that international relations can be thought of as "other worlds" (9). She contends that, "we are more likely to recognize and be able to interrogate myths in worlds in which we do not live—other 'cultures,' other times, other locations." (9). For Weber, these "other worlds" can be found in films. Other political scholars have seen the benefit of melding popular culture, particularly film, television, and even video games, with political science course content. In my past American Government and Public Policy courses, I have made reference to several television shows, such as *The West Wing*, *Newsroom*, and, recently, *House of Cards*. International relations scholars and instructors like Weber have approached the discipline through the Harry Potter books and films or TV series such as *Battlestar Galactica*, *Star Trek*, and *Game of Thrones*; sample texts include Daniel H. Nexon and Iver B. Neumann's *Harry Potter and International Relations* (2013), Anthony (Jack) Gierzynski's *Harry Potter and the Millennials: Research Methods and Politics of the Muggle Generation* (2013), Nicholas Kiersey and Iver B. Neumann's *Battlestar Galactica and International Relations* (2013) and Stephen Benedict Dyson's *Otherworldly Politics: The International Relations of Star Trek, Game of Thrones, and Battlestar Galactica* (2015).

However, visual media are not the only means that can be used to engage students in the classroom. Many of these "other worlds" were first presented to audiences as literary fiction, novels that gained so much popularity they were later adapted by Hollywood into blockbuster films. Therefore, the use of popular literature in the classroom offers students the same opportunities to delve into other worlds and cultures, while applying those concepts to their own realities. I assisted professors in graduate school who used novels such as *The Bluest Eye* (Toni Morrison, 1970), *White Teeth* (Zadie Smith, 2000), and *What Is the What* (Dave Eggers, 2006) in the classroom during my time as a graduate teaching assistant. Each of these texts was employed as a means of explaining race relations, nationalism, genocide, and other concepts in a context accessible to college students. As I have grown as an educator, I have looked for other literary fictions that would be appropriate for the classroom. Moreover, I have consulted research on critical pedagogy and critical literacy, which encourages the incorporation of popular culture into the classroom. Ernest Morrell posits, "popular culture can help students deconstruct dominant narratives and contend with oppressive practices in hopes of achieving a more egalitarian and inclusive society" (72). The Hunger Games trilogy, which was conceived from Suzanne Collins' own perceptions of war coverage and reality television, is the perfect text to challenge students to think about the political, social, and economic reality in which they live (Collins, "A Conversation").

Course Overview
The DJCE course is set up much like a traditional course. At the beginning of the semester, students are provided a syllabus outlining their assignments, the topics/issues that will be covered throughout the semester, and the reading list. The assignments include in-class participation and discussion, quizzes, a midterm and final exam, a service/social-action project, a reflection paper on the service/social-action project, and finally a synthesis Hunger Games paper and presentation. The exams and quizzes assess whether the students are doing all of the reading, if they understand the plot and characters of The Hunger Games books, and if they can apply course themes to the readings. However, the most emphasis in the course is placed on the service/action project and the paper and presentation.

As mentioned earlier, civic engagement is more than just doing a simple community service project. I could call a local animal or homeless shelter, nursing home, or food bank and set up a service project for my students. However, I believe that, as college students and young adults, students should be cognizant of and research the disadvantaged, oppressed, and needy groups in their own community. Therefore, they are required to design and implement their own service project during the semester. These projects must address a social, political, and/or economic need but also implement students' own academic and situated[1] knowledge into the projects. Amber Simmons notes, "social action projects require students to take their learning into the community to benefit the greater good through the use of their learned skills" (25). Because the students have autonomy over their projects, they are not only able to address a societal need that they feel is important, but they have also taken a step towards becoming more socially and politically cognizant of their own roles in shaping their community. It is any educator's hope that including this type of experiential component in the classroom will "allow students to express feelings and desire for change" (Simmons 25), as well as to become leaders in prompting others to become active in their community. My students have created and implemented several different types of projects: spearheading college-wide clothing drives for a local church, creating campus public service announcements about study aids and tutoring for struggling students, becoming an Ally and creating safe-zones[2] on campus, and coordinating a fundraiser for Special Love.[3] The reflection papers are designed to encourage students to think about social, political, and economic factors that led them to choose their project topic, as well as reflecting on how the project impacted their worldview. I do not require that students make connections between The Hunger Games trilogy and their service/social-action projects, but many of them still do so in their reflection papers.

The course discussions, which do involve The Hunger Games series directly, provide the impetus for students to begin thinking about how they want to frame their synthesis paper and presentation. Each week, students are assigned a portion of The Hunger Games series, as well as supplemental readings pertaining to a topic or issue relevant to the course. The topics discussed in this course are not limited to an American politics focus. Each course theme is relevant to communities and governments around the world. Therefore, I have incorporated into the course topics such as the civil rights movement; civil liberties (freedom of speech, association, religion, etc.); international human rights and war; the women's movement (domestically and internationally); the Occupy Wall Street movement; the Arab Spring; poverty and hunger; challenges to democracy; and the torture debate. Other topics related to The Hunger Games series that can easily be incorporated into the class include sex trafficking, slavery, child soldiers (Simmons), and issues of environmental justice (Burke), to name a few.

Some students are familiar with these topics through exposure from other classes or life experiences, but most have never experienced these types of injustices, nor do they imagine them happening in their own communities. For example, in Western democracies such as the United States (US), we do not expect citizens to experience extreme, abject poverty, but unfortunately it does occur. The setting of *The Hunger Games*, specifically District 12, is rural Appalachia (Collins, 41). This region of the US has a long history of poverty, and the fictional district of Katniss' birth and home are no different. What we find in "the Seam" is rampant poverty, where inhabitants experience true, sometimes debilitating hunger, disease, and poverty. Early in the series, the reader learns that Katniss has never ridden in a car before and does not have running hot water or a shower at her childhood home (something she first experiences on the train to the Capitol after the first reaping) (Collins, 42).

Throughout all three novels, Collins highlights the poverty of several districts through the emphasis she places on food. From the onset of the story, Katniss does not hide the fact that her family and those in District 12 suffer from hunger. Moreover, the reader is able to see the disproportionate amount of power held by the Capitol in Katniss' encounters with food. For example, during her first meal with Cinna, a lavish selection of food appears at the push of a button.

Katniss wonders, "What must it be like, I wonder, to live in a world where food appears at the press of a button?" (Collins, *The Hunger Games* 65). In *Catching Fire*, the reader learns that food in the Capitol is perceived so cavalierly that people drink a tonic to make them vomit so that they are able to eat more food (Collins 79–80). This particular example typically prompts the most astonishment from my classes. It is at this point that I ask them to think about the dual nature of the series' title. The actual Hunger Games is a fight to the death for the tributes, but it is a different battle for those from their districts. Not only are they rooting for the survival of a child in their district (or their own child) to win the Hunger Games, but they are also rooting for their own survival. If one of the district's tributes wins the Hunger Games, the entire district benefits with a holiday of free food and entertainment, including a Parcel Day each month, "in which food packages were delivered to every person in the district" and each household received bags of grain and cans of oil (Collins, *Catching Fire* 25). All of these examples are couched in readings and lecture material regarding poverty and hunger in the United States and abroad.

Two supplemental readings unique to this course and applicable to The Hunger Games trilogy are *Letter from Birmingham Jail* by Martin Luther King Jr. and *The Ballot and the Bullet* by Malcolm X. These two readings are assigned at the beginning of the semester and discussed in their original context early in the course. As the course progresses and the students have read further into the trilogy, we have a class discussion about the parallels between events in the texts, as well as Katniss' character and actions, and the content of the two essays by King and Malcolm X. More specifically, students are asked to draw parallels between Katniss' and the rebelling districts' struggle for freedom with that of the civil rights movement as presented from King's and Malcolm X's varying perspectives. First, the students are asked to think about how King and Malcolm X frame injustice and oppression. In each essay, King and Malcolm X acknowledge and condemn the injustices that have been committed against African American communities. King stresses the difference between just and unjust laws, which can be applied to the ways in which the Capitol inflicts unjust laws upon the districts. King notes that an unjust law is many things, including "Any law that degrades human personality" and a law that is "out of harmony with the moral law" (King). The laws of the Capitol are beyond unjust. They advocate the murder of children under the guise of history, purposefully starve citizens and deprive them of other natural resources, enforce slave labor, disproportionately punish "criminals," deny voting rights to the districts, censor communications, and much more. Malcolm X makes reference to some of the same injustices as King, but he also likens the injustices foisted upon African Americans to those associated with colonialism. In many respects, the Capitol is a colonial power controlling the colonized districts. The way in which citizens of the Capitol view the tributes demonstrates a colonial power structure. For example, Effie Trinket compares the tributes from District 12 the year prior to Katniss and Peeta's first reaping to savages (Collins, *The Hunger Games* 44), while Flavius, a member of Katniss' makeup team, notes that after an extensive beauty regimen with the team, she "almost look[s] like a human being" (Collins, *The Hunger Games* 62). Such statements are reminiscent of how the colonizers view the colonized as less than human, barbaric, etc. during the colonial era. Another approach to take when discussing these essays is through an examination of the symbolic image that King, Malcolm X, and Katniss take on through their various movements. King is a symbol of peace, shrouded in the practice of civil disobedience (King), whereas Malcolm X is a symbol of the movement that is willing to embrace violence if necessary to achieve freedom from his oppressors. Students are asked to explain which approach Katniss represents as the Mockingjay.

Once students have concluded reading the series, we discuss the future of Panem. Many students tend to note that at the end of the narrative, Panem has still not grown into the democracy that it could be. Citing President Coin's deception at the end of *Mockingjay*, students argue that while some freedoms may have been achieved through the rebellion, the fundamental facets of a true democracy, such as a free election, do not occur until Coin's assassination (Collins, *Mockingjay* 372). Interestingly, this is the point in the semester that students begin to tether democracy and justice with compassion and empathy. Many are appalled that the majority of the remaining victors—including Katniss—vote to have a final Hunger Games consisting of the prominent children of the Capitol.

These are only a few examples of the topics and readings discussed in class. As the class progresses, more readings are discussed in the context of real world application and their application to The Hunger Games books. Ultimately, they set the stage for the students' final paper and presentation. Once the course draws toward an end, students begin to work on their synthesis paper and a presentation. Students are required to create a unique analysis of the entire Hunger Games series, relative to our course content. However, the students must include an original contribution to the application of The Hunger Games series to the course themes. They are encouraged to be creative in their papers and their presentations. Many of the students have done character analyses, explaining how specific characters embody one theme of the course throughout the entire book series. For instance, one student analyzed specific characters, such as Peeta, Katniss, Gale, and Cinna, as the embodiment of democracy, justice, and civic engagement. Others separated the books into the three theme areas. For example, some students argued that *The Hunger Games* best represented the lack of democracy, *Catching Fire* further emphasized the injustices of Panem, and *Mockingjay* illustrated civic engagement through a just rebellion. The presentations have also been extremely well received and executed and are often very creative. Admittedly, many students deliver PowerPoint presentations, but others include audience participation or use a completely different medium. For example, one student, who was usually not the most engaged student, became so enthralled with the assignment that he asked if he could create a pre-recorded video presentation with the entire class rather than doing an individual presentation. I was reluctant at first, but allowed it since the class was small in number. The result was one of the best presentations I have had during my time as a college instructor. The students produced a news program, with each student acting as a journalist reporting his own presentation as a "news" story.

Success and Challenges When Teaching *The Hunger Games*

The primary purpose of the DJCE course is to encourage students to think about the course themes critically and in ways that apply to their own understanding of the world. The best way for educators to do this is through reading assignments. However, as many educators know, it is difficult to get students to read an assigned text, let alone do so as an active reader constantly interrogating the subject matter of the course in conjunction with the content of the text. Each semester that I have taught this course, the use of The Hunger Games series as active reading texts was a momentous success. I was shocked and delighted to find that each student in the course had actually completed the reading, and many had done so prior to the due dates. Several students had read ahead of their peers, completed assignments early, and were a little disgruntled when they could not discuss sections of the text that were assigned for later in the semester.[4] In addition to The Hunger Games readings, the students had also read the majority of the supplemental readings. More importantly, students had engaged both the principal and complementary texts, which was evidenced in their final presentations and papers.

Another success of the course is its relevance to multiple disciplines, and thus accessibility to students outside of the social sciences. One student stated:

> As a student in the [S]chool of [A]rts and [H]umanities taking a course in the [S]school of [S]social [S]sciences, I was really nervous that I would not be able to keep up with the other students who were political science and international studies majors. However, being able to utilize The Hunger Games series as a platform to understand democracy, justice, and civic engagement allowed me to play on my strengths as a literature major in understanding the concepts. I was able to do a character analysis to illustrate the differences between democracy and non-democracy; justice and injustice; civic engagement and selfishness.

Moreover, the series is accessible to those that may struggle with academia in general. As Morrell notes, academic curriculum is often inaccessible to many students (72). As a result, Morrell posits that educators "need to examine 'non-school' literacy practices to find connections between local literacies and the dominant, academic literacies" (72). In other words, academics should embrace popular literature and popular culture because they provide a means for students to connect topics, experiences, and realities relevant to them to the academic components of a course. Furthermore, when they are able learn concepts through a text that they deem as relevant, they are more willing to invest the time engaging the curriculum. As one of my students stated in his evaluation of the course, "nothing reaches and resonates more with college students th[a]n timely examples to which they can relate…." The student goes on to state that including The Hunger Games series as the primary texts for the course, and also requiring an application of the texts and supplemental readings in the form of a presentation, made him feel as if his time had not been wasted on something irrelevant.

While the majority of my students have embraced the inclusion of The Hunger Games trilogy in the course curriculum, there have still been challenges to adequately teaching the course material and getting students to "buy in" to the idea of using such a popular series as the primary text for the course. As William Clapton notes, some students are skeptical about the use of popular culture in an academic setting (par. 9). Even though students complain about course curriculum being dry, boring, or dense, many students still believe that a course must present curriculum in a traditional manner, with a traditional text. Others may perceive the use of texts such as The Hunger Games series as childish or "silly fun" (Clapton par. 9), rather than as a site for critical analysis. For example, one of my students recently noticed The Hunger Games books on my office bookshelf. The student initially joked that I was doing some frivolous reading while "on the job." When I told the student that they are actually the primary texts for one of my courses, the student responded with the statement, "I can't believe you assign a children's book in your class." This statement is indicative not only of what some students think about popular culture as an integral part of an academic setting, but also as to the manner in which some students limit their own understanding and intellectual growth as a result of excluding something based on their own misperceptions. However, individuals who have read the series understand that The Hunger Games is far from immature or childish reading.

A second issue that I have encountered since I began teaching The Hunger Games series in my class is student reliance on the films rather than the text itself. This was less of an issue in earlier classes, since only one or two of the films had been released.[5] However, as the adaptation of the trilogy into film draws to an end, students have attempted to rely on the films rather than the texts when drafting papers or crafting presentations. This is always a challenge when incorporating a novel or some other form of literary fiction that has been adapted to film into a course. There are several methods that can be employed to counter this shortcut. Instructors can employ quizzes and tests that emphasize facets of the reading that are not addressed in the films. Yet there is a danger to relying on these types of assessments. Students may become so focused on the plotline or minute details that they then neglect the application of the text to the overarching course concepts. But again, this can be addressed through application questions on quizzes, exams, presentations, and papers. In addition, including a writing assignment that specifically addresses the differences between the films and the text is beneficial.

Unfortunately, there is no way to counter all pitfalls of incorporating a pop culture phenomenon like The Hunger Games series into a course. One must attempt to address all possible issues as thoroughly as possible through imaginative assessments.

Conclusion

Introducing students to concepts such as democracy, justice, and civic engagement through traditional textbooks has its merit. However, taking a critical literacy approach to fostering student learning through the use of fiction is an approach that may yield benefits beyond the memorization of terms. Bringing texts such as The Hunger Games trilogy into a classroom focused solely on these concepts has the potential to cultivate a sense of action, to assist in the development of critical thinking skills, and to provide

---

the foundation for a lifetime of civic engagement. After all, the purpose of civic engagement is to develop, protect, and better one's community and prompt others to care about their fellow man. Suzanne Collins wrote The Hunger Games trilogy with the hope that her audience would question their own world. In one interview, Collins was asked what she hoped her audience would take way from the series, and she replied, "Questions about how elements of the book might be relevant in their own lives. And if they're disturbing, what they might do about them" ("A Conversation" 2). Utilizing The Hunger Games trilogy as primary texts in the DJCE classroom provides the opportunity for Collins' wishes to come to fruition. Students are challenged to think about the text in the context of their own lives and histories, while experiencing the opportunity to address the faults in their society through critical evaluation and action.

Notes

1. Situated knowledge is a phrase that is used in my field on a regular basis, particularly in feminist literature. It refers to the knowledge one gains from his or her own life experiences. For instance, I have situated knowledge about patriarchal oppression because I am a woman and have suffered some form of subordination because of my sex and gender.

2. The Allies/Safe Zone program allows people from the dominant groups in society to become active in fighting the oppression of disadvantaged groups in society. The program includes Allies that seek to fight racism, xenophobia, ethnocentrism, religious discrimination, etc. In addition, the program has grown to include several LGBT Ally groups ("Establishing an Allies/Safe Zone Program" [par. 2]). The students in my course were particularly focused on becoming LGBT Allies. This project was particularly interesting because it was spearheaded by an international exchange student from Russia who wanted to take what she had learned in the course and the Ally program back to her university in Russia the following semester.

3. Special Love is a organization that provides children with cancer and their families with support and networking opportunities ("About Us" [par.1]).

4. I consider this to be primarily an achievement of incorporating the series into the course. However, it became somewhat problematic when students "gave away" spoilers to students who had not read ahead.

5. Actually, the first Hunger Games film was set to release during the first semester that I taught the trilogy in this course. I was able to use this as an advantage. The release of the first film became an integral part of the course, and the entire class (which only consisted of eight students) took a field trip to see the movie. The students were instructed to take notes during the film on the discrepancies between the book and the film, but were also instructed to focus on whether the course concepts were conveyed differently or with greater emphasis through film.

Works Cited

"About Us." *Special Love.* Special Love, Inc., 2015. Web. 20 Nov. 2015.

Burke, Brianna. "Teaching Environmental Justice through *The Hunger Games.*" *ALAN Review* 41 (2013): 53–63. Web. 12 Nov. 2015.

Clapton, William. "Pedagogy and Pop Culture: Pop Culture as Teaching Tool and Assessment Practice." *E-International Relations.* E-International Relations, 23 Jun. 2015. Web. 12 Nov. 2015.

Collins, Suzanne. *Catching Fire.* New York: Scholastic, 2009.

_____. "A Conversation: Questions & Answers, Suzanne Collins" *Scholastic.* Scholastic Inc., n.d. Web. 18 Jul. 2015.

_____. *The Hunger Games.* New York: Scholastic, 2008.

_____. *Mockingjay.* New York: Scholastic, 2010.

Dyson, Stephen Benedict. *Otherworldly Politics: The International Relations of Star Trek, Game of Thrones, and Battlestar Galactica.* Baltimore, MD: Johns Hopkins UP, 2015.

Eggers, Dave. *What Is the What.* New York: Vintage Books, 2006.

"Establishing an Allies/Safe Zone Program." *Human Rights Campaign.* The Human Rights Campaign, 2015. Web. 20 Nov. 2015.

Gierzynski, Anthony. *Harry Potter and the Millennials: Research Methods and Politics of the Muggle Generation.* Baltimore, MD: Johns Hopkins UP, 2013.

Kiersey, Nicholas, and Iver B. Neumann, eds. *Battlestar Galactica and International Relations*. New York: Routledge, 2013.

King, Martin Luther, Jr. "Letter from Birmingham Jail." 1963. *Pullias Center for Higher Education*. Pullias Center for Higher Education/ USC Rossier, 2014. Web. 20 Nov. 2015.

Morrell, Ernest. "Toward a Critical Pedagogy of Popular Culture: Literary Development among Urban Youth." *Journal of Adolescent and Adult Literacy* 46 (2002): 72–77. Web. 12 Nov. 2015.

Morrison, Toni. *The Bluest Eye*. New York: Plume/Penguin Books, 2000.

Nexon, Daniel H., and Iver B. Neumann, eds. *Harry Potter and International Relations*. Lanham, MD: Rowman & Littlefield, 2013.

Simmons, Amber M. "Class on Fire: Using the Hunger Games Trilogy to Encourage Social Action." *Journal of Adolescent and Adult Literacy* 56 (2012): 22–34. *EBSCOhost*. Web. 12 Nov. 2015.

Smith, Zadie. *White Teeth*. 2000. New York: Vintage Books, 2003.

Weber, Cynthia. *International Relations Theory: A Critical Introduction*. 4th ed. New York: Routledge, 2014.

X, Malcolm. "The Ballot or the Bullet." (King Solomon Baptist Church. Detroit, Michigan, April 12, 1964). American RadioWorks. American Public Media, 2016. Web. 20 Nov. 2015.

RESOURCES

Chronology of Suzanne Collins' Life_____

August 20,1955	Michael John Collins marries Jane Kathryn Brady in Marion County, Indiana.
January 2,1957	Kathryn Collins is born.
August 20, 1958	Andrew Collins is born.
January 6, 1960	Joan Collins is born.
August 10,1962	Suzanne Marie Collins is born. The Collins family is living in Connecticut at this time. Collins' father is a career military man, and his various assignments necessitate several moves throughout Collins' childhood.
1968	The Collins family moves to Indiana. Collins' father, an officer in the United States Air Force, is deployed to Vietnam. As the year elapses, six-year-old Suzanne experiences a harrowing progression from a child's incomprehension of war to confusion to fear and sadness, exacerbated by accidental exposure to graphic television news footage from the war zone. This experience plants in Collins an early seed of concern about news media depictions of violence.
1969	Collins' father returns from the war so emotionally scarred that even young Suzanne is able to recognize the damage.
1974	The Collins family moves to Brussels, Belgium, when Michael Collins is given an assignment with NATO. Collins' father takes advantage of the location to teach his children about military history through field trips to castles and battlefields, pointing out the human toll

of the history behind such places. Collins completes seventh through tenth grades in Belgium. The family's next move sends them to Alabama.

1980	Collins graduates from Alabama School of Fine Arts in Birmingham with a specialization in theater.
1985	Collins graduates from Indiana University with a double major in theater and telecommunications.
1985-1987	Collins holds a variety of jobs, including reporting for a local National Public Radio station, deejaying at a country-western radio station, and data entry. In 1987, Collins heads to New York to pursue her master's degree.
1989	Collins earns an MFA in dramatic writing from New York University's Tisch School of the Arts. Her first work as a dramatist comes while working with the Classic Stage Company (an Off-Broadway group) and with a film producer.
1991-1992	Collins begins writing for children's television shows with the short-lived Nickelodeon series *Hi, Honey! I'm Home!*
1992	Collins marries Charles "Cap" Pryor, whom she met while both were students at Indiana University.
1993	Collins writes for Nickelodeon's *Clarissa Explains It All*.
1994	Collins' son, Charlie Pryor, is born.
1996-1998	Collins writes episodes of Nickelodeon's *Little Bear*.

1997-1998	Collins writes episodes of Nickelodeon's *The Mystery Files of Shelby Woo*.
1999	Collins' first published book, *Fire Proof: The Mystery Files of Shelby Woo #11,* is released.
1999	Collins' daughter, Isabel Pryor, is born.
2000-2001	Collins writes for the Warner Brothers television series *Generation O!* and meets author/illustrator James Proimos, who encourages her to write more books for children. She subsequently embarks on writing The Underland Chronicles series. Proimos also introduces Collins to his agent and would later illustrate Collins' *The Year of the Jungle*.
2001	Collins' critically acclaimed television movie *Santa, Baby!* airs.
2003	The first book of The Underland Chronicles, *Gregor the Overlander*, is published. On March 15, 2003, Collins' father dies. Collins would later note that his expertise was an invaluable resource in helping her to craft militarily realistic battle scenarios in The Underland Chronicles.
2003-2005	Collins writes episodes of the television series *Clifford's Puppy Days*.
2004	*Gregor and the Prophecy of Bane* is published.
2005	*Gregor and the Curse of the Warmbloods* is published.
2005	*When Charlie McButton Lost Power*, Collins' rhyming children's book, is published.
2006	*Gregor and the Marks of Secret* is published.

2007	*Gregor and the Code of Claw* is published.
2008	Collins' made-for-TV movie *Wubbzy's Big Movie!* airs.
2008	*The Hunger Games* is published. It receives numerous awards and accolades and would remain on *The New York Times* bestseller list for over 200 weeks.
2008-2009	Collins writes for the TV series *Wow! Wow! Wubbzy!*, which she admits in an interview is a bit of a relief from the darker storylines of her novels.
2009	*Catching Fire* is published and receives starred reviews from *Kirkus, Booklist, Goodreads*, and *School Library Journal*. It is also the recipient of two Goodreads Choice Awards, an Indies Choice Book Award (2010), and a Golden Archer Award (2012).
2010	*Mockingjay* is published and wins two Goodreads Choice Awards, as well as a Golden Archer Award (2013).
2010	Collins is selected as one of *Time* magazine's 100 Most Influential People.
2012	An action-thriller screenplay penned by Collins, *Ticket Out*, is released. The film has a limited theatrical release in Germany, Canada, and the US and is available on DVD elsewhere.
March 23, 2012	*The Hunger Games* is released in theaters. Produced by Lionsgate and made with a budget of $78 million dollars, it eventually earns a world-wide gross of $686 million.

Critical Insights

2013	*The Year of the Jungle* is published. The book is illustrated by James Proimos.
Nov. 22, 2013	*The Hunger Games: Catching Fire* is released in theaters. It earns a worldwide gross of over $864 million and is the highest grossing US film of 2013.
Nov. 21, 2014	*The Hunger Games: Mockingjay, Part 1* is released in theaters.
Nov. 20, 2015	*The Hunger Games: Mockingjay, Part 2* is released in theaters, eventually earning over $646 million worldwide.

—Compiled by Laurie Adams

Works by Suzanne Collins

Books

Fire Proof: The Mystery Files of Shelby Woo #11 (1999)
Gregor the Overlander (2003)
Gregor and the Prophecy of Bane (2004)
Gregor and the Curse of the Warmbloods (2005)
When Charlie McButton Lost Power (2005)
Gregor and the Marks of Secret (2006)
Gregor and the Code of Claw (2007)
The Hunger Games (2008)
Catching Fire (2009)
Mockingjay (2010)
Year of the Jungle (2013)

Teleplays

Clarissa Explains It All: "A Little Romance" (1993)
Clarissa Explains It All: "Blind Date" (1993) (staff writer)
Little Bear: "Duck, Babysitter/Little Bear's Band/Hop Frog Pond" (1996)
The Mystery Files of Shelby Woo: "The Alligator Mystery" (1997)
The Mystery Files of Shelby Woo: "The Hit and Run Case" (1997)
The Mystery Files of Shelby Woo: "The Smoke Screen Case" (1997)
The Mystery Files of Shelby Woo: "The Seminole Mystery" (1998)
The Mystery Files of Shelby Woo: "The Egg Mystery" (1998)
The Mystery Files of Shelby Woo: "The Spare Parts Mystery" (1998)
Little Bear: "Mitzi's Mess" (1998)
Generation O!: "Damp Sheets" (2000)
Santa, Baby! (2001)
Clifford's Puppy Days: "Socks & Snooze/Keeping It Cool" (2003)
Clifford's Puppy Days: "School Daze" (2005)
Wubbzy's Big Movie (2008)

Wow! Wow! Wubbzy!: "A Great and Grumpy Holiday/The Super Special Gift" (2008)

Wow! Wow! Wubbzy!: "Bye-Bye Birdies/Call of the Mild" (2008)

Wow! Wow! Wubbzy!: "Big Bunny Blues/The Flower Day Parade" (2009)

Wow! Wow! Wubbzy!: "Bye Bye Wuzzleburg/Wubbzy's Wacky Journey" (2009)

Ticket Out (2012)

The Hunger Games (2012) (with Gary Ross and Billy Ray)

The Hunger Games: A Reenactment—Part 1 (2013) (with Caitlin Moore)

The Hunger Games: Mockingjay—Part 1 (2014) (adaptation, screenplay by Peter Craig and Danny Strong)

The Hunger Games: Mockingjay—Part 2 (2015) (adaptation, screenplay by Peter Craig and Danny Strong)

Song Lyrics

Sting. "Deep in the Meadow." Universal Republic Records, 2012. mp3.

Howard, James N., and Jennifer Lawrence. "The Hanging Tree." *The Hunger Games: Mockingjay—Part 1 Original Motion Picture Soundtrack.* Universal Republic Records, 2014. CD.

—Compiled by Laurie Adams

Bibliography

"Award-Winning Books by Suzanne Collins." *FictionDB*. FictionDB. com, n.d. Web. 16 Sept. 2015.

Arrow, V. *The Panem Companion: An Unofficial Guide to Suzanne Collins' Hunger Games, from Mellark Bakery to Mockingjays.* Dallas: Smart Pop-BenBella, 2012. Print.

Bartlett, Myke. "Appetite for Spectacle: Violence and Entertainment in *The Hunger Games." Screen Education* 66 (2012): 8–17. *Google Scholar.* Web. 16 Sept. 2015.

Basu, Balaka, Katherine Broad, and Carrie Hintz, eds. *Contemporary Dystopian Fiction for Young Adults: Brave New Teenagers.* New York: Routledge, 2013. Print.

"Battle, Games: Cold Brutality a Common Theme." *All Things Considered.* NPR, 21 Mar. 2012. Radio.

Biography.com Editors. "Suzanne Collins Biography." *Biography.com.* A&E Television Networks, n.d. Web. 16 Sept. 2015.

Burke, Brianna. "Teaching Environmental Justice through *The Hunger Games." ALAN Review* 41 (2013): 53–63. Web. 7 Feb. 2016.

Byrne, Deirdre. "Dressed for the Part: An Analysis of Clothing in Suzanne Collins' Hunger Games Trilogy." *Journal of Literary Studies* 31 (2015): 43–62. *Ebscohost.* Web. 16 Sept. 2015.

Collins, Suzanne. *Catching Fire.* New York: Scholastic, 2009. Print.

_____. *Fire Proof: The Mystery Files of Shelby Woo #11.* New York: Aladdin-Simon & Schuster, 1999. Print.

_____. *Gregor and the Code of Claw.* New York: Scholastic, 2007. Print.

_____. *Gregor and the Curse of the Warmbloods.* New York: Scholastic, 2005. Print.

_____. *Gregor and the Marks of Secret.* New York: Scholastic, 2006. Print.

_____. *Gregor the Overlander.* New York: Scholastic, 2003. Print.

_____. *Gregor and the Prophecy of Bane.* New York: Scholastic, 2004. Print.

_____. *The Hunger Games.* New York: Scholastic, 2008. Print.

_____. "A Killer Story: An Interview with Suzanne Collins, Author of 'The Hunger Games.'" Interview by Rick Margolis. *School Library Journal*. School Library Journal, 1 Sept. 2008. Web. 6 Feb. 2016.

_____. "The Last Battle: With 'Mockingjay' on Its Way, Suzanne Collins Weighs in on Katniss and the Capitol." Interview by Rick Margolis. *School Library Journal*. School Library Journal, 1 Aug. 2010. Web. 6 Feb. 2016.

_____. *Mockingjay.* New York: Scholastic, 2010. Print.

_____. "Suzanne Collins on the Books She Loves." Interview by Tina Jordan. *EW.com: Entertainment Weekly*. Entertainment Weekly, 13 Aug. 2010. Web. 6 Feb. 2016.

_____. *When Charlie McButton Lost Power.* New York: Puffin-Penguin, 2005. Print.

_____. *Year of the Jungle: Memories from the Home Front.* New York: Scholastic, 2013. Print.

Curwood, Jen. "*The Hunger Games*: Literature, Literacy, and Online Affinity Spaces." *Language Arts* 90 (July 2013): 417–27. *Ebscohost*. Web. 16 Sept. 2015.

Curwood, Jen, Alecia Magnifico, and Jane Lammers. "Writing in the Wild: Writers' Motivation in Fan-Based Affinity Spaces." *Journal of Adolescent & Adult Literacy* 56 (2013): 677–85. *Ebscohost*. Web. 16 Sept. 2015.

Dominus, Susan. "Suzanne Collins' War Stories for Kids." *New York Times Magazine*. The New York Times, 8 Apr. 2011. Web. 16 Sept. 2015.

Dubrofsky, Rachel, and Emily Ryalls. "*The Hunger Games*: Performing Not-performing to Authenticate Femininity and Whiteness." *Critical Studies in Media Communication* 31 (2014): 395–409. *Google Scholar*. Web. 16 Sept. 2015.

Dunn, George, and Nicolas Michaud, eds. *The Hunger Games and Philosophy: A Critique of Pure Treason.* Hoboken: John Wiley & Sons, 2012. Print.

Edelstein, David. "Acting Trumps Action in a 'Games' without Horror." *NPR*. National Public Radio, 22 Mar. 2012. Web. 6 Feb. 2016.

Egan, Kate. *The World of the Hunger Games.* New York: Scholastic, 2012. Print.

Ford, Clementine. "Literature's Feistiest Feminists: How Thomas Hardy Paved the Way for The Hunger Games' Katniss Everdeen." *The Telegraph*. Telegraph Media Group, 20 Apr. 2015. Web. 7 Feb. 2016.

Frankel, Valerie Estelle. *Katniss the Caittail: An Unauthorized Guide to Names and Symbols in Suzanne Collins' The Hunger Games*. CreateSpace Independent Publishing, 2012.

Garber, Megan. "*The Hunger Games* Theme Park and the Death of the Disney Dream." *The Atlantic*. The Atlantic Monthly Group, 2 Nov. 2015. Web. 27 Nov. 2015.

Garriott, Deidre Anne Evans, Whitney Elaine Jones, and Julie Elizabeth Tyler. *Space and Place in The Hunger Games: New Readings of the Novels*. Jefferson, NC: McFarland, 2014. Print.

Hanlon, Tina L. "Appalachia in The Hunger Games Trilogy by Suzanne Collins." *AppLit: Resources for Readers and Teachers of Appalachian Literature for Children and Young Adults*. Ferrum College, 2016. Web. 6 Feb. 2016.

Hardy, Elizabeth Baird. "EBH: Don't go down in the Hole – Coal Mining Life in District 12 and in Present-Day Appalachia." *Hogwarts Professor: Thoughts for Serious Readers*. HogwartsProfessor.com, 14 Apr. 2010. Web. 6 Feb. 2016.

_____. "Let the Hunger Games Filming Begin!" *Hogwarts Professor: Thoughts for Serious Readers*. HogwartsProfessor.com, 2 Feb. 2011. Web. 6 Feb. 2016.

Henthorne, Tom. *Approaching the Hunger Games Trilogy: A Literary and Cultural Analysis*. Jefferson, NC: McFarland, 2012. Print.

The Hunger Games. Scholastic, 2016. Web. 6 Feb. 2016.

The Hunger Games. Dir. Gary Ross. Lionsgate, 2012. Film.

The Hunger Games: Catching Fire. Dir. Francis Lawrence. Lionsgate, 2013. Film.

The Hunger Games: Mockingjay—Part 1. Dir. Francis Lawrence. Lionsgate, 2014. Film.

The Hunger Games: Mockingjay—Part 2. Dir. Francis Lawrence. Lionsgate, 2015. Film.

Hunter, Nick. *Extraordinary Women: Suzanne Collins*. Chicago: Raintree-Capstone Global Library. 2014. Print.

Johnson, Naomi. "Consuming Desires: Consumption, Romance, and Sexuality in Best-Selling Teen Romance Novels." *Women's Studies in Communication* 33 (2010): 54–73. *Ebscohost*. Web. 16 Sept. 2015.

Lammers, Jayne, Jen Curwood, and Alecia Magnifico. "Toward an Affinity Space Methodology: Considerations for Literacy Research." *English Teaching: Practice and Critique* 11 (2012): 44–58. *Ebscohost*. Web. 16 Sept. 2015.

Latham, Don, and Jonathan Hollister. "The Games People Play: Information and Media Literacies in the Hunger Games Trilogy." *Children's Literature in Education* 45 (2014): 33–46. *Ebscohost*. Web. 16 Sept. 2015.

Lewit, Meghan. "Casting 'The Hunger Games': In Praise of Katniss Everdeen." *The Atlantic*. The Atlantic Monthly Group, 9 Mar. 2011. Web. 6 Feb. 2016.

Llanas, Sheila. *How to Analyze the Works of Suzanne Collins*. Edina, MN: Abdo, 2013. Print.

Miller, Laura. "Fresh Hell." *The New Yorker*. Condé Nast, 14 June 2010. Web. 29 Nov. 2015.

Muller, Vivienne. "Virtually Real: Suzanne Collins' The Hunger Games Trilogy." *International Research in Children's Literature* 5 (2012): 51–63. *Google Scholar*. Web. 16 Sept. 2015.

Neary, Lynn. "Edgy, Violent Thrillers for The Teen-Age Set." *NPR Books*. NPR, 1 Sept. 2009. Web. 7 Feb. 2016.

Nishimura, Robert. "*Battle Royale*, a Hunger Games for Grownups." *Indiewire*. Indiwire.com, 20 Mar. 2012. Web. 30 Nov. 2015.

Palen, Tim. *Tim Palen: Photographs from the Hunger Games*. New York: Assouline, 2015. Print.

Pharr, Mary F, and Leisa A. Clark, eds. *Of Bread, Blood, and The Hunger Games: Critical Essays on the Suzanne Collins Trilogy*. Series ed. Donald Palumbo and C. W. Sullivan III. Jefferson, NC: McFarland, 2012. Print. Critical Explorations in Science Fiction and Fantasy, 35.

Pulford, Adam. "'May the odds be ever in your favour': The Language of The Hunger Games." *Oxford Dictionaries*. Oxford UP, 5 Sept. 2012. Web. 7 Feb. 2016.

Ringlestein, Yonah. "Real or Not Real: The Hunger Games as Transmediated Religion." *Journal of Religion and Popular Culture* 25 (2013): 372–87. *Ebscohost*. Web. 16 Sept. 2015.

Rosen, Sarah, and David Rosen. "Representing Child Soldiers in Fiction and Film." *Peace Review* 24 (2012): 305–12. *Ebscohost.* Web. 16 September 2015.

Saunders, Jane. "What *The Hunger Games* Can Teach Us About Disciplinary Literacy." *English Journal* 103.3 (2014): 41–47. *Google Scholar.* Web. 16 Sept. 2015.

Saunders, Jane, and Gwynne Ash. "Entering the Arena: The Figured Worlds Transition of Preservice Teachers." *Journal of Adolescent & Adult Literacy* 56 (2013): 490–99. *Ebscohost.* Web. 16 Sept. 2015.

Simmons, Amber. "Class on Fire: Using the Hunger Games Trilogy to Encourage Social Action." *Journal of Adolescent & Adult Literacy* 56 (2012): 22–34. *Ebscohost.* Web. 16 Sept. 2015.

Simut, Andrei. "Dystopian Geographies in *The Year of the Flood* and *Hunger Games*." *Caietele Echinox* 27 (2014): 297–06. *Ebscohost.* Web. 16 Sept. 2015.

Skinner, Margaret, and Kailyn McCord. "The Hunger Games: A Conversation: Jungian and Literary Perspectives on Violence, Gender, and Character Development." *Jung Journal: Culture and Psyche* 6 (2012): 106–13. *Ebscohost.* Web. 16 Sept. 2015.

Strauss, Barry. "The Classical Roots of 'The Hunger Games.'" *The Wall Street Journal.* Dow Jones, 13 Nov. 2014. Web. 31 July 2015.

Sturgis, Amy H. "Not Your Parents' Dystopias: Millennial Fondness for Worlds Gone Wrong." *Reason* 46 (Oct. 2014): 46–51. Print.

Suzanne Collins. Suzanne Collins, n.d. Web. 16 Sept. 2015.

"Suzanne Collins." *Authors and Artists for Young Adults.* Vol. 86. Detroit: Gale, 2011. *Biography in Context.* Web. 7 Feb. 2016.

Taber, Nancy, Vera Woloshyn, and Laura Lane. "'She's More Like a Guy' and 'He's More Like a Teddy Bear': Girls' Perception of Violence and Gender in The Hunger Games." *Journal of Youth Studies* 16 (2013): 1022–37. *Ebscohost.* Web. 16 Sept. 2015.

Tan, Susan. "Burn with Us: Sacrificing Childhood in *The Hunger Games*." *The Lion and The Unicorn* 37 (2013): 54–73. *Ebscohost.* Web. 16 Sept. 2015.

Thomas, Mark. "Survivor on Steroids." *Griffith Law Review* 22 (2013): 361-402. *Ebscohost.* Web. 16 September 2015.

Vartian, Sylvie. "Guerrières, Chasseresses et Corps Éprouvé dans la Science-Fiction Adolescente Actuelle: Le Cas des *Hunger Games* de Suzanne Collins." *Recherches Féministes* 27 (2014): 113–28. *Ebscohost*. Web. 16 Sept. 2015.

Wilson, Leah, ed. *The Girl Who Was on Fire: Your Favorite Authors On Suzanne Collins' Hunger Games Trilogy.* Dallas: Smart Pop-BenBella, 2011. Print.

Woloshyn, Vera, Nancy Taber, and Laura Lane. "Discourses of Masculinity and Femininity in *The Hunger Games*: 'Scarred,' 'Bloody,' and 'Stunning.'" *International Journal of Social Science Studies* 1 (2013): 150–60. *Google Scholar*. Web. 16 Sept. 2015.

Yang, Jeff. "'Hunger Games' Vs. 'Battle Royale.'" *The Wall Street Journal*. Dow Jones, 23 Mar. 2012. Web. 16 Sept. 2015.

About the Editor

Lana A. Whited is editor of the *The Ivory Tower and Harry Potter: Perspectives on a Literary Phenomenon* (U of Missouri P, 2002) and coeditor, with M. Katherine Grimes, of *Critical Insights: The Harry Potter Series* (Grey House Publishing, 2015). An internationally recognized expert on the Harry Potter series, Whited has contributed essays on Harry Potter to publications such as *The Lion and Unicorn* and *Through the Looking-Glass* and annually teaches a Hogwarts Academy course in a middle-school enrichment program. A Salzburg Global Seminar fellow, Whited also was a featured panelist in 2004 at a special symposium in Trebon, Czech Republic, sponsored by the Committee on Media and Culture of the Czech Parliament. Whited is professor of English and director of the Boone Honors Program at Ferrum College in the Blue Ridge Mountains of Virginia. In 2014, she was recognized with an Exemplary Teaching Award from the Board of Higher Education and Ministries of the United Methodist Church, and she is Ferrum College's nominee for the 2016 State Council of Higher Education of Virginia's Outstanding Faculty Awards. Whited earned degrees from Emory and Henry College, The College of William & Mary, Hollins University, and the University of North Carolina at Greensboro.

Contributors

Laurie Adams followed up a stint in broadcast media with a degree in criminal justice, both fueled by an intense curiosity about what exactly makes people tick. In addition to her journalism background, Adams had three publications to her credit in the *LAE Journal* (2010), the *International Journal of Business and Social Science* (2012), and the *Council for Undergraduate Research Quarterly* (2013) prior to writing the biography of J. K. Rowling and compiling the Rowling chronology, list of works, and bibliography for *Critical Insights: The Harry Potter Series* (Grey House Publishing, 2015). She currently works as a freelance writer.

Amy Bennett-Zendzian is a lecturer in the Writing Program at Boston University, where she teaches courses on writing, fairy tales, and children's literature. She is also a book reviewer for the *Horn Book Guide*. She holds an A.B. from Cornell University, an M.A./M.F.A. in children's literature from Simmons College, and an M.A. in English and American literature from Boston University. Her main areas of research interest are fairy tales, fantasy, science fiction, and young adult literature.

Danielle Bienvenue Bray is a lecturer in the University of Georgia's Department of English. She received her Ph.D. in English with a major concentration in children's literature from the University of Louisiana at Lafayette in 2012 and is currently pursuing an M.F.A. in children's literature from Hollins University. Her recent publications include "Sissy Boy Motherhood: Male Child Mother-Figures in Middle Grades Fantasy Literature" in the *Journal of Children's Literature in Education* (Spring 2015) and "Rock Cakes and Reciprocity: Food and the Male Performance of Nurturing in Harry Potter" in *Critical Insights: Harry Potter Series* (Grey House Publishing, 2015).

Rebecca Sutherland Borah earned her B.S.Ed. and M.A. in English at Northeast Missouri State University and her Ph.D. in English from Southern Illinois University, Carbondale, where her major was composition and rhetoric, with minors in nineteenth-century English literature and gender studies. She is an associate professor of English at the University of Cincinnati, where she teaches composition with service learning and the occasional 'monsters in literature,' censorship, or Tolkien course. Her publications include "Apprentice Wizards Welcome: Fan Communities and the Culture of Harry Potter" and (with Inez Schaechterle) "More Than Girlfriends, Geekettes, and Gladiatrixes: Women, Feminism, and Fantasy Role-Playing Games." She is also known as a pop culture expert, especially when it comes to fan culture, monsters, comic books, and superheroes.

Stephanie Dror is a graduate of the Master of Children's Literature (M.A.C.L.) at The University of British Columbia, and her thesis was an ecocritical reading of young adult dystopian texts. She is currently a member of the Hans Christian Andersen Award committee with IBBY Canada as well as their membership secretary. She coauthors on the book blog *The Book Wars* and reviews children's and young adult materials for various sources, including *Quill & Quire* and the *Canadian Materials*.

Louise M. Freeman received her B.S. in biology from Emory University and her M.A. and Ph.D. in biological psychology from the University of California at Berkeley. She is currently professor of psychology at Mary Baldwin College. Her major academic interests are physiological psychology, behavioral neuroendocrinology, and applied behavioral analysis. She also has a keen interest in psychological themes in young adult fiction and has presented on *Harry Potter*, *The Hunger Games*, and *Divergent* at James Madison University, Gonzaga University, Louisiana State University, and Chestnut Hill College.

Tina L. Hanlon is an associate professor of English at Ferrum College and the Hollins University summer graduate program in children's literature. She has written essays about folktales, fantasy, and other children's stories in a variety of media. She is director of the web site *AppLit: Resources for Readers and Teachers of Appalachian Literature for Children and Young Adults* (www.AppLit.org) and a coeditor of *Crosscurrents of Children's Literature: An Anthology of Texts and Criticism* (Oxford UP, 2006).

Elizabeth Baird Hardy is a senior instructor of English at Mayland Community College (North Carolina), where she began using *The Hunger*

Games in her composition classes in 2010. She is the author of *Milton, Spenser, and the Chronicles of Narnia: Literary Sources for the C.S. Lewis Novels* (McFarland, 2006) and has contributed to a number of projects covering literary criticism and popular texts, from Harry Potter to Twilight. She frequently visits local and distant schools, libraries, and bookstores to speak on the literary value, symbolism, and Appalachian elements of *The Hunger Games*.

Jackie C. Horne earned her B.A. from Yale University and worked for a decade in children's book trade publishing. She returned to academia, graduating with an M.A. from the Center for the Study of Children's Literature at Simmons College and a Ph.D. from Brandeis University. She is the author of *History and the Construction of the Child in Early British Children's Literature*, coeditor of two volumes in the Children's Literature Association's Centennial series, and currently serves as the chair of the ChLA's Publications Advisory Board.

Todd Ide is currently a doctoral candidate (A.B.D.) in curriculum, instruction, and teacher education at Michigan State University. His research interests include examining how digital storytelling and various storytelling methods can alter the reader's understanding of a given text and the ways in which justice and equality are portrayed in children's and adolescent literature. Ide earned three degrees from Western Michigan University: an M.A. in literature/genre studies, with a thesis on *Robinson Crusoe*; an M.F.A. in fiction and creative nonfiction, with a thesis called *Loss: A Father's Story of Miscarriage*; and a B.S. in English, history, and political science/public policy. He has taught for twenty years at the secondary and post-secondary level. Ide lives in Kalamazoo with his wife and two daughters and works as an adjunct professor at Grand Valley State University in Grand Rapids, Michigan.

Lars Schmeink works as a postdoctoral researcher at the Hans-Bredow-Institute for Media Research at the University of Hamburg, where he is part of the German team of the World Hobbit Project. He received his Ph.D. in American studies from the Humboldt University in Berlin for his research on genetic engineering, posthumanism, and science fiction. In addition, he holds a master of higher education degree and has been awarded for his innovative teaching methods, which include the online teaching tool www.virtual-sf.com. He is the president of the Gesellschaft für Fantastikforschung and the editor of its member's journal the *Zeitschrift für Fantastikforschung*. His latest publications include: "Cyberpunk and Dystopia: William Gibson's *Neuromancer* (1984)" in *Dystopian Narratives: Classics, New Tendencies and Model Interpretations*; "Modern-Day Superheroes: Transgressions of Genre and Morality in *Misfits*" (with Dana Frei) in *Transitions and Dissolving Boundaries in the Fantastic*; and "Biopunk 101" in *SFRA Review*.

Amalia L. Selle completed her undergraduate education at Covenant College and her M.A. in children's literature from Hollins University. Her nine years of teaching middle-school language arts in Northwest Georgia included the delightful experience of introducing good literature, such as *The Hunger Games*, to young people. She is currently teaching high school English in Indonesia.

Amy H. Sturgis earned her Ph.D. in intellectual history from Vanderbilt University, specializes in science fiction/fantasy and Native American studies, and teaches at Lenoir-Rhyne University and Belmont University. In addition, she contributes the regular "Looking Back on Genre History" segment to StarShipSofa, which in 2010 became the first podcast in history to win a Hugo Award. In 2015, the L.A. Press Club named her Reason article "Not Your Parents' Dystopias: Millennial Fondness for Worlds Gone Wrong" the "Best Magazine Review/Criticism/Column" of the year. She has authored four books, edited six others, and published over forty essays in scholarly and popular venues, most recently in Harry Potter for Nerds II (2015), Ravenclaw Reader (2015), Star Trek and History (2013), and Lois McMaster Bujold: Essays on a Modern Master of Science Fiction (2013).

Sandra Via is assistant professor of political science at Ferrum College. She earned a doctorate in planning, governance, and globalization from Virginia Tech. Her publications include "Gender, Militarism, and Globalization: Soldiers for Hire and Hegemonic Masculinity" in *Gender, War, and Militarism: Feminist Perspectives*, a collection that Dr. Via edited with Laura Sjoberg, and "Big Blocks of Cheese and Other Lessons

on American Politics and Government: 15 Weeks in The West Wing"
(coauthored with Courtney Powell Thomas) in *Teaching Matters: Strategy and Tactics to Engage Students in the Study of American Politics.*

Index

185, 186, 187, 188, 189,
190, 191, 192, 193, 194,
196, 199, 200, 201, 202,
204, 205, 210, 212, 214,
215, 218, 219, 227, 231,
234, 235, 240, 241, 242,
243, 244, 246, 249, 250,
251, 253, 256, 257, 259,
261, 262, 266, 268, 275,
276, 277, 278
Card, Orson Scott 100
Carpenter, Susan 57, 58
Carroll, Lewis 46
Carroll, Noël 135
castaways 39
Catching Fire 10, 14, 22, 23, 29,
34, 44, 47, 53, 56, 57, 58,
59, 60, 61, 63, 68, 72, 73,
74, 75, 76, 77, 80, 84, 86,
95, 102, 109, 110, 111, 112,
113, 114, 115, 116, 117, 118,
120, 121, 129, 130, 131,
137, 147, 153, 159, 163,
165, 171, 174, 193, 194,
199, 204, 214, 215, 216,
221, 232, 240, 247, 248,
253, 256, 257, 262, 266,
268, 276, 278, 283, 290,
293, 295
Chipman, Ian 55
Cinna 29, 94, 95, 110, 115, 116,
133, 161, 164, 165, 185,
215, 230, 231, 275, 278
civic engagement 270, 271
civil rights movement 275, 276
Claflin, Sam 61
Clapton, William 280
Clark, Leisa A. 48, 69, 71, 74,
174, 237, 238, 253

Clemente, Bill 168
cognitive restructuring therapy
212, 213, 214, 216
Coin, Alma 67
Collins, Jane Brady 17
Collins, Michael 17, 19, 287
Collins, Suzanne ix, 3, 10, 13, 17,
19, 20, 21, 23, 24, 28, 47,
48, 53, 55, 56, 58, 64, 65,
66, 67, 72, 73, 74, 75, 76,
77, 82, 85, 87, 88, 92, 94,
95, 97, 100, 105, 107, 122,
123, 139, 140, 141, 159,
161, 174, 175, 195, 196,
225, 237, 238, 239, 241,
245, 253, 266, 273, 282,
283, 287, 293, 295, 296,
297, 298, 300
colonialism 277
commodity 162, 163, 164, 166,
168, 190, 191
concentration camps 41, 42
Cooper, James Fenimore 59
Crane, Seneca 260, 268
Creekmore, Billy 44, 49
Cressida, Annie 141
Crete 30, 225, 226, 228
Curtis, Jamie Lee 124

Daedalus 31
Dargus, Manohla 59, 75
d'Aulaire, Edgar Parin 47
d'Aulaire, Ingri 47
Defoe, Daniel 38
de Levita, Robin 11
Delingpole, James 56, 64, 65
de Lint, Charles 53, 62
democracy x, 5, 256, 271, 272,
275, 277, 278, 279, 281

Garriott, Deidre Anne Evans 69, 297
genocide 28, 273
Gierzynski, Anthony (Jack) 272
Gilligan, Carol 107
gladiator games 21, 28, 68, 240
Golden Age of Children's Literature 46
Golding, William 8, 19, 38
Gonsalves, Patricia 10
Gowers, Emily 29
Graves, Robert 237
Great Depression 44, 46, 175
Greek mythology viii, x, 19, 28, 29, 30, 31, 47, 63, 225, 226, 227, 228, 230, 236, 237
Green, John 51, 53, 57, 58, 59
Grossman, Lev 53, 56, 58, 61, 63, 65, 72, 73

Haines, Lise 100
Hamlet 55
Hardy, Thomas 3, 4, 32, 33
Harry Potter series x, 8, 59, 60, 70, 77, 81, 82, 136, 175, 272, 283, 284, 301, 303, 304, 305, 306
Hawthorne, Gale 35, 107, 141
Heavensbee, Plutarch 57, 95, 161, 208
Henthorne, Tom 45, 69, 74, 234
Hicks, Ray 156
hippocampus 216
Hirsch, David A. Hedrich 128
historical fiction 45
Hogwarts 3, 27, 65, 301
Holocaust, The 28, 41, 42
Horn, Jacob Jedidah 70
Hughes, Monica 100

Hugo, Victor 33
Huizinga, Johan 224
Hunger Games, The vii, ix, x, xi, 3, 4, 5, 6, 7, 8, 9, 10, 11, 12, 13, 14, 15, 16, 20, 21, 22, 23, 27, 28, 29, 30, 31, 33, 36, 37, 38, 39, 41, 43, 45, 46, 47, 48, 49, 50, 51, 52, 53, 55, 56, 57, 58, 59, 60, 62, 63, 64, 65, 66, 68, 69, 70, 71, 72, 73, 74, 75, 76, 77, 80, 84, 85, 86, 87, 88, 89, 90, 91, 92, 93, 95, 97, 99, 100, 101, 102, 105, 106, 107, 108, 109, 111, 113, 115, 117, 119, 121, 122, 136, 137, 139, 154, 158, 159, 161, 162, 163, 164, 174, 175, 176, 177, 178, 179, 181, 183, 185, 187, 188, 189, 191, 192, 193, 194, 195, 197, 204, 207, 215, 219, 221, 222, 223, 224, 225, 226, 228, 230, 237, 238, 239, 240, 248, 253, 254, 255, 256, 261, 266, 267, 268, 270, 271, 273, 274, 275, 276, 277, 278, 279, 280, 281, 282, 283, 290, 291, 293, 294, 295, 296, 297, 298, 299, 300, 304, 305, 306
hunting 3, 12, 30, 43, 107, 108, 110, 132, 136, 141, 142, 151, 177, 181, 202, 214, 230, 246
Hunt, Jonathan 57
Hussein, Saddam 66
Huxley, Aldous 37, 88, 91, 175

189, 192, 196, 197, 210,
215, 219, 233, 240, 256,
257, 258, 261, 263, 266,
277, 278, 295
Patterson, Harley x
Pavlik, Anthony 70
Pavlov, Ivan 206, 223
Pfeffer, Susan Beth 53, 73
Pharr, Mary F. 69, 74, 174, 237,
238, 253
Plato 271
Poe, Edgar Allan 124
poison 31, 126, 131, 143, 172
politics 5, 46, 105, 270, 275
Porter, Tracey 44
Postman, Neil 100
post-traumatic stress disorder ix,
6, 196, 197
pre-text 28, 39
Price, Margaret Evans 29
Proimos, James 20, 289, 291
prolonged exposure therapy 213
promos 40
Pryor, Cap 20
public sphere 105, 106
Pulford, Adam 31

Quarter Quell 31, 109, 111, 112,
114, 115, 116, 117, 158, 171,
172, 196, 204, 256

Raff, Katherine 49
Rand, Ayn 52, 90
Rayner, Rosalie 206, 223
Reaping, The 36, 37, 108, 125,
149, 153, 154, 163, 164,
168, 169, 179, 198, 215,
227, 231, 275, 277
remix 45

Riordan, Rick 51
Robin Hood 9, 30
Rockman, Connie 49
Rodin, Auguste 5
Roiphe, Katie 56, 58, 60, 65
Roman banquet 28, 29
Ross, Gary 49, 174, 178, 195, 294
Roth, Veronica 100
Rowe, Ivy 44
Rowling, J. K. 175, 303
Rubin, Courtney 9

Sae, Greasy 143, 152, 183
Salen, Katie 194, 228
Sambell, Kay 54, 81, 85
Saunders, Jane M. 7
S., Brittany 79
Schmeling, Manfred 227
Scott, A. O. 59
Scott, Whitney x
second-wave feminism/ist 106
Shaffer, Andrew 234
Shakespeare, William 31, 32, 37,
47, 49, 70
Shaw, Brent 242
Shelley, Mary 128, 137
Shilady, Jaelyn 82
Siculus, Diodorus 237
Siege of Leningrad 43
Silver, Frankie 155
Skerritt, Tom 123
Smith, Lee 44
Smith, Winston 96, 97
Smith, Zadie 273
Snow, Coriolanus ix, 17, 29, 34,
38, 67, 71, 86, 90, 95, 96,
97, 98, 99, 111, 115, 116,
119, 131, 132, 134, 137,
143, 172, 190, 250, 254,